The Forgotten Farmers

The Story of Sharecroppers in the New Deal

This book is the 1964 award winner of the Agricultural History Society

The Forgotten Farmers

The Story of Sharecroppers in the New Deal

David Eugene Conrad

GREENWOOD PRESS, PUBLISHERS
WESTPORT, CONNECTICUT

Library of Congress Cataloging in Publication Data

Conrad, David Eugene.
    The forgotten farmers.

    Reprint. Originally published: Urbana : University
of Illinois Press, 1965.
    Includes bibliographical references and index.
    1. Share-cropping. 2. Agriculture--Economic
aspects--Southern States. 3. Southern Tenant
Farmers' Union. I. Title.
[HD1478.U6C6 1982]   333.5'63   82-955
ISBN 0-313-23358-6 (lib. bdg.)   AACR2

Reprinted in 1982 by Greenwood Press,
A division of Congressional Information Service, Inc.
88 Post Road West, Westport, Connecticut 06881

Printed in the United States of America

10 9 8 7 6 5 4 3 2 1

To Beverly

Contents

chapter one

The American Peasants

One of the most abiding problems of men on earth has been the struggle over the control and use of land. Since ancient times, slavery and tenancy have been the means of oppressing those who till the soil. In the United States, despite the large amount of land and the relative ease of acquisition, slavery and tenancy fastened themselves on the agricultural system, especially in the South. By 1930 more than half of all Southern farmers did not own the land they farmed, and nearly three out of four cotton farms were operated with tenant labor. Moreover, cotton farms accounted for one-fourth of all farms in the country and half of Southern farms.[1] There were 1,831,470 tenant farmers in the

[1] W. A. Turner, *A Graphic Summary of Farm Tenure,* U.S. Department of Agriculture Misc. Pub. No. 261 (Washington: U.S. Government Printing Office, 1936), pp. 1–3.

South in 1935, about 63 per cent of all tenants in the nation. Tenants produced roughly two out of three bales of cotton in the United States.[2] Tenancy had been on the rise in the South and in the nation since 1900. The national tenancy rate increased from 35 per cent in 1900 to 43 per cent in 1935. It ranged from 70 per cent in Mississippi to 6 per cent in Massachusetts. In 1900 the part of American farm land operated by tenants was less than one-third of all cultivated land, but by 1935 it was 45 per cent. Nor was tenancy confined to Negroes, as was often supposed. The rate of white tenancy rose alarmingly after 1900 to the point that 46 per cent of all white farmers in the country were tenants in 1935. Among Negro farmers, 77 per cent were tenants, but this figure had been fairly constant since 1900. About half of all Negro tenant farmers were at the lowest level of tenancy, sharecropping, and 29 per cent of white tenants were croppers. Other statistics indicate that it was becoming increasingly difficult to climb out of tenancy,[3] that farms were changing hands with amazing rapidity, that more and more land was being mortgaged,[4] and that farmers as a class were gradually losing control of the land.[5]

As early as 1917, former President Theodore Roosevelt showed concern about developments in land tenure when he wrote an article in the *Ohio Farmer* entitled "Will Our Farmers Become a Tenant Class?"[6] The statistics indicate an affirmative answer and also that the Great Depression was hastening the process. What happened to the ideal of farm ownership? Thomas Jefferson dreamed of an intelligent, independent electorate made up mostly of freeholding farmers. That dream became American dogma, but it was lost somewhere in the twentieth century. Forty-two per cent of farm families owned no land in 1940, and every year 40,000 more joined their ranks. National land policy during the

[2] U.S. Bureau of the Census, *United States Census of Agriculture: 1925. The Southern States*, II (Washington: U.S. Government Printing Office, 1925), 108.

[3] U.S. Bureau of the Census, *Statistical Abstract of the U.S., 1941* (Washington: U.S. Government Printing Office, 1942), pp. 681–685.

[4] E. Hjalmar Bjornsen, "Farm Debt and Farm Foreclosures," Bureau of Agricultural Economics, *The Agricultural Situation*, XXIV, No. 2, February, 1940 (Washington: U.S. Government Printing Office, 1940), 18–21.

[5] Turner, *A Graphic Summary of Farm Tenure*, p. 1.

[6] Theodore Roosevelt, "Will Our Farmers Become a Tenant Class?" *Ohio Farmer*, CIV (October 13, 1917), 314.

nineteenth and twentieth centuries was dedicated to individual ownership of family-size farms,[7] and yet in 1936 President Franklin D. Roosevelt was forced to admit that "we have fallen far short of achieving that ideal." [8]

The President's pronouncement came only after careful study of farm tenancy by several government agencies and a special committee. For years, many of the key men in the federal government concerned with land problems had been gravitating toward the conclusion that something was basically wrong with the national land tenure system. They did not come out and say it, but they implied in their writings that a change was needed. What they had in mind was not clear—perhaps communal ownership for some groups, perhaps guaranteed tenure, perhaps governmental limitations on the freedom of farmers to mortgage and sell their land. One official blamed "freedom of disposition," or the unlimited right of the landowner to sell the land even if it was not in his own best interest, for much of the trouble. He felt that it led to land speculation and tenancy.[9]

Farm tenancy existed in all parts of the United States during the 1930's, but it was most numerous in the Southern states, especially in cotton areas. Cotton farms were mostly small and low in value, averaging less than half the size and a third of the worth of other types of farms in the nation. Three out of four cotton farmers were tenants, chiefly because cotton lent itself to tenancy better than any other American crop.[10]

Cotton is a tropical plant which was adapted to the mildly tropical parts of the United States. It thrives on hot weather and moderate, timely moisture. Since frost is deadly to cotton and the growing season is long, it cannot be grown profitably north of the line where there are fewer than 200 frost-free days each year. Thus, in the 1930's the "Cotton Belt" covered most of Texas, southern Oklahoma, Arkansas, Louisiana, Mississippi,

[7] Paul V. Maris, "Farm Tenancy," *Yearbook of Agriculture, 1940*, U.S. Department of Agriculture, 76th Cong., 3rd Sess., House Doc. 695 (Washington: U.S. Government Printing Office, 1940), pp. 887–888.

[8] Franklin Roosevelt, *Farm Tenancy, Message from the President Transmitting the Report of the Special Committee on Farm Tenancy*, 75th Cong., 1st Sess., House Doc. No. 149 (Washington: U.S. Government Printing Office, 1937), p. 1.

[9] L. C. Gray, "Our Major Land Use Problem and Suggested Lines of Action," *Yearbook of Agriculture*, 1940, pp. 404–409.

[10] Turner, *A Graphic Summary of Farm Tenure*, pp. 1–3.

Alabama, Georgia, South Carolina, North Carolina, western Tennessee, and northern Florida.[11] Since it was the big money crop of the South, cotton monopolized the richest land—the alluvial soils of the numerous river valleys and the fertile prairies of Texas and Oklahoma. Yet it was also the crop of the small upland farmer who scratched out an existence on marginal and submarginal land.[12]

Where cotton culture was the most intensive, tenancy was the greatest. The Mississippi Delta, the Black Belt of northern Mississippi and Alabama, and the Piedmont Plateau of South Carolina were areas where tenant farmers far outnumbered landowners, and these were also the centers of cotton production. There were 890 counties in the country, mostly in the South, where there were more tenants than landowners.[13] Texas had the most tenants, but Mississippi had the highest rate of tenancy. In Mississippi, there were more than twice as many tenants as owners. More than half of the tenants were Negroes, but they had one million less acres of land than white tenants. Negro and white sharecroppers, on about equal terms economically, made up 40 per cent of the farm population of Mississippi but occupied farms worth only 23 per cent of the total value of farms in the state.[14]

Southern tenancy, like slavery before the Civil War, was an institution "peculiar" to the South. It was not only an economic but a social and political order, the origins of which lay clearly in slavery and the plantation system.[15] In order to operate effectively, a plantation must have abundant and fertile land, cheap, docile labor, social as well as economic management of the labor, and an imperishable crop with a ready market. When emancipation of the Southern slaves took place after the Civil War, the cheap labor and the social and economic controls were removed. This situation forced planters to seek ways to return the workers to the soil. They tried year-long wage contracts, but the Negroes did not understand contracts and refused to work for a year without pay. If the Negroes were paid for shorter work

[11] Rupert Vance, *Human Factors in Cotton Culture* (Chapel Hill: University of North Carolina Press, 1929), pp. i and 14.
[12] *Ibid.*, pp. 14–23.
[13] Turner, *A Graphic Summary of Farm Tenure*, pp. 1–25.
[14] Bureau of Census, *Statistical Abstract, 1941*, p. 689.
[15] Vance, *Human Factors in Cotton Culture*, pp. 34–37.

periods, they often left after the first pay day and did not return until their money was spent. Under the Black Codes passed by the Southern states soon after the War, Negroes could be imprisoned for vagrancy and their labor bought by planters, but these codes were wiped out when the federal government imposed radical Reconstruction on the South.[16]

For years, large tracts of land lay vacant in the South until gradually a solution to the labor problem was found—sharetenancy. The plantations drifted quite naturally into it. The Barrows plantation in Georgia is a good example. It consisted of 1,000 acres and had about twenty-five Negro families. For several years following emancipation the field hands worked in two gangs under Negro foremen and received a portion of the crop in lieu of wages. But after a while the two squads split into smaller groups and there was much squabbling and inefficiency. At that point Barrows reorganized the plantation and divided the land into family tenant tracts. Each family worked its own piece of land and the gang system was abandoned. One by one, the workers moved their cabins from where they were grouped behind the plantation house to their own tract. The method of sharing the crop was replaced by rent, paid in cotton to the landowner.[17] Under this new plantation system, soon common throughout the South, planters maintained the necessary cheapness and docility of labor, and social and economic control. Wrote one apologist in 1927: "The slave was probably predestined to be what he has since very largely become—a peasant farmer." [18]

This explanation of how emancipated slaves became tenant farmers does not apply to the 1,202,174 white tenants in the South in 1935. The traditional rationale in the South for the existence of white tenants was that they were "poor whites," an ignorant, shiftless, lazy class of people for whom tenancy would be a step up. But there were never enough "poor whites" in the South to account for the millions of white tenants and their

[16] Arthur F. Raper, *Preface to Peasantry* (Chapel Hill: University of North Carolina Press, 1936), pp. 96–98.
[17] D. C. Barrows, "A Georgia Plantation," *Scribner's Monthly*, CXX (April, 1881), 830–835.
[18] Robert E. Park, "The Anti-Slavery Movement in England," *American Journal of Sociology*, XXXIII (September, 1927), 290–291.

families.[19] Many of these fell into tenancy because they could not afford to buy land. Others were jobless urban workers who moved to farms during times of depression.[20] Some were former landowners who lost their farms because of crop failure, low cotton prices, laziness, ill health, poor management, exhaustion of the soil, mechanization of agriculture, excessive interest rates, or inability to compete with tenant labor. Many tricks of nature could cause a cotton farmer to lose his crop and perhaps his farm: drought, floods, boll weevil, untimely rain, frost, hail, high winds, root rot, and many other plant diseases.[21]

As the Southern tenancy system developed, it became stratified into economic and social classes. There were fundamentally three types of tenants with many variations: the cash-tenant, the share-tenant, and the sharecropper—often simply called "cropper." The cash-tenant was at the top of the tenancy heap. If any tenant was in a position to move into ownership, it was usually the cash-tenant. He owned his own work animals and implements and was able to provide for himself and family throughout the year and to buy fertilizer and feed. He paid a fixed cash rent each year, all profit above rent and operating going into his own pocket.

The share-tenant was next in status. He owned most of the necessary work animals, tools, and machinery and could furnish seed, feed, and two-thirds or three-fourths of the fertilizer. Some share-tenants could provide for their families during the crop season, but when they could not the landlord extended credit. For use of land and house and the privilege of gathering wood for fuel, the share-tenant paid one-fourth or one-third of the crop, depending on how much the landlord had augmented his work animals, implements, seed, and fertilizer.

The lowliest tenant was the sharecropper. He had only the labor of himself and his family to offer. The landlord furnished land, house, fuel, half the fertilizer, work animals, implements, supervision, and the necessities of life, on credit. The sharecropper paid half of his crop in rent.[22]

[19] Bureau of Census, *Statistical Abstract, 1941*, p. 687.

[20] Edmund de S. Brunner and Irving Lorge, *Rural Trends in Depression Years* (New York: Columbia University Press, 1937), pp. 1–11.

[21] Vance, *Human Factors in Cotton Culture*, pp. 80–107.

[22] S. A. Goldenweiser and E. A. Boeger, "A Study of the Tenant Systems of Farming in the Yazoo-Mississippi Delta," *United States Department of*

A tenant who was neither cash- nor share-tenant but a little of both was the standing renter. He paid rent in a fixed amount of produce and furnished everything he needed to make a crop. His social and economic status was usually slightly below a cash-tenant and above a share-tenant, but it could be considerably lower when he was a "bale-a-plow" tenant. Under this arrangement used on some large plantations, the tenant farmed only about twenty acres, received nearly everything needed to make a crop including a plow, and paid a bale of cotton per year in rent.

A high percentage of cash-tenancy in an area reflected the disintegration of the plantation system. Where the plantations were strong, sharecropping was likely to be most prevalent, and there was much competition between white and black croppers, to the detriment of both. In reality, the sharecropper was little more than a wage hand being paid in kind, and the statutes of some Southern states recognized him as such rather than a tenant. Cropper farming, requiring close supervision by the landlord and obedience and servility by the tenant, gave small reward to individual initiative and self-expression. Essentially, it was a form of debt peonage.

Share-tenancy was considered in parts of the South to be an exclusively white institution. It developed in the mountain and Piedmont areas of the Old South before the Civil War and was still most prevalent there in the 1930's. Often, white farmers on a plantation would be in this status while black ones would be sharecroppers. Cropper farming was a child of the Reconstruction period [23] and was most common in the Piedmont, Black Belt, and Delta. White sharecropping was not as intense in the Delta and was more widespread throughout the Cotton Belt than Negro cropping. Also, there were considerable numbers of white croppers on tobacco farms in Kentucky, Tennessee, and Virginia.[24]

The most unfortunate of Southern farm workers was the day laborer or wage hand who had a precarious existence without any assurance of work, food, or housing from one day to the

Agriculture Bulletin 337 (Washington: U.S. Government Printing Office, 1916), *passim*.

[23] Raper, *Preface to Peasantry*, p. 149.
[24] Turner, *A Graphic Summary of Farm Tenure*, p. 31.

next. Many planters might have preferred this type of labor except that it required continuous outlays of cash throughout the growing season and allowed less control of workers.[25]

Despite the extent of tenancy, it was not until the Great Depression of the 1930's that it became recognized as a serious national problem. Writers like John Steinbeck, James Agee, and Erskine Caldwell wrote about it, and the tragedy of tenancy was depicted in plays, best-selling novels, and movies. Several government agencies made extensive studies of the problem. It was ironic that tenancy did not become a celebrated cause until the entire country was in serious economic difficulties, but the reason for this was that liberal writers, trying to show the need for action in the Depression, used the most extreme examples of privation and poverty in the country—the Southern tenants.

Southern tenancy was a vicious, self-perpetuating system. On a tenant plantation [26] the workers were little more than serfs, held to the land by debt, ignorance, poverty, and dependence on the landlord. That was the way the planter wanted it. He could not afford to let his tenants become too independent or self-reliant because he would lose control over them and this would cut his margin of profit. The plantation system taught the tenant certain things—how to plow, hoe and pick cotton, fix wagon wheels, build makeshift houses, slaughter animals, and cook turnip greens—but it could not allow tenants to rise above this menial level. In the Black Belt, to give a Negro a formal education was to "ruin a good nigger."

What kept the tenants from escaping? Could they not seek others jobs? Some did, but they were the aggressive ones. The ordinary tenant knew nothing but farming and could not imagine himself doing anything else. And then it was hard to escape. If a tenant had debts, and most did, the state laws in many Southern states practically tied him to the land until the crop was made. Moreover, there was a sort of gentlemen's agreement among

---

[25] Raper, *Preface to Peasantry*, pp. 146–147.

[26] In 1910 the Bureau of the Census began using the term "tenant plantation" which it defined as "a continuous tract of land of considerable area under the general control or supervision of a single individual or firm, all or part of such tract being divided into at least five small tracts which are leased to tenants." U.S. Bureau of the Census, *Thirteenth Census of the United States: 1910. Agriculture,* V (Washington: U.S. Government Printing Office, 1911), 878.

planters that they would not hire tenants from another plantation without the consent of the planter concerned. The tenant who "slipped off" to escape his debts faced flogging, murder, or lynching, especially if he were a Negro.

With plantation labor virtually trapped on the land, there ensued an endless game where the planter tried to get all he could from the tenant and the tenant all he could from the planter. Although the tenant usually made little or no profit at the end of the season, he had at least made a living through the year by buying on credit at the plantation store. Tenants habitually took all the credit they could get, and the planter was saddled with the worry of preventing them from getting deeper in debt to him than they could hope to pay. Landlords were often dictatorial and autocratic, but tenants also learned tricks to get what they wanted.[27]

The hopeless part of the tenancy system was that there was no room for improvement. The landlord was forced to depend on unstable, irresponsible, inefficient labor. If he attempted to improve the quality of his tenants by raising their standard of living, he was likely to drive himself into bankruptcy. His profits depended on the poverty of his tenants. On the other hand, most tenants were probably paid as much as they were worth to the landlord considering what they produced. The fact that the most unscrupulous landlords were the ones who made the best profits led the cotton economy into a vicious downward spiral, the final outcome of which seemed destined to be a class of subhuman people—serfs or worse who were completely dependent and who would be a definite liability to the landowner and the country in general.[28]

It was generally true that the exploitation of the cottonfield workers was in direct proportion to the size of the plantation. Often the owners of the great plantations were absentee landlords, syndicates, or corporations, some European, who hired managers to run the plantations. These managers were expected to show a profit each year; if cotton prices were down, they had to make the profit from their tenants.[29]

[27] Raper, *Preface to Peasantry*, pp. 171–173.
[28] Harold Hoffsommer, "The AAA and the Sharecropper," *Social Forces*, XIII (May, 1935), 494–502.
[29] Howard Kester, *Revolt Among the Sharecroppers* (New York: Covici-Friede Publishers, 1936), pp. 38–39.

Cotton plantations were such marginal operations that they were forced to exploit the soil as well as the workers. Planting cotton as they did every year on every available square foot of land, even up to the front door of the tenant shacks, eventually caused the soil to wear out. In parts of the Carolinas and Georgia, the plantation system had run its course, leaving in its wake a barren land and broken people. When the land began to play out, planters and more alert tenants left. All that remained were decadent tenant families, made so by generations of poverty, lack of education, poor food, blind prejudice and hard work. According to Arthur Raper, who made a study of them in Georgia, they were now ready for permanent "peasantry." [30]

The attitude of planters toward their tenants, especially in the Old South, has been called "paternalistic," but it is hard to imagine a father exploiting his children the way a planter did his tenants. True, many planters looked upon their tenants as "childlike" people who would starve to death without supervision, and often it was to the planter that a tenant turned when he had a problem or was in trouble. Most planters felt that tenants would not tend gardens or cows if they had them and could not be counted on to do anything on their own initiative. Some even held back part of their tenants' annual pay knowing they would spend it foolishly if paid all at once. The typical planter believed that keeping tenants on the ragged edge of privation was the best way to make them work. The fear of hunger was the only thing that would drive them into the fields. "The man working for food not only works regularly," explained one Georgia planter, "he works gladly; he takes orders cheerfully, is seldom sullen—all in all, he's the most satisfactory farm worker." [31]

Like his ante-bellum prototype, the planter had social control over his workers. On some plantations, community and family matters were subject to his review. Many planters, for instance, would not allow couples to live together without being legally married. The planters determined all holidays and customarily gave an annual picnic-barbecue for their workers. Some provided primitive schools and churches for tenants and others helped support such endeavors. [32]

[30] Raper, *Preface to Peasantry*, p. 4.
[31] *Ibid.*, pp. 157–159.
[32] Vance, *Human Factors in Cotton Culture*, pp. 77–78.

Race relations played an important role in the plantation system. White supremacy was the gospel of Southern life. The Ku Klux Klan, although waning, was still active during the 1930's, and plantations were the best place to find "unreconstructed rebels." In Georgia, Sherman's march to the sea was mentioned daily. A Negro did not question the word of a white man in anything; he did what he was told to do, and he did it in a servile manner if he cared much for his personal safety. To the typical Southern white, the only likeable Negro was one who "knew his place."

Politically, the most Democratic part of the nation was probably the least democratic. Negro office holders were practically unknown, and most Negroes were prevented from voting. In public schools, money spent on the education of white students varied from six to sixty times the expenditure for colored children.[33]

The bane of the tenant, and yet the blessing, was the "commissary" or plantation store where he could buy tools, utensils, food, and some clothing. Some planters required their tenants to use the commissary, and most extended credit for food, fertilizer, and clothing only through their own store. From the time the season began until the crop was made, the tenant was likely to be completely dependent on the commissary for "furnish," or food and clothing. Planters made good profits from their stores. According to one Georgia landowner, there was only one way for a planter to make money using hired labor, and that was to have a commissary and keep the books himself, "making sure that at the end of the year he has gotten it all, and his labor has 'just lived,' as one would say." [34]

Prices at the commissary were often considerably higher than at stores in town, and there was a limit set on each tenant's credit. However, if one man's crop looked promising, his credit limit was raised; another who was sick or whose cotton was infested with boll weevil or Johnson grass might find his ability to buy food severely restricted. All commissaries charged interest on their advances, ranging from 10 to 60 per cent per annum.[35]

[33] Raper, *Preface to Peasantry*, pp. 4–6.

[34] Kester, *Revolt Among the Sharecroppers*, pp. 42–43.

[35] Arthur F. Raper and Ira De A. Reid, *Sharecroppers All* (Chapel Hill: University of North Carolina Press, 1941), pp. 22, 38–39, 42, 68–69.

"Settlement day," after the cotton was picked and ginned and when the landlord settled with his tenants, was keenly anticipated all season long by the tenants. Parents whose children asked to buy things told them, "Jus' wait 'til settlement day." During the weeks of the brutal labor of picking, as the great day approached, the tenants grew more and more excited. Most tenants in the lower levels had no idea what was coming to them. They knew whether they had made a good crop or not, and perhaps they had some idea of cotton prices, but most of them kept no account of their credit. Many did not know enough arithmetic even to approximate what their settlement should be. They simply hoped for the best. When they were disappointed, they tended to blame their landlord for cheating them. This was warranted in some cases but not in others. Ordinarily, the tenant was a poor judge of whether or not he had been cheated.[36]

In addition to half of the proceeds from the cotton and cotton-seed taken in payment of rent on settlement day, the landlords on tenant plantations deducted the year's "furnish" with interest, any advances of cash or charges for breakage, a fee for supervision and management usually amounting to 10 per cent of the advances at the commissary, and a charge for the use of plantation roads and ditches which was ordinarily 10 cents per acre farmed.[37]

Before the depression, in the years when crops were good, most tenants cleared at least a few hundred dollars on settlement day. A few lucky ones in the higher levels got a thousand or more. But during the depression, many tenants finished the year in debt, and many had debts of more than one year's standing. Estimates of average tenant income varied from $103 [38] to $459 per year.[39]

A survey of three large Arkansas plantations conducted by the

[36] *New York World-Telegram*, February 28, 1935, p. 2; and T. J. Woofter, *Landlord and Tenant on the Cotton Plantation*, Works Progress Administration Monograph No. 5 (Washington: U.S. Government Printing Office, 1936), p. 82.

[37] Kester, *Revolt Among the Sharecroppers*, pp. 49–50.

[38] Hoffsommer, "The AAA and the Sharecropper," *Social Forces*, XIII, 494–495.

[39] Cotton Section, Agricultural Adjustment Administration, "Arkansas Plantation Study," National Archives, Washington, D.C., Record Group 145, Records of the Agricultural Adjustment Administration. Hereinafter cited as NA, RG 145.

Cotton Section of the Agricultural Adjustment Administration and the University of Arkansas found that actual cash income of tenants was about $300 in 1934 including government benefits. One of the three plantations grossed $132,004 that year, of which the tenants got only $29,842.[40] Tenants in the East studied by the Works Progress Administration averaged $309 per family, or about $73 per capita. They were able to spend only $13 per month for food, fuel, medicine, and clothing while awaiting settlement.[41] The Farm Security Administration, in spot studies in Mississippi, Alabama, and Arkansas found tenant income to be about $132, only one-fourth as much as that of corn tenants in Nebraska.[42] Sociologist Arthur Raper, in a classic study of two cotton counties in Georgia, learned that Negro tenant families spent only $92 for food, clothing, and tobacco in 1934 and white families $161. Another authority, Rupert Vance, told the National Country Life Conference in 1938 that "unless one has actually observed the way tenants live, the meaning of such low incomes is hard to visualize." [43]

Each year after a settlement was made, tenants began to move. Perhaps they were dissatisfied with their profits, perhaps they were evicted, or more likely they were simply hunting for the better place they seldom found. During the cold, rainy months of December and January the highways and roads of the South were clotted with displaced tenant families, their wagons and junk cars loaded with pitiful belongings and dirty, underfed children. But for all their trouble, moving seldom raised the status of tenants and often lowered it.

The mobility of some tenants was amazing, especially sharecroppers. Statistics gathered by the Cotton Section of AAA showed that a considerable percentage of tenants had moved six or seven times since they started farming and a few had lived on as many as fifteen farms.[44] The average tenure of tenants in two counties in Georgia was 3.7 years for Negroes and 2.9 for

[40] *Ibid.*

[41] Woofter, *Landlord and Tenant on the Cotton Plantation*, p. 83.

[42] Carl Taylor, Helen Wheeler, and E. L. Kirkpatrick, *Disadvantaged Classes in American Agriculture*, Farm Security Administration Social Research Report No. 8 (Washington: U.S. Government Printing Office, 1938).

[43] Country Life Conference, Lexington, Kentucky, 1938, *Disadvantaged People in Rural Life* (Chicago, 1938), p. 3.

[44] AAA, Cotton Section, "Arkansas Plantation Study," NA, RG 145.

whites. Among Negro sharecroppers, the tenure was only 2.8 years and among whites only 2.4.[45] An extensive study by AAA of 13,575 tenant families on relief revealed that 40.6 per cent made some type of move in 1934.[46] Admittedly, relief tenants were not representative of all tenant families, but one source estimated that 43 per cent of all tenants were on relief in 1935.[47]

Every group which studied the tenancy problem during the 1930's was appalled by it. A special commission appointed by Arkansas Governor J. M. Futrell in 1936 found "illiteracy, poverty, wretchedness, with destruction to health and character." [48] Norman Thomas, traveling through cotton country, saw worn-out people going to work on worn-out land and commented that there were "few drearier sights in the world." An independent study sponsored by a group of prominent citizens [49] and conducted by Rupert Vance of the University of North Carolina and Charles S. Johnson of Fisk University gave credence to the worst things being said about tenancy. Their report concluded that although cotton farmers in the South contributed a billion dollars annually to the world economy, they were "the most impoverished and backward of any large group of producers in America." [50] President Roosevelt's Commission on Farm Tenancy in 1936 found that one-fifth to one-fourth of the nation's farm population lived in extreme poverty, were chronically undernourished and subject to pellagra, malaria, and hookworm, were often without medical care, and were usually poorly clad.[51]

Tenant housing, by all accounts, was the worst in the land. Houses were usually two-room, clapboard shacks, unpainted,

[45] Raper, *Preface to Peasantry*, p. 61.
[46] "Agricultural Adjustment Administration-Federal Emergency Relief Administration Survey," File 119, NA, RG 145.
[47] Hoffsommer, "The AAA and the Sharecropper," *Social Forces*, XIII, 494–495.
[48] Governor's Farm Tenancy Commission, *Findings* (in the files of the National Agricultural Workers' Union, Washington, D.C.), 1936.
[49] This group included William Green of the American Federation of Labor, Clark Howell, editor of the *Atlanta Constitution*, Governor Frank O. Lowden of Illinois, William Allen White, editor of the *Emporia Gazette*, and Gen. Robert E. Wood, President of Sears, Roebuck and Company.
[50] Charles Johnson, Edwin Embree, and W. W. Alexander, *The Collapse of Cotton Tenancy* (Chapel Hill: University of North Carolina Press, 1935), p. 1 and *passim*.
[51] President's Committee on Farm Tenancy, *Report*, 75th Cong., 1st Sess., House Doc. No. 149 (Washington: U. S. Government Printing Office, 1937), p. 1.

weatherbeaten, and in the process of falling down. Wind and rain came through holes in the roofs and walls. Plumbing was unheard of and outhouses were considered a luxury. A tenant's personal possessions usually consisted of a few rickety chairs, a table, a bed or two, a few ragged quilts, a broken washstand, some boxes, a few dishes, a pig or a dog, and once in a while, some chickens.[52] It was generally recognized that if a tenant hoped to get ahead, he had to acquire work animals, implements, and a wagon. The best way to do this was by such sidelines as raising cows, chickens, and pigs and taking extra jobs.[53] And yet 60 per cent of the Negro tenants studied by Raper in Georgia owned neither mules nor horses, 31 per cent had no cows, 17 per cent no pigs, and 10 per cent no chickens.[54]

Tenants worked from dawn to dusk, or from "can to can't" as they said in the Arkansas Delta. On most plantations, a bell rang at dawn summoning the workers to the fields, and those who did not respond were severely disciplined. Children began working in the fields when they were six; women worked each day until time to fix meals or do housework. The hardest work was picking the cotton at the end of the season. James Agee describes this as "simple and terrible work" which required "all the endurance you can draw up against it from the roots of your existence." [55]

Tenant children attended school sporadically in schools which were usually open less than half the year. Throughout the rural South, schools were customarily closed during the cotton picking season. The average attendance of the children of 349 tenant families in Arkansas was only 3.8 months in 1934.[56] Hundreds of one-room Negro schools had no windows or desks. While most white children in rural areas could ride to school in buses, most Negro and some white students had to walk. Rural teachers were poorly paid and inadequately trained. Their salaries were below $30 per month in many counties.[57] A high percentage of adult

[52] Kester, *Revolt Among the Sharecroppers*, pp. 40–41, 43–46.
[53] Texas Division of Public Welfare, *Studies in Farm Tenancy in Texas*, University of Texas Bulletin No. 21 (Austin, 1915), p. 36.
[54] Raper, *Preface to Peasantry*, pp. 81, 86.
[55] James Agee and Walker Evans, *Let Us Now Praise Famous Men* (Boston: Houghton-Mifflin, 1960), pp. 326–348.
[56] AAA, Cotton Section, "Arkansas Plantation Study," NA, RG 145.
[57] Raper and Reid, *Sharecroppers All*, p. 24.

tenants were illiterate, and all but a few were totally incapable of absorbing, correlating, or critically examining any idea or physical fact beyond the simplest and most obvious.[58]

The diseases of malnutrition, filth, and immorality were always with tenants. Their diet of cornbread, molasses, and sowbelly (fat salt pork), eaten three time a day, caused pellagra. Their lack of sanitation led to malaria, typhoid, and many other diseases. Working in the fields barefooted gave them hookworms. Immorality caused their venereal disease rate to be high.[59] Families were big but the birth rate was even higher. The tenants studied by Raper averaged about six living children, but the death rate was 10.8 per cent among white tenants and 20.4 per cent for Negro sharecroppers.[60]

The prospect of ever escaping tenancy seemed so dim that when tenants got a few dollars they tended to spend them on things they wanted instead of necessities. What they wanted most was a car, and a surprisingly high percentage of tenants in the Old South owned some sort of old jalopy.[61] During the late 1940's and the 1950's, a story circulated through the country of how the Russian government decided to let their people see the film *The Grapes of Wrath* because it showed the failure of American capitalism but had to cancel it when their people were amazed to learn that the "Okies" [62] had their own cars. This story gave great comfort to certain Americans who liked to think that even the poorest people in America were better off than the average Russian. But Steinbeck's novel also tells what it cost the "Okies" to buy their cars. Few tenants in Oklahoma had cars; so they had to sell everything accumulated in a lifetime of work—animals, plows, harness, cooking utensils, and most tragic of all, their tenuous right to the land because when they lost these things they lost their status as tenants.[63]

Literary travelers in the South during the 1930's taxed their

[58] Agee and Evans, *Let Us Now Praise Famous Men*, p. 306.
[59] Kester, *Revolt Among the Sharecroppers*, pp. 41–42.
[60] Raper, *Preface to Peasantry*, p. 70.
[61] *Ibid.*, pp. 157–161, 174–176.
[62] "Okies" was a name applied to displaced tenants and small farmers who migrated from Oklahoma to California in the 1930's.
[63] John Steinbeck, *The Grapes of Wrath* (New York: Viking, 1939), pp. 83–89. The used-car lot scene, described in these pages, is one of the most striking and poignant in depression literature.

talents to describe tenancy. English author Naomi Mitchison wrote, "I have traveled over most of Europe and part of Africa, but I have never seen such terrible sights as I saw yesterday among the sharecroppers of Arkansas." [64] Frazier Hunt, reporter for the *New York World-Telegram,* commented that cotton pickers reminded him of Chinese coolies working in the fields; however, he added that he had seen no children working in China as he had in the South.[65]

Erskine Caldwell, whose literary reputation was built on writing about the seamy side of Southern rural life, pulled out all the stops:

Near Keysville [Georgia] a two-room house is occupied by three families, each consisting of man and wife and from one to four children each. . . .

In one of the two rooms a six-year-old boy licked the paper bag the meat had been brought in. His legs were scarcely any larger than a medium sized dog's leg. . . . Suffering from rickets and anemia, his legs were unable to carry him for more than a dozen steps at a time . . . his belly was swollen several times its normal size. His face was bony white. He was starving to death.

In the other room of the house, without chairs, beds, or tables, a woman lay rolled up in some quilts trying to sleep. On the floor before the open fire lay two babies, neither a year old, sucking the dry teats of a mongrel bitch.[66]

James Agee and Walker Evans, a New York magazine writer and a government photographer on leave from the Farm Security Administration, probably reached the greatest literary heights in *Let Us Now Praise Famous Men.* For weeks they lived with the families of Bud Woods, George Gudger, and Fred Rickets, white tenant farmers in Alabama. They ate abominable food, slept in a bed crawling with bedbugs, fleas, and lice, and in general tried to live as tenants lived.

In the introspective and tortured writing of Agee and the stark photographs of Evans are to be found the closest, most painful description of the human suffering caused by tenancy. The reader comes to know the three families as people—how they lived and what they felt. He meets Annie Mae Gudger who looks fifty years old but is only twenty-seven. He knows little

[64] Statement given to Howard Kester. Quoted by Kester, *Revolt Among the Sharecroppers,* p. 51.

[65] *New York World-Telegram,* July 30, 1935.

[66] "Bootleg Slavery," *Time,* March 4, 1935, pp. 13–14.

Valley Few Gudger (Squinchy), aged twenty months, who is so sickly he will probably not live out the year.[67] And the reader concludes that the only alternatives for a tenant were complete misery or complete insensibility.

[67] Agee and Evans, *Let Us Now Praise Famous Men*, p. 81 and *passim*.

chapter two

The Agricultural Adjustment Act

Like the entire economy, American agriculture in 1933 was in danger of complete collapse. Farm prices, which had never completely recovered from the postwar depression of 1920–1922, plunged to such depths in the Great Depression that some crops were not worth the cost of harvesting. During the 1920's, a hard core of farm leaders such as George N. Peek, Chester Davis, Charles Brand, and M. L. Wilson fought continuously for some sort of relief for agriculture through federal legislation.[1] The various McNary-Haugen Bills proposed during the 1920's were designed to raise farm prices artificially to a level of "parity" so

[1] Edwin Nourse, Joseph Davis, and John D. Black, *Three Years of the Agricultural Adjustment Administration* (Washington: The Brookings Institution, 1937), pp. 3–5.

that farmers would have their fair share of the national income,[2] but the bills were killed by two Presidential vetoes. The agrarians also turned their attention to the export-debenture plan, a different approach to the same goal, but it too met with little success.[3] Pressure from farmers eventually forced Congress to pass the Agricultural Marketing Act of 1929, which had the support of the Hoover Administration. The purpose of this measure was to promote effective merchandising of agricultural goods and to stabilize prices by making government loans on farm surpluses to cooperatives. Stabilization corporations were also provided to deal with unusual surpluses. After this program had lost nearly $350 million Congress abandoned it as a failure.[4]

In the Presidential election of 1932, the successful candidate, Franklin D. Roosevelt, emphasized the need for farm legislation,[5] and during the lame-duck session of Congress which met after the election, friends of agriculture in Congress made serious efforts to pass helpful legislation. But the strong likelihood that President Hoover would veto destroyed hopes for a farm bill during that session.[6] Other obstacles were a lack of agreement among farm leaders and agricultural experts on what should be done, the refusal of the President-elect to reveal his intentions until he entered office, and the fact that the Senate could not make reasonable progress until certain members left office.[7]

Franklin Roosevelt became President on March 4, 1933. In his inaugural address he called for "definite efforts to raise the values of agricultural products and with this the power to purchase the output of our cities." [8]

Roosevelt's agricultural advisers, Henry Wallace, Rexford Tugwell, Henry Morgenthau, and others had been at work for some time on a new farm bill which they planned to get passed in the

[2] Gilbert C. Fite, *George N. Peek and the Fight for Farm Parity* (Norman: University of Oklahoma Press, 1954), pp. 60–63.

[3] Chester C. Davis, "The Development of Agricultural Policy Since the End of the World War," *Yearbook of Agriculture,* 1940, pp. 308–312.

[4] Harold G. Halcrow, *Agricultural Policy of the United States* (New York: Prentice Hall, 1953), p. 260.

[5] *New York Times,* September 15, 1932, p. 1.

[6] George N. Peek, *Diary,* January 5, through February 1, 1933. (Papers in the Western Historical Manuscripts Collection, Columbia, Mississippi.)

[7] *New York Times,* March 5, 1933, sec. 21, p. 1.

[8] *Ibid.,* sec. 1, p. 3.

special session of Congress which began on March 4.[9] They proposed that the bill contain parts of four major farm proposals so that Congress would not be forced to choose one over the other. This was an especially appealing idea politically since each plan had its own powerful supporters. Roosevelt laughed and said, "Well, we can try." [10] The President then ordered Wallace, his new Secretary of Agriculture, to call a meeting of farm leaders, lock himself in a room with them, and not come out until they had agreed on a program for agriculture.[11]

Wallace got the conference of farm leaders to agree to most of the Administration's ideas. A memorandum adopted by the conference called for parity prices and asked that the President and the Secretary of Agriculture be given powers to lease land to curtail production, "regulate and supervise" agricultural marketing, implement a plan whereby surplus cotton owned by the government could be sold to cotton farmers at less than the cost of production, levy a tax on agricultural products, and assume all powers necessary to put the plans into effect.[12]

George Peek later described the farm bill as a "hodgepodge of conflicting notions compromised into a bill which had to be passed in order to get action." [13] Russell Lord termed it "an omnibus measure, but a fantastically elastic omnibus." With journalistic license he wrote, "The measure as drawn sought to legalize almost anything anybody could think up." [14]

The real authors of the farm bill, despite the pretext of the farm leaders' conference, were Wallace, Tugwell, and Mordecai Ezekiel. Also consulted were George Peek, Henry Morgenthau, General Hugh Johnson and Bernard Baruch. The legal drafting was done by Frederick Lee and Jerome Frank. The bill was completed five days after the farm leaders' conference.[15] How-

[9] Henry A. Wallace, *New Frontiers* (New York: Reynal and Hitchcock, 1934), pp. 162–163.

[10] Rexford G. Tugwell, *The Democratic Roosevelt* (Garden City, New York: Doubleday, 1957), p. 275.

[11] Russell Lord, *The Wallaces of Iowa* (Boston: Houghton-Mifflin, 1947), p. 328.

[12] *New York Times*, March 12, 1933, p. 1.

[13] George N. Peek, *Why Quit Our Own* (New York: D. Van Nostrand Co., Inc., 1936), p. 14.

[14] Lord, *The Wallaces of Iowa*, p. 330.

[15] Wallace, *New Frontiers*, p. 164, and Louis Bean (USDA economist), interview with author, August 1, 1959.

ever, it must be added that most of the basic ideas in the bill had been proposed many times before, some of them in previous sessions of Congress.

On March 16, Wallace and Tugwell went to the White House to hand the President the final draft of the bill.[16] Roosevelt, his imagination stirred by the concepts of the proposals, had already written a longhand message to accompany the bill to Congress.[17] The measure was introduced in the House that same day. Thus the agricultural recovery bill, which, in Tugwell's words, was drafted "over a weekend, sponsored by a hastily convened meeting of farm leaders, and approved within a few days," was ready for legislative approval.[18]

In truth, the bill was one of the most imaginative and far-reaching measures ever seriously considered by Congress. Behind its radically different programs was an intent to intervene in the economy on the side of the underdog which marks a major turning point in the philosophy of the American government. In the years since, few ideas have developed in connection with the farm problem which were not contained in the Agricultural Adjustment Act of 1933 [19] and its amendments. The principle of parity for farmers, the guiding light of the bill, remains today as a key feature of farm programs, whether Democratic or Republican.

The avowed purpose of the Agricultural Adjustment Act was "to relieve the existing national economic emergency by increasing agricultural purchasing power, to raise revenue for extraordinary expenses incurred by reason of such emergency, to provide emergency relief with respect to agricultural indebtedness . . . and for other purposes." [20]

Title I declared a state of emergency in agriculture partly because of "a severe and increasing disparity between prices of agricultural and other commodities" and added that this disparity was destroying the purchasing power of farmers and impairing

[16] Peek, *Diary*, March 16, 1933, Peek Papers.

[17] Arthur M. Schlesinger, Jr., *The Coming of the New Deal*, Vol. II, *The Age of Roosevelt* (Boston: Houghton-Mifflin, 1959), p. 29.

[18] Tugwell, *The Democratic Roosevelt*, p. 276.

[19] This name for the act did not appear until it was placed in the *United States Statutes at Large*. While being considered by Congress, it was known as "the farm relief bill."

[20] U.S., *Statutes at Large*, XLVIII, Part I, 35.

agricultural assets supporting the national credit structure. The bill committed the government to three basic policies: to raise farm prices to parity,[21] to correct "present inequalities" gradually but as rapidly as national needs would permit, and to "readjust" farm production to a level which would be fair to both farmers and consumers.

The Secretary of Agriculture was given the power to reduce production for market through acreage control of any basic commodity by making agreements with the producers, or by other voluntary methods. He was authorized to provide rental or benefit payments to farmers who reduced production on any basis which he deemed "fair and reasonable." Also, the Secretary could enter into marketing agreements with processors or commercial handlers of agricultural commodities as a means of raising prices.

To provide for the rental and benefit payments to cooperating farmers, a tax was placed on the "first domestic processing" of agricultural commodities. The tax was to be set by the Secretary of Agriculture based on the difference between the farm price and the parity price. However, this tax level was to be approached gradually. In addition, the Secretary could adjust the tax if it appeared to be causing an accumulation of surpluses or seriously impeding traffic in a certain commodity. The tax was to be collected only on the portion of the commodity to be consumed domestically. Cotton ginning was specifically exempted. To avoid profiteering, a rather weak provision authorized the Secretary to publish information regarding the cost and prices of processors.

A provision which drew much political fire was one allowing the Secretary to appoint officers and administrators in all salary brackets under $10,000 per annum. This meant that these employees would not be subject to regulations of the Civil Service Commission. The Secretary could also establish state and local committees or associations of producers, and he could permit cooperative associations of producers to receive rental and benefit payments for their members. Otherwise, rental and benefit payments would be made directly to producers. The

[21] The act defined parity as farm prices which would give "a purchasing power with respect to articles that farmers buy equivalent to the purchasing power of agricultural commodities in the base period." The base period was defined as August, 1909, to July, 1914 (except for tobacco).

act did not specify how this would be done and it did not make it clear whether the payment would be made to the producer personally. Moreover, the law did not clearly define a "producer" —a notable omission since a "processor" was defined. If the bill had specified that producers were to be paid individually and if it had defined sharecroppers and share-tenants as producers, much of the difficulty later encountered in administering the law might have been avoided.

With the approval of the President, the Secretary could make such regulations "with the force and effect of law" as were necessary to carry out the provisions of the act. He could also assess penalties not to exceed $100 for violations of his regulations. Decisions on rental and benefit payments were subject to review only by the Secretary of Agriculture and the Secretary of Treasury. In order to assist in enforcement, the Secretary was given powers to require information from individuals and concerns and to hold hearings to obtain pertinent information.[22]

For the purposes of the act, basic agricultural commodities were defined as wheat, cotton, field corn, hogs, rice, tobacco, and milk and its products. The sum of $100 million was to be appropriated for rental and benefit payments until proceeds from the processing tax became sufficient. The President was given the power to terminate the act or any part of it when he deemed the national economic emergency over.[23]

Henry Wallace and others looked upon the Agricultural Adjustment Act as the culmination of the farm legislation battles of the past twelve years—a final victory for old war horses like George Peek and other farm leaders.[24] And there is much truth in this view. Yet, in some ways the act was not what the old-line farm leaders had been fighting for at all. Old ideas such as export dumping and the guaranteed cost of production were not present. Instead, the new bill followed the economics of scarcity and provided for acreage reduction—ideas quite abhorrent to some farm leaders.

President Roosevelt's message to Congress emphasized the experimental character of the bill. The President asserted that

[22] U.S., *Statutes at Large*, XLVIII, Part I, 35–36.
[23] *Ibid.*, pp. 36–41.
[24] Wallace, *New Frontiers*, pp. 150–159; and Chester Davis to author, October 1, 1959.

"deep study and the joint counsel of many points of view went into the bill," but he said, "I tell you frankly that it is a new and untrod path. . . ." The unprecedented conditions of the country called for "the trial of new means" to rescue agriculture. Roosevelt urged Congress to speedy action because planting time was coming soon. He promised that if a "fair administrative trial" of the measure failed to produce the hoped-for results, he would "be the first to acknowledge it" and to advise Congress accordingly.[25]

The 73rd Congress, to which Franklin Roosevelt submitted the agricultural recovery bill, was overwhelmingly Democratic. That party held 60 seats in the Senate and 310 in the House. The Republicans had only 35 senators and 117 representatives. The Farmer-Labor Party had one senator and five representatives.

Like many other Congresses, the 73rd was at times ruled by the Western and Southern agrarian elements. This was due in part to the single party system in Southern states which allowed representatives and especially senators to be re-elected many times and to build up seniority. Thus the Southerners and Westerners were able to dominate key committees. In the Senate, all the important chairmen were Southerners or Westerners.[26]

In such a Congress, an Administration farm bill which contained most of the current schemes for relieving farm distress had every chance of passing. And yet there were congressmen who had their own ideas about what kind of farm legislation should be passed, and there were those who resented executive usurpation of congressional bill-writing functions. Moreover, the Republican minority, although sincerely wishing to do something for the farmers, was not anxious to see the Democrats get all the credit for saving them.

Consideration of the bill began in the House on March 21. It lasted two days, during which supporters of the bill mentioned repeatedly that they expected it to be amended in the Senate while opponents complained bitterly of the ban on amendments in the House.[27] The vote on the farm relief bill came late on March 22. For all the violent opposition voiced by speakers in

[25] U.S., *Congressional Record*, 73rd Cong., 1st Sess., 1933, LXXIII, Part I, 528.
[26] *Ibid.*, p. 142
[27] *Ibid.*, pp. 750–762.

the short time allotted, the opponents polled only ninety-eight votes. With 316 representatives voting for the bill, it passed by better than a three-fourths majority.[28] Thus the Administration's agriculture bill, without a word changed, passed the House after two days of debate and only six days after the President transmitted it.

Undoubtedly, much of the opposition to the farm bill was partisan, but much of it was also sincere—the result of serious economic and constitutional objections. Even so, because of limitations on debate and amendments, the opposition had little opportunity to form. The only organized resistance came from the Republicans, and a large part of this was sheer partisanship. Had full debate and amendments been allowed, it is possible that a strong movement might have developed among Northern and urban Democrats which, combined with Republican strength, could have posed a threat to the bill.

Judging from the speed with which the measure passed and the casual way exact provisions were discussed in the House, most supporters of the bill took it largely on faith. They felt if agriculture was to be saved the time had come to give the President the powers he requested; moreover, they had been told by some of the agricultural experts that the bill would work. Add to this the heavy pressure from home to vote for the measure, and it is clear why so many legislators voted for it. However, few cast their votes gladly and many expressed misgivings. The big factors in their minds were the need for action and the absence of any alternative.

Democratic leaders felt when the farm bill passed the House that it would be radically changed or even completely rewritten in the Senate. Senator Ellison D. Smith, Chairman of the Agriculture Committee, announced he would oppose the bill as passed by the House, except for the part containing the cotton-option plan.[29] If the Administration hoped to ram the agriculture bill through the Senate as it had in the House, it was due for disappointment. Although the senators were under great pressure from home to act swiftly, many would not allow the bill to pass without due consideration and amendment. In the Senate there is no limitation on debate.

[28] *Ibid.*, p. 766.
[29] *New York Times*, March 23, 1933, pp. 1 and 3.

Before the bill came to the floor, there were five days of hearings before the Committee on Agriculture and Forestry. The purpose was to examine the House bill and make a report to the Senate. The chairman of the committee, Ellison D. "Cotton Ed" Smith, revealed at the beginning of the hearings a conversation with the President in which Roosevelt emphasized the experimental nature of the bill. The President said, according to Smith, that he intended to enforce it only one year. Roosevelt indicated that if certain features of the bill worked, he would continue with them; otherwise, he would terminate the entire act. Rexford Tugwell, present at the hearings in his capacity as Assistant Secretary of Agriculture, gave marketing agreements as an example of one part of the bill the Administration might wish to retain permanently.[30]

The witnesses at the hearings were Administration officials, farm leaders, and businessmen. Secretary of Agriculture Henry Wallace appeared first. He explained that the Administration was dedicated to the principle of restoring the purchasing power of farmers. To accomplish this, he asked for "broad and flexible" powers, and urged the senators to speedy action because the planting had already started.[31]

Throughout the hearings, little attention was given to the problems or position of tenant farmers under the proposed act; however, on one occasion committee members inquired of Wallace how tenant farmers and landlords would be paid for reducing acreage under the domestic allotment plan. The Secretary replied that this would be a matter of administrative regulation, presumably by him. When Senator George Norris, Republican of Nebraska, suggested that rental payments be split between landlord and tenant the same way the crop was usually divided, Wallace tacitly agreed. Another senator asked point blank if tenants would have the same "advantages" as landlords under the act, and Wallace replied, "Of course, that is a matter of regulation." With this somewhat nebulous assurance, the senators dropped the matter.[32]

One of the star witnesses was George N. Peek. He told the

[30] U.S. Senate, *Hearings before the Committee on Agriculture and Forestry on H.R. 3835*, 73rd Cong., 1st Sess. (hereinafter cited as Senate, *Hearings on H.R. 3835*), pp. 49–50.

[31] Senate, *Hearings on H. R. 3835*, pp. 148, 128–131.

[32] *Ibid.*, p. 38.

committee in his emphatic manner that it would be a mistake to reduce production by the domestic allotment plan and that the plan would probably not work anyhow. He charged that one of the greatest reasons for low farm prices was profiteering by the processors and handlers of agricultural goods. To remedy this, he placed faith in the licensing and market agreement features of the bill. When a senator asked him if he favored the bill as a whole, he said yes.[33]

John Simpson, president of the National Farmers Union and also representing the Farmers' National Holiday Association, followed Peek to the stand. He flayed the Administration's bill, saying it was a price-fixing measure which would yield the farmers less than half the cost of production. Simpson attacked the basic idea of reducing farm surpluses. The problem, he said, was not overproduction but underconsumption. The only overproduction in the country was in "empty stomachs and bare backs." [34]

On March 27, Ed O'Neal, president of the American Farm Bureau Federation, wrote all members of the committee requesting that he be allowed to testify. He protested that John Simpson's presentation before the committee did not reflect the views of the thirty-four farm leaders who attended the conference called by the Secretary of Agriculture on March 10. O'Neal stated that the conference formulated and agreed upon the principles which were written into the Administration's farm bill. But he did not get a chance to testify because the hearings ended the day after he wrote the letter.[35]

In executive session the Agriculture Committee voted to report the Administration's bill favorably and Chairman Smith did so on April 5. Two days later he began an explanation of its complicated provisions. According to Senate protocol, he also acted as floor manager for the measure.[36] Smith's key role was unfortunate for those desiring speedy passage because, although he favored the bill, he had many reservations. "Cotton Ed," having

[33] *Ibid.*, pp. 74–83, 104.
[34] *Ibid.*, pp. 104–116.
[35] O'Neal to Elmer Thomas, March 27, 1933. *Thomas Collection*, Division of Manuscripts, University of Oklahoma Library, "Legislation File," 73rd Cong., "Agricultural Legislation."
[36] U.S., *Congressional Record*, 73rd Cong., 1st Sess., 1933, LXXIII, Part II, 1281.

entered the Senate in 1909, was the ranking Democrat.[37] In some ways he fitted the standard definition of a Southern demagogue. He was an outspoken advocate of white supremacy, the poll tax, and states' rights, and an opponent of antilynch laws. When a Negro rose to deliver a prayer at the 1936 Democratic National Convention, Smith stalked out, muttering, "The man is black— black as melted ink." [38] Three things were sacred above all else to him: game birds, cotton, and, during elections, Southern womanhood.[39] He was proud of being a cotton planter, with tenants on his South Carolina plantation, and he often introduced bills in the Senate to benefit cotton farmers, hence his nickname, "Cotton Ed." In the early 1920's, Smith had been a member of the Farm Bloc.[40]

As Smith explained the farm bill to the Senate, many senators asked questions concerning its operation. Often he was forced to answer that in matters of specific execution, all would depend on the decisions of the Secretary of Agriculture. Senator Simeon Fess, Republican of Ohio, finally remarked rather hopelessly: "Are we not embarrassed in not knowing what is likely to be done? Is not that one of the weaknesses of the bill?" Cotton Ed could only answer that "those who represented the authors of the bill" thought it necessary to hand over discretionary powers to the Secretary. Some senators were genuinely alarmed at this prospect, and worse yet, they realized that because of tremendous pressure from the public, the press, and farmers, the bill was sure to pass.[41]

When Senator Smith finished his less-than-enthusiastic presentation of the bill, Senator Joseph T. Robinson of Arkansas took the floor to offer the major Administration arguments for the bill. As the majority leader, Robinson was a power in the Senate and in the Democratic Party. In 1928 he had been the party's candidate for Vice-President, and more than any other senator

[37] *Congressional Directory,* 73rd Cong., 2nd Sess., p. 160.

[38] James M. Burns, *Roosevelt: The Lion and the Fox* (New York: Harcourt, Brace and Company, 1956), p. 341.

[39] John A. Rice, "Grandmother Smith's Plantation," *Harpers,* CLXXVII (November, 1938), 579.

[40] Theodore Saloutos and John D. Hicks, *Agricultural Discontent in the Middle West 1900–1939* (Madison: University of Wisconsin Press, 1951), pp. 321–341.

[41] U.S., *Congressional Record,* 73rd Cong., 1st Sess., 1933, LXXIII, Part II, 1390–91.

he spoke for the Roosevelt Administration. In his early career, Robinson had been state representative, United States representative, and governor of Arkansas before going to the Senate in 1913. He was a skillful speaker and parliamentarian who looked more like a New York banker than an Arkansas politician.[42] To the poverty-stricken sharecroppers of his home state, he was "Greasy Joe" Robinson.[43]

Robinson emphasized parity prices for farmers as the basic idea of the farm bill. He explained, however, that the Secretary of Agriculture intended to push farm prices up to parity levels gradually, since precipitous action might harm the national economy. To calm the fears of consumers, Robinson asserted that the bill would not necessarily cause a great increase in the cost of living. Doubling the price of cotton, he explained, would add no more than two cents to the cost of a dollar cotton shirt, and if the price of wheat rose three-fold it would add only one cent to the cost of the wheat in a loaf of bread.

In answer to charges made by Republicans that the bill authorized an "army of taxgatherers" and other employees, Robinson declared that the existing machinery, supplemented by the state land-grant colleges, experimental stations, and county agents could administer the act. And farmers would be asked to execute "their end of the program." [44]

After Robinson finished, the Senate began several days of rather aimless debate in which Senators Smith and Huey P. Long were the star performers. Long, the "Kingfish" and virtual dictator of Louisiana, had been in the Senate only one year. Most sophomore senators wisely stay out of the limelight, but Huey Long loved it. When addressing the Senate he seemed to aim his remarks more at the galleries, especially the reporters' section, than at his fellow senators. In his short time in the Senate the "Kingfish" had acquired many cordial enemies, especially among other Southern senators. During consideration of the farm bill he was fighting an attempt to oust him from the Senate which originated from a group of Louisiana citizens led by a former governor.

Long was one of the most violent critics of the farm bill. He

[42] *Congressional Directory*, 73rd Cong., 2nd Sess., 1934, p. 6.
[43] *Sharecroppers Voice*, May, 1935.
[44] U.S., *Congressional Record*, 73rd Cong., 1st Sess., 1933, LXXIII, Part II, 1393–97.

felt that the real New Deal reformers had been "sold out" and that someone ought to "go down to the White House and tell the President what [had] happened." He charged the Administration's farm bill was "a half-baked scheme that comes out of the penman who was left . . . by Mr. Arthur Hyde [Hoover's Secretary of Agriculture] when he left office." The "penman" was Mordecai Ezekiel, and one of Long's favorite ways of entertaining the galleries was to read selected obscure passages from the pen of the Department of Agriculture economist. Once Long had the Senate clerk read a fantastically complicated equation included by Ezekiel in a pamphlet on computing the parity price for hogs.[45] While reading the clerk was interrupted by laughter, and Senator Burton K. Wheeler, Democrat of Montana, called out, "Mr. President, are they still talking about hogs?" Huey Long said, "Mr. President, this is a table relating to hogs. It clears the matter up." Evidently most of the hilarity had a Republican flavor and was at the expense of the farm bill because Majority Leader Robinson intervened to remark sourly, "it is perfectly manifest that higher mathematics has not much recognition in this body." Nonetheless, the subject of Ezekiel's "hogarithms" came back many times in later debate to plague the supporters of the bill.[46]

On April 11, Chairman Smith began offering amendments suggested by the Agriculture Committee. Most of them were minor, designed to correct defects in wording or to delineate more carefully the powers granted. But one committee amendment was of great importance—the cost-of-production plan. This was a scheme whereby minimum prices, no less than the cost of production, would be set by law on seven basic commodities. Opposed by the Administration, this idea had many supporters, and the effort to include it in the bill was the first real rebellion in the Senate against the Administration's railroading tactics.

When the Senate voted on the cost-of-production amendment, it carried forty-seven to forty-one. Eighteen Midwestern Republicans voted for the amendment and thirteen others against. Pas-

[45] "The regressive equation is as follows: (1) $\log X_u = - 0.9443 \log X_1 + 0.15888 \log X_2 - 0.21986 \log X_3 - 0.23675 \log X_4 - 0.07250 \log X_5 + 2.23777 \log X_6 + 0.4759 \log X_7 + 0.02659 \log X_8 + 1.63099 \log X_9 - 1.9443 \log X_{10}$."

[46] U.S., *Congressional Record*, 73rd Cong., 1st Sess., 1933 LXXIII, Part II, 1473–1637.

sage of the amendment was an important setback to the Administration's hopes of speedy passage of the farm bill exactly as submitted to Congress. Moreover, it opened the door for possible drastic revision of the bill.[47]

After the cost-of-production fight, the Senate returned to consideration of the entire farm bill, with partisan tempers now beginning to show occasionally. As the senators expressed themselves, the patterns of their support and opposition emerged. Proponents of the bill placed faith in it to accomplish overall agricultural recovery and were willing to accept obvious inequities to consumers. They argued that, although the bill might cause higher prices to consumers for agricultural goods, the increase would return purchasing power to farmers and allow them to buy more goods and services, thus stimulating the entire economy and making higher agricultural prices a lesser burden to consumers.

Raising prices was only a short-range goal to the supporters of the bill. The Administration spokesmen believed its real value lay in its salutary long-range effect on the entire economy. It was obvious to them that the nation could not recover as long as 40 per cent of the population, the farmers, were permanently depressed. And if agricultural recovery required drastic action, the end would justify the means. The opponents of the bill divided into two general groups: those who felt it would not work, and those who believed that whether it would or not, it was not worth trying because of the immediate hardship to consumers and because of the threat to the American system of government. The opponents charged, for example, that the bill, in authorizing the employment of personnel not under Civil Service, would make possible the organization of a tremendous political machine which could tip the balance of political power in some states. Also, they condemned the bill because it was designed to raise the price of food and clothing at a time when millions were ill-fed and poorly clothed.[48]

When the senators had finished their speeches about the farm bill in general, Majority Leader Robinson began pushing toward final passage. When Robinson began offering the perfecting amendments, he opened the door for general amendments from

[47] *Ibid.*, pp. 1636–37.
[48] *Ibid.*, pp. 1790–95.

the floor. Many new amendments were presented, some of which would have drastically changed the bill. One of the amendments offered at this time was a package of political dynamite. It became the greatest threat of all to the Administration's bill. Characteristically, it came from Huey Long and was an attempt to inject monetary inflation into the bill as a means of aiding farmers and the entire country.[49]

For twelve days the Senate debated various schemes to achieve inflation while the Administration stewed over the fate of its farm bill. When it became evident that some sort of inflationary amendment to the farm bill would pass, President Roosevelt wisely decided to let the senators have their own way. With the backing of the Administration, Senator Elmer Thomas of Oklahoma introduced an amendment authorizing the President to place money in circulation through the purchase of government bonds by the Federal Reserve system, to issue fiat money up to $3 billion if needed, to accept silver in payment of international war debts and issue silver certificates on the silver thus acquired, and to lower the gold content of the dollar.[50] Senator David Reed, Pennsylvania Republican, despaired that the amendment embodied "every variety of unsound money that the wit of man can suggest," [51] but it passed over the principal opposition of New England Republicans.[52]

While the Senate moved toward a vote on the Thomas Amendment, it worked concurrently on other amendments in order to clear the way for a final vote on the farm bill as soon as the Thomas Amendment passed. There were nine more days of dilatory debate, but at last on April 28, the Senate was ready to vote. The Thomas Amendment having passed earlier that day, the entire bill was engrossed and read a third time. Then, on the final vote, the bill passed sixty-four to twenty, with eleven not voting. There were five "pairs" which would have meant five more votes for each side had the votes been cast. Sixteen Re-

[49] *Ibid.,* pp. 1741–42.
[50] Elmer Thomas, "Forty Years a Legislator" (Unpublished manuscript in *Thomas Collection,* University of Oklahoma Library; and *Thomas Collection,* Correspondence and Papers, 73rd Cong. File, "Inflation Amendment to Farm Bill").
[51] U.S., *Congressional Record,* 73rd Cong., 1st Sess., 1933, LXXIII, Part II, 2308.
[52] *Ibid.,* pp. 2551–52.

publicans, mostly from New England, voted against the bill, and they were joined by only four Democrats.[53]

On May 3, the House of Representatives voted on the eighty-five amendments passed by the Senate. All but one were turned down by a margin of 307 to 86. Thus, it was necessary to send the bill to a conference committee. After four days of hard work, the conference made its report. The senators gave in on six of the Senate amendments and the representatives on sixty-seven. The remaining twelve required compromises. When these were worked out, the result was a bill not vitally different from the original Administration measure, except for the Thomas Amendment.

The conference committee was able to reach agreement on every point but the cost-of-production amendment. On that score the House conferees remained adamantly opposed, and the matter was submitted to the House. There, the conference report was adopted, and after a short but heated debate, the cost-of-production amendment was voted down 109 to 283 with 40 not voting. It was an important victory for the Administration.[54] The Senate grudgingly voted to accept the bill without the cost-of-production plan. The same day the bill was signed by the President.[55]

Five days earlier, on May 5, President Roosevelt had explained to the American people in a fireside chat the principles behind the new legislation. He blamed the economic plight of the country on a lack of planning. The new concept was to bring farming and industry into a partnership with the government. This was not to be a partnership in profits, and it did not imply government control. The partnership would be achieved through mutual planning and "agreements" enforced by the government.[56]

The nation seemed to regard the signing of the AAA with guarded optimism. On the Cotton Exchange there was a spurt of trading in futures and a rapid increase in prices, but almost immediately a reaction of profit-taking set in and the market closed only slightly higher. The next day it dropped considerably. The security and commodity markets slowed down, and specula-

[53] *Ibid.*, pp. 2552–62.
[54] *Ibid.*, pp. 3060–79.
[55] *Ibid.*, pp. 3060–73, 3114–23.
[56] *New York Times*, May 8, 1933, pp. 1–2.

tive activity and fluctuations were curtailed. Milo Reno, president of the Farmers' National Holiday Association, condemned the farm act as unsatisfactory, but canceled the nationwide farmers' strike scheduled for May 13.[57]

The Agricultural Adjustment Act was a hastily written and experimental measure, although parts of it had long been advocated by agricultural reformers. Its objectives were not as radical as the means used to reach them. It was passed at a time when the normal legislative processes were not in operation and by a Congress which had grave misgivings and suspected that the law was unconstitutional. The reason for strong support was that something—anything—had to be done for agriculture. The Congressmen were also under tremendous public pressure to "back the President" in the emergency. The extraordinary discretionary and even lawmaking powers were grudgingly handed over to the Secretary of Agriculture in the hope that he could do what Congress had been unable to do—accomplish agricultural recovery.

To some people, like George Peek, who was to be its first administrator, the act was a simple measure to raise farm prices, but to the advocates of a "planned economy" in the New Deal it was part of the great goal of eliminating from the American scene the harmful inflation-deflation cycle. To the planners, the act was "a new charter," a departure into the realm of Franklin Roosevelt's "partnership" between government and industry. In this partnership, the government would regulate the production, flow, and sale of food and fiber to make supply meet demand and no more. Surpluses would be eliminated. Prices would be determined by what was fair for all. Exploitation and unfair competition would be ended. Antitrust laws would no longer be needed because the government would become the trust.

These radical ideas were not presented in Congress in arguments for the farm bill. Had this been done, it might not have passed. Instead the measure was pictured as what the farmer needed and what the President and the majority of the people wanted. Few senators and representatives could oppose that combination, although many wanted to.

The Agricultural Adjustment Act gave the President and the Secretary of Agriculture the most comprehensive powers yet granted in time of peace. The Secretary was offered a whole

[57] *Ibid.*, May 13, 1933, pp. 1, 3, 17, and May 14, 1933, p. 14.

cluster of farm relief schemes, any one of which he could enforce or ignore as he saw fit. He could have had others, including the cost-of-production plan, had he wanted them. He had power to raise and lower processing taxes, to make regulations with the force of law, to adjudicate appeals from his own decisions, to raise tariffs, to regulate the planting, harvesting, and marketing of commodities through contracts and agreements, to hire and fire employees at will, and to spend money earmarked for his use without regard to budgets or appropriations. To say the Secretary was made the "Czar of Agriculture" is to take only a little literary license. It is difficult to escape the conclusion that Congress handed over these great powers because it did not know what else to do.

Throughout the writing, consideration, and passage of the Agricultural Adjustment Act the consequences for millions of tenant farmers and sharecroppers were hardly mentioned. Many hours and thousands of words were used in weighing the probable effects on farmers in general, consumers, processors, manufacturers, and even farmers in the Philippines and Puerto Rico, but little heed was given to the possible tragic results of the bill on the lower classes of farmers. Not a voice was raised to protest that drastic acreage reduction might mean the difference between a bare living and no living at all for marginal and submarginal farmers. No one warned that it would bring the eviction and displacement of thousands of tenant farmers and sharecroppers and the firing of many farm hands. But sharecroppers and hired hands had little representation in the high councils of the Department of Agriculture or, for that matter, in the 73rd Congress. As it turned out, this was the blind side of the Agricultural Adjustment Act.

chapter three

The Cotton Programs

Even while the first draft of the Agricultural Adjustment Act was being prepared, Secretary Wallace and President Roosevelt gave thought to administration of the act. They decided to create a new agency under the Department of Agriculture, to be called the Agricultural Adjustment Administration. The selection of a head for the agency was important. The administrator must be extremely capable, sympathetic with the goals of the law, and acceptable to Congress and farm leaders. Wallace felt the logical choice was George N. Peek,[1] who somewhat reluctantly accepted.[2]

Before assuming responsibility as Administrator, Peek wanted it understood that the power granted to the Secretary of Agricul-

[1] Wallace, *New Frontiers*, pp. 168–169.
[2] Peek, *Diary*, April 5, 1933, and April 7, 1933.

ture by the Adjustment Act should be transferred to him and that he should have free access to the President in disputes.[3] Wallace agreed to delegate responsibility "insofar as that can be done," but he made it clear that he and the Department of Agriculture had final responsibility. He felt that if there was a difference of opinion, he and Peek should go to the President together.[4]

When Peek took over as Administrator on May 15, he began surrounding himself with many of the men who had been with him in the fight for farm parity during the 1920's. To head the Division of Information and Publicity he picked Alfred D. Stedman. Chester C. Davis, his lieutenant in the McNary-Haugen fight, became Chief of the Production Division. Oscar Johnston, a Southern cotton plantation manager, was chosen Head of the Finance Division.[5]

But Peek appears to have had little to say about who headed two other divisions under him. The Consumers' Counsel was largely the creation of Secretary Wallace. One day while walking across a street near the huge South Agriculture Building in Washington, he remarked to Louis Bean, an economic adviser, that along with the attempt to raise agricultural prices someone should look after the interests of the consumer. Bean suggested Frederick Howe, an old-line progressive who had once led a campaign against the high cost of living, and Wallace approved.[6]

Peek also had no part in choosing the General Counsel of AAA. Wallace wanted Jerome Frank, a protégé of Felix Frankfurter, whose appointment was being urged by Rexford Tugwell. But Peek found Frank objectionable because ". . . he had no experience with farm organizations or farmers . . . he had been a city lawyer, and . . . his personality was such as not to inspire the confidence of farm leaders." Peek asked President Roosevelt to have Frank transferred to another department. The President agreed, but Wallace prevailed on both men to let Frank stay. Later, Peek reasoned that Assistant Secretary Rexford Tugwell was behind the desire to keep Frank in AAA.[7]

At a conference on July 17, Wallace and Peek decided that AAA would endeavor to keep its organization small and would

[3] Peek to Wallace, May 12, 1933. Peek Papers.
[4] Wallace to Peek, May 12, 1933. Peek Papers.
[5] Fite, *George N. Peek and the Fight for Farm Parity*, p. 284.
[6] Louis Bean, interview with author, August 10, 1959.
[7] Peek, *Why Quit Our Own*, pp. 21–22.

turn over "duties of a continuing nature" to the Department of Agriculture, particularly those that might go on after AAA went out of existence.[8] The two men had different ideas on the organization of AAA. Wallace wanted a separate division for each commodity which would handle both production and marketing problems with production clearly being the paramount concern. Peek placed faith in marketing agreements to accomplish the goals of the act; so he proposed two sets of commodity sections, one to handle marketing and the other production. The two men took their problems to President Roosevelt, who resolved the question in favor of Peek.[9] This created a situation where two sets of workers, each responsible to different chiefs, worked on wheat, cotton, and corn-hogs. In the course of practical operation, it became apparent that marketing agreements were effective in raising prices only for a limited number of commodities, namely, dairy products and fruits and vegetables. In the other commodities there seemed little use of separate divisions to handle marketing, and these marketing divisions were eventually abolished.[10]

Secretary Wallace felt that some of the old war horses of the farm movement now in AAA, such as Peek, Brand, and Davis, would have to "modify" their long-held ideas to fit the world situation. Peek and Brand, for instance, would have to change their views concerning the need for export sales at less than domestic prices, or "dumping." [11] But George Peek had no intention of changing his views. Soon after he took over as Administrator he issued a crisp statement of policy which said: "The sole aim and object of this Act is to raise farm prices." During his seven months in office he never deviated from this restricted concept of AAA which conflicted sharply with that of Wallace and Tugwell that AAA was the agricultural phase of a planned economy. Mistrusting the "planners" in the Legal Division, of which there were many, Peek arranged that his own salary be paid to Frederick Lee, who would serve as his personal legal aide.[12]

AAA worked closely with already existing agencies in the

[8] Record of Council Meeting, July 17, 1933. Peek Papers.
[9] As indicated by Table 1.
[10] Nourse, Davis, and Black, *Three Years of AAA*, pp. 51–57.
[11] Wallace, *New Frontiers*, pp. 168–169.
[12] Lord, *The Wallaces of Iowa*, pp. 342–345.

Department of Agriculture. The Bureau of Agricultural Economics, which for years had been aiding agriculture through research and education, provided AAA with statistical information. The technical bureaus of the Department such as Plant Industry, Animal Industry, and the Division of Crop and Livestock Estimates supplied their records and expert knowledge. For help in field work, AAA sought the assistance of the Extension Service, especially the county agents and teachers of vocational agriculture.[13]

Wallace was determined not to build up a bureaucracy. His decision to use county agents as local administrators reflects this determination. Also, in keeping with M. L. Wilson's [14] ideas of democratic local control, Wallace decided to leave many decisions to county associations of farmers organized for the purpose. State committees made up mostly of AAA or Extension Service employees would form the link between the county associations and Washington. Wallace hoped the county associations would become forums where farmers could express their desires which would be transformed into programs in Washington. This plan worked to some extent with the farmers of the Midwest, but Southern cotton farmers showed little initiative in planning their own programs.[15]

Theoretically, the centerpiece of the entire administrative system was the county association. When a grower signed a production control contract, he automatically became a member of his county association. These associations were organized with a board of directors, president, vice president, secretary, and treasurer. Often the important post of secretary was held by the county agent. In some counties, the agents serving merely as sources of information and advice. In other counties, the local organizations were so apathetic that the agents became the administrators.[16]

The job of the county association was to supervise production

[13] Nourse, Davis, and Black, *Three Years of AAA*, pp. 51–54.
[14] M. L. Wilson was a former Montana State College professor who served during the 1920's as head of the Division of Farm Management in the Department of Agriculture. With John D. Black and Beardsley Ruml he formulated the domestic allotment plan before the crash of 1929. Schlesinger, *Coming of the New Deal*, p. 36.
[15] Nourse, Davis, and Black, *Three Years of AAA*, pp. 68–75.
[16] *Ibid.*, pp. 68–78.

TABLE 1

FIRST ORGANIZATION OF AAA

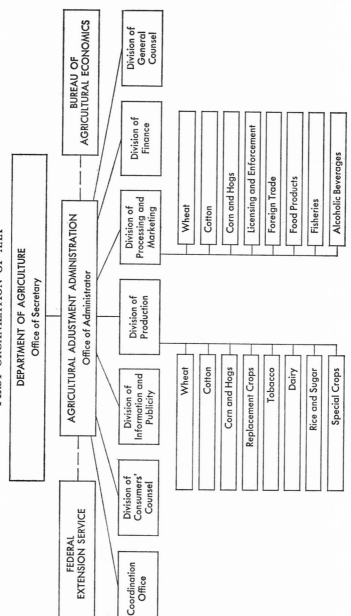

control. This responsibility was delegated to an allotment committee, usually called the county committee. The members were either chosen by the county agent, or elected by the board of directors or the association members. The committee's first task was to check data concerning past production submitted by farmers in applying for contracts. Later, it was charged with seeing that acreage reduction was carried out and with making adjustments in acreage allotments. In most agricultural areas, three-man community committees were set up to break down acreage allotments and check compliance. The various committeemen received per diem for their services.[17] Farmers could complain about any inequities arising out of the program to their community or county committee and could appeal to state boards of review created for that purpose.[18]

But AAA did not leave the checking or compliance solely to county and community committees. The Commodities Division in Washington chose supervisors of compliance from a list of nominees submitted by the county committees. The supervisor's job was to visit every contract farm to determine that the terms had been carried out. They had to certify compliance before the county committee could clear the contract for payments of benefits from Washington. They were paid by the committees out of funds allotted to them for benefit payments; however, they were not under control of the local committees and reported directly to Washington.[19]

The days and nights of late spring and early summer, 1933, were hectic ones in the Department of Agriculture. The halls of the huge USDA building on the south side of the Mall in Washington were crowded with farmers, processors, distributors, manufacturers and representatives of cooperatives, each wanting immediate benefits for his own particular interest. While the lawyers were drawing up marketing agreements for the milk sheds of the larger cities, the Wheat and Cotton Sections were planning their programs and the higher-ups were putting the finishing touches on the organizational structure of AAA.[20]

It was late spring before AAA had formulated its acreage re-

[17] USDA Form Cotton 4, December 18, 1933, NA, RG 145.
[18] Cully Cobb to Senator Joseph Robinson, April 29, 1935, NA, RG 145.
[19] Nourse, Davis, and Black, *Three Years of AAA*, pp. 68–77.
[20] Wallace, *New Frontiers*, p. 172.

duction programs for the major commodities.[21] By that time the cotton had been planted and was beginning to sprout. The situation looked desperate with 13 million bales—three years' supply —already on hand. In 1932, cotton had dipped to a pathetic price of five cents per pound or about half of parity, and prospects were even worse for 1933 if something was not done. For several weeks Wallace and his advisers were led astray by a few experienced cotton traders who liked cheap cotton because it improved their positions on the international market, but when Wallace realized these traders had only selfish interests he worked out an effective, if drastic, course of action.

The plan was simple. The AAA would pay farmers to plow under 10 million acres of cotton, a fourth of the crop, so that the market would be less glutted at the end of 1933. Growers would be induced to plow up by benefit payments sufficiently large to be attractive. The money for these payments would come from the processing tax on cotton. The big question was whether farmers could be induced to plow under their own cotton. The agricultural leaders knew they had at least one factor working in their favor—the threat of five-cent cotton in 1933 if acreage were not reduced.[22]

There were some cogent arguments against the cotton plow-up presented at the time the proposal was made. One was the obvious fact that if a fourth of the crop were destroyed, approximately one-fourth less labor would be needed to cultivate and harvest what was left, and one-fourth less ginning would be done. The whole cotton economy would be operating at only three-fourths of capacity. Reports from county agents indicated that landlords were worried about being able to keep their tenants if acreage were reduced.[23] The leaders of AAA took this into consideration, but they were so anxious to get some kind of cotton program under way, and they were so dedicated to the idea of increasing prices through enforced scarcity, that they went ahead with their plans.[24]

[21] *Ibid.*, p. 172.
[22] *Ibid.*, pp. 172–173.
[23] A. L. Schoffner to C. B. Schwab, May 26, 1933, File 31, NA, RG 145.
[24] Henry I. Richards, *Cotton Under the Agricultural Adjustment Act* (Washington: The Brookings Institution, 1934), and Calvin Hoover, "Human Problems in Acreage Reduction in the South," hereinafter cited as "Hoover Report," Landlord-Tenant File, NA, RG 145, pp. 17–19.

The next problem was to work out the details of the plow-up. How would the arrangements be made with farmers? How would they be paid for plowing their cotton? How would their compliance be checked? Part of the procedure for payment had been provided by Congress. The Agricultural Adjustment Act included some special provisions concerning cotton. Because of the operation of the Farm Board and the Cotton Stabilization Corporation, the government already had on hand millions of bales of cotton which the Act transferred to the control of the Secretary of Agriculture. The Act authorized the Secretary to offer to sell this cotton to cotton farmers at a very low price in return for reducing their cotton acreage. For every pound of cotton a producer agreed by contract not to produce, the government could sell him a pound of surplus cotton. The producer signing such a contract had the option of buying the cotton any time before January 1, 1934, at the average price paid by the government or of allowing the government to sell the cotton for him, in which case he would receive only the profit from the sale. The producer was not liable for any loss if the sale price was less than the average price paid by the government.[25]

How could cotton farmers benefit by having an option to buy cotton from the government? The entire plan was predicated on the economy of scarcity. If the 1933 crop was appreciably reduced, the price of cotton would rise. Cotton farmers could buy government cotton at less than what it would have cost them to raise it, and sell at the higher prices brought about by enforced scarcity. In addition to the cotton option plan, the leaders of AAA decided to offer payment in cash to the farmers who signed plow-up contracts if they preferred it.[26] AAA set the benefit payments for destruction of the cotton at $7 to $20 an acre, depending on the average yield of acres destroyed. If the farmer elected to be paid in cotton options, he received from $6 to $12 in cash per acre plus an option to buy an amount of cotton equal to that destroyed at six cents per pound. The government agreed to sell the option cotton for the farmer at any date designated by him and to turn over to him all money received in excess of six cents per pound plus administrative costs. These transactions were handled by an organization under control of

[25] U.S., *Statutes at Large*, XLVIII, Part I, 33–34.
[26] Johnston, Memo to Mr. Cobb, August 20, 1933, NA, RG 145.

AAA called the Cotton Pool. The head of this agency, a Mississippi planter named Oscar Johnston, was active in formulating cotton policies within AAA.

Those farmers who were willing to agree to reduce acreage signed an "Offer to Enter into Cotton Option-Benefit or Benefit Contracts." They were told that "only if a large majority of cotton farmers agree to help can the plan be carried out." [27] The leaders of AAA felt that farmers would have to agree to destroy at least 3,500,000 bales for the program to be effective.[28]

The way the cotton program was set up, the producer would save the work and expense of harvesting, ginning, and marketing the cotton on his "contracted acres," but he would lose the income from the cottonseed. Wallace, Davis, Peek, Cobb, and Johnston saw it as an advantage that the labor costs of contract signers would be reduced, and although it occurred to them that this might work a severe hardship on farm workers, they did not allow it to affect their plans. They decided, however, not to let any farmer reduce his acreage more than 50 per cent in order that the effect on his farm workers would not be completely disastrous.[29]

Of the two plans for payment for acreage reduction, the cotton option plan was a far better deal for the producer if he did not need all of the money immediately. Producers with tenants were in a favorable position to take advantage of the option plan because they needed no large outlay of cash to get their crop harvested, this being the responsibility of their tenants.

The Cotton Section of the Commodities Division of AAA had charge of planning and implementing the cotton plow-up. Head of the section was Cully Cobb, former editor of the *Southern Ruralist* published in Atlanta, and onetime Assistant Director of Extension in Mississippi. Cobb came from a Tennessee farm family and was educated at Mississippi A. and M. College, now Mississippi State University. He was a capable administrator, familiar with the Southern scene and not anxious to reform it radically.[30] His two assistants, E. A. Miller and W. B. Camp, were of the same type, with Southern agricultural college extension

[27] Richards, *Cotton Under AAA*, pp. 1–6.
[28] *Yearbook of Agriculture, 1934* (Washington, 1934), p. 29.
[29] Cobb, Memo to Chester Davis, November 15, 1933, NA, RG 145.
[30] Cobb to author, June 13, 1961.

service backgrounds. Cobb also brought five regional consultants from various parts of the Cotton Belt into the section to advise in the processing of the cotton contracts.

A Rental and Benefits Audit Unit was organized in AAA to handle, analyze, check and tabulate the contracts received in all the commodity programs.[31] This unit grew to such proportions that it employed as many as 3,000 people. Since it was housed in one big building, it was often called "the factory." [32] The state extension offices, county agents, and county and community committees rounded out the organizational structure set up to administer the cotton program.[33]

The first sign-up campaign began in mid-June, 1933. George Peek spoke over the Columbia Broadcasting System to explain the plow-up.[34] In addition to the 733 county agents in cotton producing counties, 247 emergency agents and 22,000 volunteer workers participated in the huge task of explaining and negotiating the acreage reduction contracts. Governors of cotton states proclaimed a "Cotton Week." The program was explained in newspapers and at county and community meetings. President Roosevelt said in a press release, "every cotton grower should go along . . . for the benefit of the whole country . . . [and] to reduce an over-supply of cotton and thereby obtain a better price for what he grows." [35]

Farmers who signed the contracts, or "offers" as they were called before they were approved by AAA, estimated their 1933 production and offered to plow under part of it. One member of each local committee was required to inspect each farm and estimate the yield. If he and the farmer could agree on the probable yield, both signed the contract offer. The papers were then reviewed by the county committee, although many committees let the county agent or clerks handle this. The approved contracts were signed by the county agent and forwarded to Washington.[36] By July 19, Administrator Peek was able to pronounce the sign-up a success. He told a national radio

---

[31] Cotton Section, File No. 31, NA, RG 145.
[32] Nourse, Davis, and Black, *Three Years of AAA*, pp. 59–60.
[33] See Table 2.
[34] Radio remarks of George N. Peek, CBS, June 19, 1933, Peek Papers.
[35] Richards, *Cotton Under AAA*, pp. 18–20.
[36] *Ibid.*, pp. 17–28.

audience that the nation's farmers had taken a long step on the trail to "practical and sensible planning for agriculture." [37]

In Washington, the Cotton Section carefully examined the offers, especially the reasonableness of yield estimates, and the large offers. Most of them were accepted, although many had to be returned first for more information.[38] Altogether, AAA made 1,030,433 contracts which removed 10,487,991 acres from production with an estimated yield of 4,489,467 bales. Counting both cash payments and advances on cotton options, AAA paid out $161,771,697 to farmers for the plow-up.[39]

The wide acceptance of the cotton plow-up by farmers and the general public was a tribute to the adaptability of Americans and their faith in the New Deal. When farmers first heard of the program their reaction was sheer amazement, but after it was fully explained they found it attractive. It guaranteed at least six cents a pound for cotton that would not have to be harvested, and it offered opportunity for considerable profit through the option plan, depending on how much cotton prices rose. To the big planters and landowners the idea was particularly appealing because all the payments would be made to them and they could collect on debts from their tenants before giving them their share of the benefits.

But to the simple minds of tenant farmers, there seemed something basically wrong with plowing under cotton. One Georgia planter took his tenants out late in the summer of 1933 to mark off the acreage to be plowed. The tenants helped him silently, and when he left they sought the shade of a Chinaberry tree. One of them said, "You know, I ain't never pulled up no cotton stalks befo', and somehow I don't like the idea." Another groaned, "I been feelin' sorter funeral-like all afternoon." A third relieved the gloom somewhat by saying, "Let's swap work that day; you plow up mine, and I'll plow up yours!" [40]

Publicly, leaders of AAA were enthusiastic about the plow-up, but privately some of them had mixed emotions. The farm-bred Secretary of Agriculture saw the program as an amazing demonstration of what a united people could do when there seemed

[37] Radio remarks of George N. Peek, CBS, July 14, 1933, Peek Papers.
[38] Cotton Section, File No. 31, NA, RG 145.
[39] *Yearbook of Agriculture, 1934*, p. 722.
[40] Raper, *Preface to Peasantry*, pp. 243–246.

TABLE 2

LOCAL, STATE, REGIONAL, AND NATIONAL STRUCTURE OF AAA

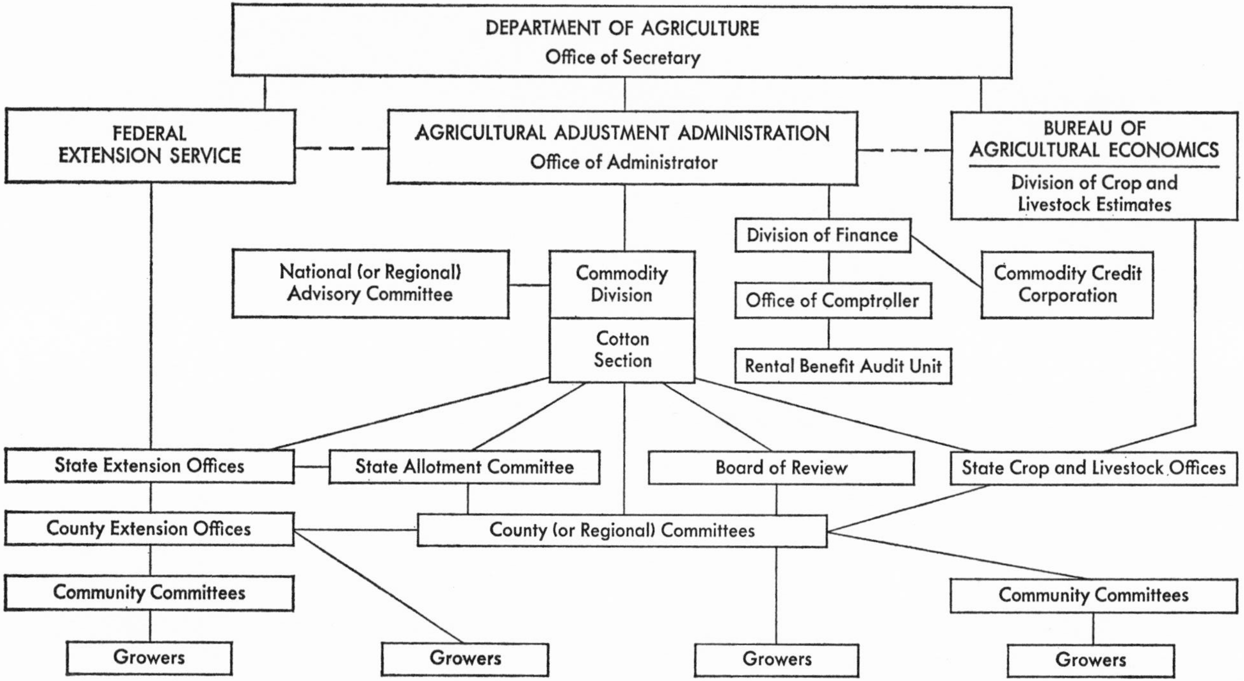

to be no alternative. He consoled himself that the 1933 crop would be worth more, including AAA benefit payments, than the larger 1932 crop; nevertheless, he grieved over the destruction of a growing crop. To him it was a "shocking commentary on our civilization." He could tolerate it only as a cleaning up of the wreckage from the old days of unbalanced production. "Certainly," he wrote later, "none of us ever want to go through a plow-up campaign again, no matter how successful a price-raising method it proved to be." [41]

In truth the plow-up was only moderately successful at raising prices. The average price received by producers of cotton was 6.52 cents per pound in 1932 and 9.72 cents in 1933 (cotton had reached 35.4 cents in 1919). Production in 1933 was 13,047,000 bales, actually slightly greater than the 13,002,000 bales in 1932.[42] Critics of the New Deal have used these statistics to discredit the cotton program, saying that, although farmers plowed under millions of acres, they used more fertilizer on the remaining land and produced as much as ever. This assumption seems unwarranted since the use of fertilizer was only slightly greater in 1933 than in 1932 and not nearly as much as usual.[43] Also, if a farmer used extra amounts of fertilizer on his remaining cotton, he violated the 1933 cotton contract. The reason for the increased cotton production in 1933, despite AAA's efforts, was that 1933 was a better year for cotton than 1932. Production per acre was up even in those areas of Oklahoma and Texas where fertilizer was never used, and it might well have reached 17 million bales, as it did in 1931, without AAA's plow-up.[44] Department of Agriculture economists estimated that the 1933 acreage reduction had added a quarter of a billion dollars to the season's income of cotton growers. They based this estimate on gross income including benefit payments compared to five and one-half cent cotton without the program.[45] Wallace and the AAA chiefs had no illusions about the plow-up. They knew it was only a stopgap measure and that a long range program spanning several years

[41] Wallace, *New Frontiers*, pp. 173–175.
[42] *Yearbook of Agriculture, 1934*, p. 459.
[43] *Yearbook of Agriculture, 1935*, p. 734.
[44] Richards, *Cotton Under AAA*, pp. 64–65.
[45] Peek, "The First Four Months Under the Farm Act," *New York Times*, September 17, 1933. Peek Papers.

would be necessary to adjust cotton production to demand, and to raise prices to parity.

Considering the scope of the plow-up and its radical departure from past policies, the program was remarkably well administered. The county agents and committeemen checked zealously to see that the cotton was plowed under as agreed, and reports of chiseling were scarce. No checks were mailed by AAA until word came from the county committee that the cotton had been destroyed. There was a lag of about one month between the time AAA received the report of compliance and the mailing of the check, and occasionally processing at the local level took considerable time. Thus, it was late September before federal money began to flood into the cotton country. By that time, many farmers had begun to complain about the slowness of payments.[46] Meanwhile, cotton prices peaked at 10.6 cents per pound in July and declined to 8.8 cents in mid-September. Consequently, farmers and politicians grew restless and began bringing pressure for some sort of price-fixing for cotton.[47]

Oscar Johnston, AAA's Director of Finance, suggested that the government loan farmers ten cents a pound on their 1933 crop using the cotton as security. This would allow farmers to hold the cotton off the market until the price rose to ten cents or, if it did not, give the cotton to the government for cancellation of the loan. President Roosevelt, under pressure from the cotton states, ordered Jesse Jones, Chairman of the Reconstruction Finance Corporation, to begin making the loans. Accordingly, Jones set up the Commodity Credit Corporation with Lynn P. Talley, his assistant in RFC, as the Director, and Oscar Johnston as Assistant Director. The CCC loaned about $160 million on 4.3 million bales of 1933 cotton, part of which was option cotton held by 1933 contract signers. This technique of supporting prices proved eminently successful and was soon adopted for other commodities.[48]

The 1933 cotton program was put into effect with such speed that little thought was given to the special problems raised by farm tenancy in the South. AAA's actions toward tenants in 1933 seem to have been dictated by the lack of a clear general tenant

[46] T. Roy Reid to Wallace, January 10, 1934, NA, RG 145.
[47] Richards, *Cotton Under AAA*, pp. 70–71.
[48] *Ibid.*, pp. 94–95; and Schlesinger, *Coming of the New Deal*, p. 61.

policy. With no guide lines, administrators tended to fall easily into the pattern of the Southern tenant system, and the 1933 program served only to perpetuate that evil in all of its forms.

However, the Administration had early warning of the possible consequences of framing a cotton program without giving consideration to tenants. George McClellan, a Washington attorney who had been with the Crop Production Loan Unit of the Farm Board, wrote in April, 1933, to President Roosevelt that in the absence of safeguarding provisions, the Agricultural Adjustment Act would allow landlords to lease their land to the government for a safe and sure rental and leave tens of thousands of tenants and their families to "idleness and beggary." Said McClellan, "No group of Americans are as voiceless and undefended as these small farm tenants." [49] His letter was referred by Louis Howe to Secretary Wallace.[50]

McClellan recommended that cotton contracts contain provisions preventing landlords from decreasing the number of their tenants or increasing the acreage farmed by them, and that violations be punished by withholding rental payments to the landlords. It was important, according to McClellan, that no payment be made before July 15 in order that the government might cancel payments to contract violators.[51]

Wallace referred McClellan's recommendations to Mordecai Ezekiel, who advised the Secretary that there were probably considerable grounds for the lawyer's fears concerning tenants. Ezekiel reported that some Southern farmers had already told him that when they rented part of their land to the government they would readjust by having fewer tenants to handle the remaining acres. Ezekiel commented that this would have "exceedingly unfair consequences." He suggested that the Secretary write McClellan that his point of view would be taken into account in making cotton policies.[52] Paul Appleby, Assistant to the Secretary, wrote a letter to this effect,[53] but unfortunately, most of McClellan's ideas were soon lost in the rush to get the

[49] McClellan to Wallace, April 4, 1933, NA, RG 16. An earlier letter to Roosevelt is described in this letter.
[50] Howe to McClellan, March 22, 1933, NA, RG 16.
[51] McClellan to Wallace, April 4, 1933, NA, RG 16.
[52] Ezekiel, Memo to the Secretary, April 6, 1933, NA, RG 16.
[53] Appleby to McClellan, April 10, 1933, NA, RG 16.

1933 cotton program under way. Some of them were eventually incorporated into the 1934-35 program.

The 1933 cotton contract did not even mention tenants. It required producers to obtain the consent of all "lien holders" and "persons who appear to have an interest in the crop" before agreeing to the plow-up, but it did not specifically take into account tenants and sharecroppers. Following accepted Southern practices, only landowners were allowed to sign the 1933 contracts, but most of them worked out arrangements with their tenants before signing. The Adjustment Administration instructed landlords to divide the payments received for the plow-up among their tenants according to the interest each tenant held in the crop. Thus, a sharecropper was to receive one-half of the payments, a share-tenant two-thirds or three-fourths, and a cash-tenant all.[54]

The idea of making payments to landlords and letting them disburse the money to their tenants originated with the Cotton Section and was approved by Chester Davis as Chief of the Commodities Division, by Peek, and by Wallace. The men of the Cotton Section had intimate knowledge of the tenancy system of the South, and they knew it would be disturbing to the normal workings of the system if the government made payments directly to tenants.[55] In this they were right. The tenants had no legal claim on the crop in most states, and the relationship with their landlord was often paternalistic. Tenants were normally dependent on the landlord in most economic matters, so it seemed only natural to the Cotton Section that the landlords should receive the tenants' share of the benefit payments. In addition, they knew that landlords would resent the government's dealing directly with tenants, especially if such dealings provided the tenants with a separate income which would make them less dependent.[56]

Frankly, the Cotton Section saw things from the landlords' paternalistic point of view.[57] Many landlords, they knew, felt a duty to maintain their tenants even though they were financially unable to do so. A survey of 809 landlords in Alabama showed

[54] USDA, Form No. Cotton 1a, *Cotton Acreage Reduction Contract, 1934–1935*, NA, RG 145.

[55] Cobb, Memo to Mr. Christgau, September 8, 1934, NA, RG 145.

[56] Calvin Hoover, *Hoover Report*, NA, RG 145.

[57] Paul Appleby, Memo to Mr. Cobb, December 27, 1934, NA, RG 145.

that 89 per cent of them felt this way. Like most Southerners, the men of the Cotton Section regarded tenants and croppers as a class apart, incapable of making wise decisions or handling affairs in their own best interests. In the same Alabama study, 40 per cent of the landlords opposed granting relief to tenants because they might learn they were not completely dependent on the landlords and because it might raise their standard of living and improve their bargaining position. The feeling was common among landlords and in the Cotton Section that it would be better not to give the tenants and croppers money since they would only spend it foolishly on things like phonographs and used cars when their families needed the necessities of life.[58]

In their own way, Cully Cobb and others in the Cotton Section were concerned about the welfare of tenants and croppers. When an early proposal was made that the most economical method of reducing cotton acreage would be to reduce the number of tenants and croppers, they objected on the grounds of the obvious disastrous social effects. They felt the tenants would be better off if they stayed on the farm where the landlords would "more or less" take care of them; therefore, they decided to deal primarily with the landlords and let them handle their own tenants fairly, hoping that local public opinion would lend support to the feeling of obligation.[59] This is a curious line of reasoning if one stops to analyze it. If the same idea were followed elsewhere by the federal government, it might have turned relief money over to employers in the hope they would be placed under a moral obligation to give jobs to needy people.

In addition to the reasons already cited for dealing through the landlords, there were administrative factors involved. The Cotton Section was appalled by the prospect of having to process more than a million cotton contracts with landowners. Had contracts been made also with tenants and croppers, the number would have been much higher.

But the most compelling reason for favoring the landlords over the tenants was that unless AAA got the voluntary cooperation of the landlords the cotton program would fail. Chester Davis,

[58] Hoffsommer, "The AAA and the Sharecropper," *Social Forces*, XIII, 497–498; Raper, *Preface to Peasantry*, pp. 157–159; and Cotton Section, "Resume of Tenant Problem," January 9, 1934, NA, RG 145.

[59] Richards, *Cotton Under AAA*, pp. 111–112; and Johnston, Memo to Chester Davis, January 26, 1935, NA, RG 145.

then Head of the Production Division, put it this way: "Our problem . . . was to go the limit in protecting sharecroppers on the land while getting the contract signed. If it wasn't signed, we had no program." [60]

Thus, AAA took a course of action which perpetuated and even strengthened the Southern tenancy system[61] largely because of the exigency of the moment. A program was needed to destroy part of a standing crop. This would be hard enough to sell to the farmers involved without making it more unpalatable by threatening to disturb relations with their tenants.[62] There was probably no course open to AAA but the one it took, for in a program where the benefits went with the land there was little place in the scheme of things for landless farmers.

Much more thought and work concerning tenants went into planning the 1934 cotton program, but by then the die was cast. A large part of the 1934 plan was formulated by Oscar Johnston, who was asked by Peek to take part in the planning conference. Later this seemed a sinister choice to some tenant farmer groups because Johnston was one of the biggest planters in the South. But at the time it was only natural for Peek to choose Johnston in view of his broad experience in cotton. Johnston drafted a preliminary outline of the cotton program which was considered at several high-level conferences and generally accepted. The plan was then presented at three public producers' meetings in Dallas, Atlanta, and Memphis, with Cully Cobb, J. Phil Campbell, and Johnston each presiding over one of these meetings. When the three men returned to Washington reporting general acceptance of the plan, the Cotton Section began a draft of the contract. Alger Hiss, Principal Attorney of the Legal Division, provided legal counsel and Oscar Johnston served as general adviser.[63]

Basically, the idea in 1934 was for the government to rent 15 million acres of cotton land to keep it out of production, which would leave only about 25 million acres in cultivation. The

[60] Davis to author, June 15, 1959; and Calvin Hoover, *Hoover Report,* NA, RG 145, 16.
[61] Committee on Minority Groups in the Economic Recovery, "Foreword" and "Conclusion" of the Rosenwald Study, NA, RG 145, 18.
[62] Calvin Hoover, *Hoover Report,* NA, RG 145, 17.
[63] Memo to Chester Davis (Johnston), January 26, 1935, NA, RG 145.

leaders of AAA also decided that in 1935 they would reduce acreage by 10 million acres and negotiate the 1935 contracts at the same time as those of 1934.[64]

In return for taking his land out of production a farmer received a rental payment based on the average yield of lint cotton computed from figures supplied by the farmer. The rental was three and one-half cents per pound, but could not exceed $18 an acre. In addition, the contract signer received a "parity" payment of "not less than one cent per pound" of the "farm allotment," which was computed by multiplying 40 per cent of the total acreage of the farm times the average yield of the farm in the years 1928–32.[65] Forty per cent was the usual percentage of total production used domestically. This was in keeping with the Adjustment Act, which provided that prices would be artificially raised only on the portion of the crop which was to be consumed at home.

The rental payments were made in two equal installments, the first between March 1 and April 30, just before planting time, and the second between August 1 and September 30, just before harvest. The timing of the payments was devised to reduce the credit needs of cotton farmers. Half of the payment was made before there was any proof that the signer really intended to reduce acreage. This was done in an effort to increase the farmers' purchasing power, but it could create havoc if many farmers decided not to live up to their part of the bargain after they had received half the money.[66] Another weakness of the program was revealed when a landlord refused to deal fairly with his tenants. Although this violated the contract, AAA's severest punishment was to withhold all payments—no great penalty when the landlords had already received half of what was due them.[67]

Any "owner, landlord, cash-tenant or managing share-tenant who operates or controls a cotton farm" could sign a 1934–35 contract if his farm was normally planted in cotton or if he had fulfilled a 1933 contract. A cash-tenant could sign without the owner of the land signing if he could furnish evidence of a lease. The determination of who qualified as a "managing share

[64] USDA, Form Cotton 4, December 18, 1933, NA, RG 145.
[65] USDA, Form No. Cotton 1a, *Cotton Contract*, 1934–1935, NA, RG 145.
[66] Richards, *Cotton Under AAA*, pp. 108–109.
[67] Hoover, *Hoover Report*, NA, RG 145.

tenant" was left to the county committees. An owner and any type of tenant could enter a "side agreement" concerning payments if both were willing. This was an important provision because quite often the owner was in a position to pressure his tenants to make such agreements.

The land taken out of production by the contract was called the "rented acres." Each contract signer was given an allotment of acreage which he could rent to the government. The allotment was based on 40 per cent of production in the base period of 1928 to 1932 and was determined by the county committees. However, decisions of the county committee could be appealed to the state committee and ultimately to the Cotton Section of AAA. The rented acres could be used to plant soil-improving or erosion-preventing crops such as peas, clover, vetch or lespedeza, or the soil could lie fallow or be used to grow food or feed crops for consumption on the farm. The producer could not include waste, gullied, or eroded land in the rented acres. He could not increase the total acreage planted over 1932 and 1933 including rented acres, nor could he increase the acreage planted in any basic commodity or the number of livestock kept for sale or profit.

The contract signer was required to allow any authorized agent of AAA access to his farm and to any records pertaining to the production and sale of cotton and had to expressly waive any right to have such records kept confidential.[68]

The tenant provisions of the 1934–35 contract were the most fateful action taken by AAA concerning tenants. During the planning conferences, the basic question was raised as to whether the contracts should contain any provision for nonmanaging share-tenants and sharecroppers, or whether matters should be left completely to landlords as in 1933. This prompted Cully Cobb to make a series of recommendations concerning landlord-tenant relations which were generally accepted. However, Alger Hiss objected to them, saying they gave inadequate protection to tenants.[69]

Hiss got nowhere with his objections in the planning conference; so he took this problem to his boss, Jerome Frank. He

[68] USDA, Form No. Cotton 1a, *Cotton Contract, 1934–35*, NA, RG 145; and USDA, Form Cotton 4, December 18, 1933, NA, RG 145.
[69] Johnston, Memo to Chester Davis, January 26, 1935, NA, RG 145.

reported to Frank that certain provisions in the contract proposed by Cobb were "not legally enforceable." For instance, Cobb's proposals required landlords to keep the normal number of tenants on the farm in 1934 and 1935 "insofar as possible." Hiss felt this phrase was vague and a matter of opinion left to the landlord which the government could not successfully challenge even in court. In addition, Cobb recommended that a landlord could evict any tenant who became a "nuisance" or a "menace," and again the determination was left to the landlord. Hiss also questioned Cobb's idea of making parity payments to landlords and requiring them to make a "proper distribution thereof" to their tenants. He said it was improper and "contrary to the traditional method of handling government funds" to pay money to one private individual for payment to other private individuals.

To remove some of the defects he found in the proposed contract, Hiss suggested a sentence be inserted to read, "The determination of the Secretary that any . . . violation or misstatement has occurred shall be final and conclusive." This left matters of opinion up to the Secretary; he would have the final say, for instance, on whether a tenant had actually been a "menace" or a "nuisance."

All of Hiss's recommendations, in the form of a legal opinion, were approved by Jerome Frank but disapproved by Chester Davis.[70] Because of the disagreement, Davis called to Washington D. P. Trent of Oklahoma, one of the outstanding state Directors of Extension, to serve as Assistant Director of the Commodities Division. Trent was an expert on tenancy and participated in conferences with Cobb, Davis, Hiss, and Johnston, but still they could not agree. Finally, the matter was submitted to Administrator Peek, who turned it over to his Executive Council made up of the heads of departments. The council settled most points in favor of the Cobb-Johnston position and instructed Alger Hiss to draft tenant provisions for the contract in accordance with their decisions.

When Chester Davis presented the final draft of the contract to George Peek for his approval, he pointed out that a provision in it requiring landlords to keep the normal number of tenants

[70] Hiss, Memo to Mr. Frank, January 26, 1935, NA, RG 145; and Hiss, Legal Memo Re Draft of 11/5/33 of Cotton Contract, November 3, 1933, NA, RG 145.

was not legally enforceable. Also, he recommended adoption of Hiss's suggested sentence which made the Secretary final arbiter in matters of opinion concerning the contract. Peek approved Hiss's sentence, and this might have been a fearful weapon in forcing compliance with the contract had AAA chosen to make it such. Final approval of the contract was made at a conference of Peek, Fred Lee, Cobb, Hiss, Trent, Davis, Frank, and Wallace[71] in October, 1933.

In all of these deliberations, there was no one to represent sharecroppers and tenant farmers. Alger Hiss did what he could to protect them legally, but he had little effect on policy decisions. The ones who won the fight were Cully Cobb, Oscar Johnston, and Chester Davis—practical men whose primary concern was planning an effective program to limit cotton production and raise prices. Cobb and Johnston, because of their background, tended to favor landlords, perhaps unconsciously. It was inconceivable to them that payments should be made directly to sharecroppers and nonmanaging tenants. This would disturb the whole Southern economy. It is little wonder that a citybred, Harvard lawyer like Alger Hiss was able to do no more to protect landless farmers, and that despite his efforts, the 1934–35 contract remained a remarkable piece of pro-landlordism.

Most of the tenant provisions in the contract were found in paragraph 7, which became famous during the next two years.

The producer shall . . . endeavor in good faith to bring about the reduction of acreage contemplated in this contract in such a manner as to cause the least *possible* amount of labor, economic, and social disturbance, and to this end, *insofar as possible,* he shall effect the acreage reduction as near ratable *as practicable* among tenants on this farm; [he] shall, *insofar as possible,* maintain on this farm the normal number of tenants and other employees; [he] shall permit all tenants to continue in the occupancy of their houses on this farm, rent free, for the years of 1934 and 1935, respectively (*unless* any such tenant shall so conduct himself as to become a nuisance or a menace *to the welfare of the producer*); during such years [he] shall afford such tenants or employees, without cost, access to fuel to such woods lands *as he may designate;* [he] shall permit such tenants the use of *an adequate* portion of the rented acres to grow food and feed crops for home consumption and for pasturage for domestically used livestock; and for such use of the rented acres [he] shall permit the *reasonable* use of work animals and equipment in exchange for labor.[72]

[71] Johnston, Memo to Chester Davis, January 26, 1935, NA, RG 145.
[72] USDA, *Cotton Contract, 1934–35,* NA, RG 145. Author's italics.

Obviously, the paragraph was full of good wishes for the tenants, but it was purposely made unenforceable by qualifying phrases. Actually, Oscar Johnston and Cully Cobb did not intend that the paragraph should be enforceable. It's purpose, they felt, was to place a moral obligation on landlords to look after their own tenants and permit them to share in the government benefits.[73]

As in 1933, the contract provided that rental and parity payments would be made only to contract signers, who were to distribute the money among their tenants and croppers on a basis of acreage. The contract specified that this was not intended to establish the right of any tenant to such payment; it was done only to obligate the producer to pay his tenants a "proportionate benefit." At any time within thirty days after distribution of benefit payments, AAA could require a producer to show written receipts for his payments to tenants of money or "supplies and other benefits." In the event a producer refused to make distribution to his tenants or croppers, or refused to show the receipts of such payment, he agreed in the contract to forfeit all payments, and pay the government twice the amount due his tenants and croppers. The idea was that the money would then be paid directly to the tenants and croppers; however, this provision was never enforced.[74]

Following the rule that the benefits went with the land, sharecroppers and nonmanaging share-tenants received none of the rental payments. Cash-tenants got all of the rentals, and managing share-tenants half. Parity payments were divided according to the tenant's share in the crop. Cash-tenants got all, share-tenants, both managing and nonmanaging, received their usual two-thirds or three-fourths, and sharecroppers one-half. The sharecroppers' share also depended on the portion of the farm which they normally farmed.[75]

Thus, the best a sharecropper could hope for was half of the parity payment, or half-a-cent per pound of cotton normally grown for domestic consumption. His landlord got the other half-cent of the parity payment plus a rental of three and one-

[73] Johnston, Memo to Chester Davis, January 26, 1935, NA, RG 145.
[74] R. N. Elliott, Acting Comptroller General of U.S., to Wallace, March 10, 1937, Records of the Solicitor, NA, RG 16.
[75] USDA, Form No. Cotton 1a, *Cotton Contract, 1934–35*, NA, RG 145.

half cents per pound of cotton not grown.[76] As one critic of the
program pointed out, this was "a curious eight to one division." [77]
The overall effect was that a cropper whose landlord did not
reduce acreage got his usual half of the entire crop, but one
whose landlord had a 1934–35 contract got half of 60 per cent
of the crop and one-eighth of the benefit payments on the
remaining 40 per cent. Indeed it was bad news for a tenant
when his landlord signed a cotton contract. Significantly, the
tobacco contracts were more favorable to tenants. Sharecroppers,
for example, got one-half of all payments.[78] Table 3 indicates
statistically the extent to which the cotton contracts favored
the landlord over nonmanaging share-tenants and sharecroppers.

The chiefs of AAA had faith in AAA's voluntary programs to
raise cotton prices in 1934, but many Southern farmers were
resentful of the fact that those farmers who had not voluntarily
reduced acreage in 1933 had benefited handsomely by the
increase in prices. Throughout the South there was sentiment for
some sort of compulsory program, and when indications of this
feeling reached the Department of Agriculture, Secretary Wallace ordered 41,000 questionnaires mailed out to farmers in the
South asking if they favored "compulsory control . . . to compel
all producers to cooperate in the cotton adjustment programs." [79]
The answer was overwhelmingly in favor of compulsion, 95
per cent of the 25,000 replies being affirmative.[80] Later, Senator
Thomas P. Gore, a Democrat from Oklahoma, charged in the
Senate that the questionnaire was rigged, saying that of the
41,000 queries, 21,000 went to people who were in some way
employees of the government and were therefore prejudiced in
favor of compulsion.[81] Actually, Gore was mistaken in his statistics but seemingly correct in his assumptions: all of the 41,000
were in some way employees of the government. One thousand
of them were county agents; 10,000 were county committeemen;

[76] George Bishop to Senator Joseph Robinson, January 10, 1934, NA, RG
145.

[77] Norman Thomas, *Plight of the Sharecropper* (New York: Covici-Friede
Publishers, 1934), p. 30.

[78] Calvin Hoover, *Hoover Report*, NA, RG 145, pp. 6–8.

[79] USDA, "Questionnaire on Cotton Reduction Plans," 1934, NA, RG 145.

[80] Richards, *Cotton Under AAA*, p. 120.

[81] U.S. Senate, *Hearings Before the Senate Agriculture Committee*, "Confirmation of Rexford Tugwell," 73rd Cong., 2nd Sess., 1934, p. 149.

and 30,000 were official crop reporters who received small stipends for reporting crop and climatic conditions.[82]

TABLE 3

HYPOTHETICAL INCOMES (1934)
Landlords and Nonmanaging Share-Tenants (½ Share)

BASIS: 40 acres farmed by one tenant, cotton prices at 6.5 cents per pound in 1932 and 12.6 cents per pound in 1934, taken from the *Yearbook of Agriculture*, 1935, p. 426. Previous and 1934 production of 200 pounds of lint cotton per acre.

ASSUMPTIONS: That without AAA's cotton programs prices would have remained at the 1932 level in 1934.

	Landlord with no Contract but with Prices Raised by AAA Program		With 1934–35 Contract		With no AAA Program	
	Landlord	Tenant	Landlord	Tenant	Landlord	Tenant
Rental Payments (based on 3.5 cents per pound on 40% of acreage)			$112			
Parity Payments (based on 1 cent per pound on 40% of acreage)			$16	$16		
Sale of Cotton (see "Assumptions" above)	$504	$504	$302.40	$302.40	$260	$260
Total Income	$504	$504	$430.40	$318.40	$260	$260

CONCLUSIONS: Tenants' income was increased 22.4%; landlord's income was increased 65.5% by AAA's cotton program. Landlords who did not sign cotton contracts were better off than those who did and their tenants were much better off.

Congress responded to the pressure from the Cotton Belt in April, 1934, by passing the Bankhead Cotton Control Act. The measure provided that if two-thirds of all cotton farmers agreed

[82] Richards, *Cotton Under AAA*, p. 122.

to it in a referendum, a tax of 50 per cent of the average market price would be placed on all cotton ginned by a farmer over his given allotment. In many ways, this idea was the progeny of M. L. Wilson's domestic allotment plan. The Bankhead Act was to apply only to 1934, and for that year the maximum amount of cotton exempt from the tax was fixed by the law at 10 million bales. All farmers were to be sent certificates for the amount of tax-free cotton allotted them. When their cotton was ginned they could present these certificates and get the bale tag, which was required on all cotton bales.

Anticipating that what they were passing might be unconstitutional, Congress inserted in the Bankhead Act a statement that "it is *prima facie* presumed that all cotton and its processed products will move in interstate or foreign commerce." This, Congress hoped, would bring the act clearly under the powers to regulate interstate and foreign commerce granted to Congress by the Constitution.

The act instructed the Secretary of Agriculture to take into account recent droughts and other unusual conditions in computing allotments. Penalty for violation of the act was set at $1,000 or six months in prison, or both. The Secretary was authorized to make regulations necessary to carry out the act, and maximum penalty for violation of these was $200. The act instructed the Secretary to make regulations "protecting the interest of sharecroppers and tenants in the making of allotments and the issuance of tax exemptions certificates." [83]

Using the questionnaire sent to 41,000 people as temporary farmer approval, AAA set the Bankhead plan in motion. By July, 1934, Cully Cobb was able to announce that county committees had been set up throughout the South to decide how much of the county allotment of tax-free cotton would be given to each farmer. These committees had instructions to base their decisions on acreage and previous production. In order to obtain their exemptions, farmers had to apply to their county committee. Landowners, cash tenants, and managing share-tenants who operated a separate farm might submit an application jointly with their landlords, or the committee might allow them to sign separately if the circumstances seemed to warrant.[84]

[83] U.S., *Statutes at Large*, XLVII, Part I, 598–607.
[84] USDA, Press Release, July 17, 1934, NA, RG 145, and Davis to Robinson, August 29, 1935, NA, RG 145.

The allotment for all cotton states, including California and Missouri, was 10,460,251 bales.[85] Most states exceeded their quota in actual production, but the drought-stricken states of Texas, Oklahoma, Louisiana, and Arkansas fell short by almost 1.5 million bales. Although other states exceeded their quotas, the net result was that national production failed to reach the national quota by 745,000 bales. In the drought states, the tax exemptions served as a form of crop insurance, because farmers were able to sell the exemptions they did not need to growers in other parts of the country who did.[86]

The Bankhead controls proved so popular that Congress renewed them for 1935. Perhaps because of criticism of the limited referendum used in 1934, AAA decided this time to submit the matter to all cotton farmers for approval. The voting took place in December, 1934. Not since carpetbag days had so many Negroes voted in the South; said one gray-haired Georgia Negro, "We don't vote much, but we likes to." But still less than half the 2,600,000 eligible cotton farmers participated.

Throughout the South, the pattern in the election was for the landlords to encourage and occasionally threaten their tenants to vote for the controls. In Georgia, planters told their tenants that if the Bankhead plan failed to pass, they would plant no cotton next year. "Nothing could be worse than five- and ten-cent cotton," announced one; "the Bankhead Bill has given us twelve-cent cotton, and the folks working with me had better vote for it." The outcome of the election was ten to one, 1,060,226 to 99,650, in favor of the Bankhead controls. Only Oklahoma and California, of the seventeen cotton states, failed to pass the measure by the desired two-thirds margin.[87]

With the 1934–35 contract, commodity loans, and the Bankhead controls, the pattern of AAA's cotton program during the early New Deal was set. The elements were present for either fair or unfair treatment of sharecroppers and nonmanaging tenants. Much depended on how the programs were administered.

[85] Congress had authorized 10,000,000 bales of 500 pounds each. The average weight of cotton bales was 478 pounds, so AAA converted the original allotment into 478-pound bales.

[86] USDA, *Yearbook of Agriculture, 1935*, p. 696; and Cobb to Robinson, August 26, 1935, NA, RG 145.

[87] *Newsweek*, December 22, 1934, p. 7; Raper, *Preface to Peasantry*, p. 249; and Cobb, Memo to Chester Davis, January 5, 1935, NA, RG 145.

chapter four

AAA's Tenant Problems

By the fall of 1933, hundreds of painfully scrawled letters from tenants were arriving each month in Secretary Wallace's office. Some complained of receiving no payment for the plow-up: "Sire I write you concern of my account and plowing up. I plowed up suppose to bee 13 acrs at $12.75 per acer and ploud up my intire crop so you let me here from you at once so I will no what to do. . . . "[1] Another wrote:

first we will call you attan to crop year 1933 Began of the Reduction By destroying of a said amount of cotton By which plain [plan] would are was Rental acres to u.s. government its splended perpious was to aid the shear croper as well as the landlord.

. . . Mr. James Robb [the landlord] . . . has never give we the agricultural workers of Widner Ars. not one dime of our Rightful Part. and now he is going around this week baging [bragging] and

[1] Robert Allen to H. C. Malcom, December 5, 1933, NA, RG 145.

Perswading and making us sign a Blank Claiming for us to get our mony there are miny Bean forsted to sign some kind Blank is with his saying for us to be Paid for destroying crop of 1933. Mr Wallas without a dout this is true We. are a great number. . . . We can Remember now Mr Robb did Beat and crikle [cripple] and knock and Put on the country [county] farm his labor he run the great farm of Widner. Ark. Called Wheeler.[2]

Still another: "Dear Sir: Is it lawful that Dr. Tailor should buy cotton that hasn't been pledged or appraised, and plow said cotton up and not allow his croppers to plow up because they did not want to take $6 per acre when they were suppose to have one half of said crop. There are 5 croppers here [who] have not been allowed any part of our crop."[3]

One cropper told how his landlord had promised to pay him $17 per acre for the plow-up but was now willing to pay only $12. He said he had plowed under eight acres of cotton and produced six bales plus 600 pounds on his remaining seventeen acres, which the landlord marketed for him. He claimed he had received nothing for his crop and that the landlord refused to settle with him.[4]

Other tenants complained that their settlement for the plow-up had not been fair. A group of Alabama croppers stated: "In 1933 we plowed up our cotton—and on many plantations we received no benefit whatever for this. When payments were allowed us—we were forced to allow it to be applied on our accounts. . . . In many cases we were given credit for one-third of the payments [they were entitled to half]. . . . The plantation owners argued that since we did not have to pick the cotton plowed under we were not entitled to one half. . . . We were cheated on that deal."[5]

From Texas came a report from a man who identified himself only as a homeowner in a small town that landlords were requiring sharecroppers "to make and gather the crop and set aside one fourth of the entire crop to pay loans and taxes." The writer said this practice was "forcing the white tennant [sic] out of homes on the farm."[6] A leader of a tenants' organization sent

[2] Bladning [Sic] to Wallace, April 20, 1935, NA, RG 145.
[3] W. J. Franks to H. C. Malcom, August 14, 1933, NA, RG 145.
[4] Lem Peterson, affidavit taken by H. C. Malcom, November 28, 1933, NA, RG 145.
[5] A. D. Gath, et al., to Wallace, December 12, 1934, NA, RG 145.
[6] H. J. Turner to Wallace, December 26, 1933, NA, RG 145.

a list of sharecroppers who had received no payment and demanded to know, "What is your department doing to try to stop such 'rackets' and give the man who tills the soil a break. These planters are not such big devils that you need be afraid to crack down on them." [7]

There is no accurate way to determine the extent of landlord chiseling in 1933. The Agricultural Adjustment Administration reviewed only 2,759 landlord-tenant complaints in three years,[8] but this means little because the machinery for processing complaints in 1933 was inadequate and many tenants did not understand their rights or were afraid to assert them.

One proven case was the Twist Brothers Plantation of Cross County, Arkansas. The Twists failed to get the consent of their tenants to plow up cotton and made no distribution of payments. After more than a year of investigation, AAA stopped further payments to them until they made proper settlement.[9] Another case was that of E. H. Polk of Phillips County, Arkansas. Before the plow-up, he told all of his sharecroppers that the government was going to pay him $11 per acre to plow up the cotton and agreed to split the money with them if they complied. In reality, Polk had chosen the cotton option plan and the $11 per acre was his initial payment. He received an additional $6 per acre from his option cotton which he did not split with his croppers.[10] It seems likely that many landlords followed the same practice. Also, data gathered by the Arkansas Labor Bureau indicated a large number of landlords took the plow-up money due tenants and applied it on old debts going back as far as 1930.[11]

A tenant was lucky if he received any cash from the 1933 plow-up. The AAA's policy of paying all benefits to landlords allowed them to collect on old debts before settling with tenants. This practice did not violate the 1933 contract; moreover, AAA considered its responsibility to extend no further than to guarantee that the payments were applied to debts.[12] A tenant who received

[7] J. R. Butler to W. B. Camp, August 13, 1935, NA, RG 145.

[8] Cobb, Memo to the Secretary, March 11, 1937, Landlord-Tenant File, NA, RG 145.

[9] Margaret Bennett, Memo to Mr. Frank, December 19, 1934, NA, RG 145.

[10] Chester Davis, Memo to the Secretary, September 27, 1934, NA, RG 145.

[11] W. D. Ezell to T. Roy Reid, December 4, 1934, NA, RG 145.

[12] Calvin Hoover, *Hoover Report*, NA, RG 145.

his share, either in cash or canceled debts, was still worse off than one whose landlord had not signed a 1933 contract. The tenant on a contract farm received three cents a pound for cotton plowed under while the tenant of the noncooperating landlord got five cents if his cotton sold for the average price. Two additional cents a pound may not seem like much, but it made a difference of 40 per cent in a large part of the annual income of the tenant.[13]

The Bankhead cotton control program in 1934 was also open to abuse. The Bankhead Act instructed the Secretary to make provisions "protecting the interest of sharecroppers and tenants," [14] indicating that Congress had become more aware of such problems. The Adjustment Administration complied by setting up regulations that cotton exemption certificates, the forms which allocated to each grower the number of bales he could market free of tax, would be issued to landlords and tenants in the proportion in which they were to share in the crop, and that the tenant's share of exemptions would be computed without regard to current or past debts. However, it was not obligatory that certificates be issued separately. A landlord could get his tenants to sign an agreement making him trustee for the certificates and thus received all of them. This arrangement was obviously put in the regulations to be used on those plantations where the tenants were incapable of handling monetary matters, or where the landlord thought this was the case. Trustees were required to make a "final report and accounting" of their distribution of certificates.[15]

By mid-1934, reports were appearing in newspapers and letters were pouring into AAA's offices in Washington to the effect that landlords were forcing their tenants to sign trustee agreements and then taking all the tax exemptions for themselves.[16] Many tenants believed that since they had not signed cotton contracts in 1934 they were not bound by the Bankhead Act and did not need tax exemptions. For this reason, and because of sheer ignorance,[17] many tenants had not applied for tax exemptions.

[13] Raper, *Preface to Peasantry*, pp. 243–246.
[14] U.S., *Statutes at Large*, XLVIII, Part I, 589, 606.
[15] Chester Davis to Robinson, August 29, 1935, NA, RG 145.
[16] *Chicago Daily News*, October 4, 1934; and H. L. Mitchell to W. B. Camp, August 13, 1934, NA, RG 145.
[17] Alvin Nunnally to Wallace, July 31, 1934, NA, RG 145.

Officers of a tenant organization wrote Cully Cobb that "very few if any" croppers had applied because the croppers had not been informed it was necessary. Whether this was "thru design or ignorance on the part of [AAA's] representatives" the tenant leaders were not prepared to say. They asked Cobb to send someone to explain the law,[18] but he sent only the pertinent regulations.[19]

Under the Bankhead Act, farmers who did not produce their quota of cotton could sell the tax exemptions at four cents per pound to other producers. There were rumors throughout the Cotton Belt that kinship and friendship played an important part when some county committees made the allocations of certificates. To some observers it seemed that those farmers with "connections" did not reach their quotas and sold their exemptions to neighbors who went past theirs. Naturally, few tenants had "connections." [20]

The tenant difficulties under the 1934–35 cotton contract were the most serious encountered by AAA. In the early spring of 1934, D. P. Trent, AAA's troubleshooter in matters of tenancy, feared there would be difficulties under the 1934 contract and decided to take a field trip to make a firsthand check. He drove through eastern Arkansas, where a large part of the trouble under the 1933 contract had originated. He talked with lawyers, businessmen, landlords, and tenants, and asked people at random what they thought of the government's cotton program, and whether they knew of any injustices to tenants or had heard of a tenant's organization. The answers were varied and confusing, but Trent concluded that there must be some fire where there was so much smoke. He returned to Washington, conferred with Cobb and the two decided to seek the advice of the Directors of the Extension Service in Southern states. In writing the directors, Trent said: "I think we all agree that there are a considerable number of tenants who will not receive the benefit payments intended for them unless some definite and prompt action is taken." [21]

[18] Mitchell, Nunnally, and Butler to Cobb, August 15, 1934, NA, RG 145.
[19] Cobb to Mitchell, August 23, 1934, NA, RG 145.
[20] Raper, *Preface to Peasantry*, pp. 243–246.
[21] Trent to Extension Directors of Southern States, April 12, 1934, NA, RG 145.

The advice from the directors was that the AAA should make its intent to protect the rights of tenants perfectly clear to all district and county agents and others who handled tenant matters. Accordingly, Chester Davis sent out a letter in May, 1934, calling on all "who are to assist with the landlord-tenant problem" to be patient and fair-minded and to use good judgment. Davis quoted long passages from the Adjustment Act and pointed out that the Act was designed to benefit all farmers. He stated flatly that this included all classes of tenants. However, he added that the purpose of AAA was to deal with the acute agricultural emergency and not to solve a "deep-seated social problem." The AAA, Davis said, did not intend to interfere in the normal relationship between landlord and tenant, but it was going to make sure that the benefits of the Adjustment Act were received by all farmers in fair and equitable proportion.

Davis instructed that cotton contracts be administered so that all types of tenants would receive the portion of "rental and parity payments specified in the contract," and that no one should be allowed to withhold from tenants what was rightfully theirs or secure for themselves a larger share of the benefits than provided in the contract. "The Agricultural Adjustment Administration," Davis explained, "is obligated to see to it that these programs do not operate to the disadvantage of tenant farmers." He noted that signs were already appearing that landlords were violating the 1934 contract by evicting tenants, converting them from tenants to wage hands, withholding benefit payments from them by various devices, refusing to grant the status of managing share-tenant, and raising rents.[22]

The Administrator decided also to take further precautions. He instructed Trent to set up special machinery to investigate and take action concerning tenant complaints. Trent recruited seven men from the Southern extension services and assigned each to investigate and make adjustments in their states. This group was known as the Adjustment Committee.[23]

Davis' precautions were well-founded. Once the 1934 program was in motion, a veritable deluge of mail hit Washington from both tenants and landlords. One of the most frustrating problems was that of the managing share-tenant. The 1934–35 contract

[22] Chester Davis to District Agents and Others, May 5, 1934, NA, RG 145.
[23] Trent, Memo to Chester Davis, December 28, 1934, NA, RG 145.

defined such a tenant as "one who furnished work stock, equipment and labor and who manages the operation of the farm," but this definition only seemed to add to the confusion. Senator Joseph Robinson called the Cotton Section in Washington to ask what a managing share-tenant was. Nobody in the cotton states, he said, had ever heard of it. George Bishop, a consultant, explained that no one in the Cotton Section knew for sure either, but as near as he could interpret it was "the old third and fourth renter who furnishes [provides for] himself and produces cotton and pays a third of the feed or cash rent for feed and one fourth of the cotton for rent." [24]

So much misunderstanding resulted from the original definition of a managing share-tenant that Administrator Davis was forced to issue a new detailed definition. He said it was a share-tenant who occupied a distinct tract of land which had its own cropping system and was operated independently of any other tract, even if it was part of a larger land holding. Such a tenant directed his own labor "without direct supervision" by the owner. However, for an owner to visit the farm occasionally to give instructions on planting and harvesting did not constitute "direct supervision." [25]

It was a crucial matter whether tenants were managing share-tenants or not. If they were, they could sign a 1934–35 contract and be eligible for rental as well as parity payments. If not, they got only parity payments. Final determination was left to the county committee or occasionally, a field adjustor from AAA. Landlords were extremely reluctant to concede the status because it meant fewer benefits for themselves. They reasoned that no tenant was entitled to a rental payment—rent should go to the owner of the land. This opinion was also shared by the key men in the Cotton Section.[26] The problem was one of semantics. The term "rental" was misleading since the government was not renting the land to use it but to take it out of production. Had it been called a "nonproduction payment" or something like that, the landlords might have resisted paying part of it to their tenants less vigorously.

When Oscar Johnston went to Memphis in December, 1933, to

[24] Bishop to Robinson, January 10, 1934, NA, RG 145.
[25] Chester Davis to District Agents and others, May 5, 1934, NA, RG 145.
[26] Bishop to Robinson, January 10, 1934, NA, RG 145.

explain the 1934 program to producers, he was questioned by landlords who feared they would have to share rental payments with their croppers. Johnston informed them that if a landlord signed a contract at a time when he had no agreements with his tenants, he would not have to share rentals. But if the landlord already had agreements with managing share-tenants, they would be entitled to half of the rental money. The meaning must have been clear to all landlords present that they should sign the 1934–35 contract before making arrangements with their tenants.[27]

An example of other subterfuges used by landlords to avoid granting the status of managing share-tenant was submitted to the Legal Division of AAA. A landlord gave leases which specifically denied a managing share-tenant relationship and stated that the tenant was not entitled to any rental payments.[28] This practice was not uncommon throughout the South.

Because of its importance to the people involved and the difficulty in interpreting the definitions, the determination of who was a managing share-tenant often called for Solomon-like judgment. One field adjustor was so dismayed by a case that he reported: "This seems to be another of those cases where the landlord has not relinquished the authority to manage, but is not very active in his management. Landlord says he manages; tenants say they manage. Take it or leave it. You may be wrong either way you decide." The adjustor finally decided in favor of the landlord on the basis that since he employed a riding boss, all of his tenants could not be managing.[29]

Making rental and parity payments to one million contract signers in 1934 and trying to assure proper settlement with tenants was a big headache for AAA. Simply mailing out that many checks was a problem. Cully Cobb was instrumental in inducing the Treasury Department to allow the use of check-writing machines,[30] and for a time the Rental and Benefits Audit Unit of the Cotton Section had to work in three shifts, twenty-four hours

[27] Johnston, Address at Municipal Auditorium, Memphis, Tennessee, December 11, 1933, NA, RG 145.
[28] Frank to Gatlin, March 22, 1934, NA, RG 145.
[29] Margaret Bennett, Memo to Mr. Frank, Exhibit "B," February 4, 1935, NA, RG 145.
[30] Cobb to author, June 13, 1961.

a day to make the payments without delay.[31] In the Comptroller's "factory," a room half a block long, 1500 employees with hundreds of business machines labored to turn out 80,000 checks per day.[32]

Before any checks were mailed, Chester Davis, following through on his instructions for equitable distribution, called a conference in Washington of Extension Directors and other USDA officials from cotton states to devise a method of assuring compliance with the cotton contracts.[33] The conference decided to require landlords to sign a certificate of compliance with the cotton contract. In advising Secretary Wallace of this action, Chester Davis assured him a "fair distribution" would be made of 1934 benefits. It was decided to mail a form to contract signers which they would fill out and sign, indicating whether they had followed the regulations in distributing payments to tenants. The Legal Division drafted a form, but the Cotton Section objected to its length and wrote a shorter one. After seeing the form proposed by the Cotton Section, Jerome Frank said it would make it "next to impossible" to determine if the landlord had complied with his obligation. Any unfairness by the landlord, said Frank, could be covered up easily because the form lumped together the cash settlement made by the landlord and the cancellation of tenants' "furnish" debts. If landlords used the "furnish" to pay government benefits to their tenants, Frank felt the government had a right to see that fair prices were charged;[34] therefore, he wanted them itemized. Frank ordered Francis Shea, Head of his Opinions Section, to prepare a memorandum stating the legal aspects of forcing compliance with the contract in the distribution of payments to tenants. He told Shea to include a statement about how "we boasted" in the literature put out to explain the cotton program that tenants and croppers would be treated fairly. He also wanted a statement to the effect that action could be taken without going to court against a landlord who canceled old "furnish" debts instead of making cash payments.[35]

The Cotton Section saw things altogether differently. Cully Cobb had made plans to supply landlords with instructions on

[31] E. A. Miller to Rep. Marvin Jones, November 22, 1934, NA, RG 145.
[32] Wallace, *New Frontiers*, pp. 187–188.
[33] USDA, News Release, May 24, 1934, NA, RG 145.
[34] Frank, Memo to Mr. Trent, November 5, 1934, NA, RG 145.
[35] Frank, Memo to Mr. Shea, November 2, 1934, NA, RG 145.

how to distribute parity payments and a standard receipt to be used. Also, the Section told landlords that within thirty days after the receipt of parity payments, they might be required to give a complete accounting of their distribution. The purpose of this was to gain better compliance from landlords. Cobb did not intend to make a blanket demand for accounting and did not plan to have his section audit all accountings made. To do so, he said, would be a "colossal and expensive task." He and his section saw the purpose of the certificate of compliance as providing a basis for investigation in case of disputes. Cobb rejected Frank's idea of having every landlord itemize his distribution. He felt this would result in a "negative reaction" among landlords.[36]

The fight over the certificate of compliance had been simmering for months when Acting Administrator Victor Christgau, whose sentiments lay more with Frank, ordered Cobb to develop a form which would "assure the proper distribution" and yet not be any more complicated than necessary.[37] Accordingly, Cobb had his section draft a new form.[38] When this was submitted to Chester Davis, he turned the matter over to D. P. Trent, Assistant Director of the Commodities Division, for a decision between the Legal Division's long form and the Cotton Section's new short form. Trent knew he held a hot potato, but he was a man with tender conscience concerning tenants. Although the final decision would be made by Davis and Wallace, he knew they would probably follow his recommendations. He also knew that AAA had received "great many criticisms" because the tenants' share of rental payments had been so small. The agency had answered the complaints by saying tenants would receive parity payments later. Trent felt that if AAA did not assure that tenants received their parity payments, there would be "a new flood of criticisms." The cotton contract did not permit a tenant to pledge part of his parity payment to his landlord, but Trent was fully aware that most tenants would use their parity checks to pay what they owed their landlords, and he felt the debts should be paid. But because of the criticism it might bring, Trent believed AAA should not allow landlords to appropriate

[36] Cobb, Memo to Chester Davis, October 26, 1934, NA, RG 145.
[37] Christgau, Memo to Mr. Cobb, November 13, 1934, NA, RG 145.
[38] Cobb, Memo to Chester Davis, October 26, 1934, NA, RG 145.

the tenants' share of parity payments to settle debts without the tenants' consent. Therefore, Trent recommended that landlords be instructed that the purpose of the cotton program was to increase purchasing power to all farmers including tenants, and that landlords were not to apply tenants' parity payments on old debts. Moreover, he argued that payments be applied on current debts only by agreement with the tenants.[39] A statement to this effect appeared later in AAA's instructions to landlords for distribution of parity payments.[40]

In further recommendations, Trent acknowledged Jerome Frank's belief that landlords should be required to give a detailed accounting of their settlement. However, the Cotton Section had improved its short form to the point that Trent thought it was adequate, so he recommended its use. In line with Cully Cobb's reasoning, he agreed that the Legal Division's long form would be difficult to administer and distasteful to landlords.[41] Davis and Wallace approved Trent's recommendations.[42] The Cotton Section won this battle, having surrendered only on the point that tenants would have to agree to applying their parity payments on current debts. And yet Trent had done all he could to help the tenant.

In the certificate of compliance as it was finally sent out, the landlords were required to certify that in keeping with paragraph 7 of the contract they had reduced acreage ratably among tenants, that all tenants had been allowed to continue living in their houses rent-free for the year, that each tenant had been given the use of an adequate portion of the rented acres on which to grow food and feed, and that tenants were permitted reasonable use of work animals to farm the rented acres in exchange for labor. Any exceptions to these provisions were to be noted by the landlord. County committees and supervisors were required to check all phases of compliance and sign the certificate along with the landlord. Cully Cobb remarked with some justice that this was going "about as far as possible in protecting the rights of tenants." [43]

Despite AAA's good intentions, the withholding of tenants'

[39] Trent, Memo to Mr. Bower, November 8, 1934, NA, RG 145.
[40] USDA, Form No. Cotton 35A, November 26, 1934, NA, RG 145.
[41] Trent, Memo to Chester Davis, November 12, 1934, NA, RG 145.
[42] Davis, Memo to the Secretary, November 22, 1934, NA, RG 145.
[43] Cobb, Memo to Chester Davis, January 5, 1935, NA, RG 145.

parity payments by landlords, either in payment of debts or out-and-out cheating, was probably widespread. The unfavorable publicity about this which Trent had feared continued to appear in newspapers and liberal magazines, and AAA took careful note of it.[44] However, reports from tenants that they had been cheated were not always reliable. Few tenants adequately understood what was due them and they tended to be guided by what other tenants got. Some landlords in making their distribution of benefits "ratably" took into account the fertility of land and previous production. Thus one tenant with twenty acres might receive more than another with twenty, and the other tenant might feel cheated.[45] In addition, the benefit checks of tenants who had signed trustee agreements, whether or not they knew what they were signing, were sent to the landlords and could quite properly be applied on current debts. Such tenants might receive no cash from the government and feel that they had been wronged. Often they had no legitimate complaint under AAA's regulations.[46]

In cases where it was proven that a landlord refused to distribute benefit payments, his contract was suspended and no payments were made until he submitted proof of compliance. If the landlord refused to comply, his contract was canceled by the Secretary. However, this worked a hardship on the tenants of that landlord, since their payments were also stopped when the contract was canceled. The Legal Division became concerned with this problem and began trying to get administrative approval for making separate payments to producers who voluntarily reduced their acreage although they had no contract.[47] Approval for this policy was never obtained.

There were many landlords who fully complied with the contract in distributing benefits to tenants. One such was Oscar Johnston, of the Delta and Pine Land Company. Perhaps he was forced to be "more Catholic than the Pope" by his high position in AAA, but Johnston wrote Cully Cobb in 1937 that he had been holding money for three years for some of his tenants who had left without collecting it. He had tried diligently to learn their

[44] Various clippings and extracts, Landlord-Tenant File, NA, RG 145.
[45] W. D. Ezell to T. Roy Reid, December 5, 1934, NA, RG 145.
[46] Reid to Wallace, January 10, 1935, NA, RG 145.
[47] Robert McConnaughey to T. B. Thibodeaux, August 31, 1934, NA, RG 145; and W. T. Watkins to Alger Hiss, April 18, 1934, NA, RG 145.

present addresses but could not. They owed him money and he asked if he could cancel the debts with the money he was holding. Cobb, who was a stickler for rules once they were made, wrote Johnston that he could not.[48]

The everyday routine of processing tenant complaints, and the possibility that some of them were unfounded, seems to have enured some people in AAA to the human tragedy with which they were dealing. But occasionally a letter got out of channels and into a place where it could cause an immediate reaction. Such a letter was received by Jerome Frank from a Negro in Ashdown, Arkansas, who was afraid to sign his name and had mailed it on a train because "they are hard on us about writing Washington, D.C." It said simply: "Please, Sir, fix it so farmers poor people can get the money that is put out, if you will please, Sir, help us. We need clothes. Some need bed clothes and we are hungry." [49]

The problem which proved the greatest thorn in AAA's side was evictions. Paragraph 7 of the 1934–35 contract required the landlord to maintain on his land the normal number of tenants and to permit all tenants to live rent-free in their houses during the two years.[50] And yet it was inherent in cotton acreage reduction that fewer tenants would be needed. During the debates in Congress over the Adjustment Act, Senate Majority Leader Joe Robinson had told his colleagues that landlords could not rid themselves of the cost of production by "turning men out," and he doubted if they would even if they could.[51] Apparently, the senator did not understand Southern landlords as well as he thought. Even before the 1934 contracts were signed, there were numerous evictions. During the season there were others, and after the 1934 crop was in, a great wave of them developed.

The pressures on a landlord were great to discharge some of his tenants. About 40 per cent of his acreage lay fallow, and yet if he kept the same number of tenants his operating expenses for the year would be almost as great. If he evicted tenants he would not have to support them, he would not have to split government benefit money with them, and he could use the rented acres for his own purposes. AAA's rental checks, coming early in the

[48] Cobb to Johnston, March 8, 1937, Landlord-Tenant File, NA, RG 145.
[49] Anonimous [*Sic*] to Jerome Frank, November 23, 1934, NA, RG 145.
[50] USDA, Form No. Cotton 1a, *Cotton Contract, 1934–35*, NA, RG 145.
[51] U.S., *Congressional Record*, 73rd Cong., 1st Sess., 1935, LXXIII, 1237.

season as they did, gave him money with which to hire day workers or wage hands to cultivate and harvest the crop. Such workers had no rights under the contract, so with them the landlord could return to the relation he wanted with his labor, one in which the government did not interfere. Only those landlords who sincerely wished to comply with their contract, who feared to violate it, or who felt a paternalistic responsibility toward their tenants, resisted the temptation to evict. Fortunately, they were in the vast majority.[52]

However, those landlords who made evictions caused great personal tragedy for the tenant families involved. Since fewer tenants were needed throughout the South, there was no place for dispossessed tenants to go but to the road or to the towns and cities to try to get on relief. Travelers in the South saw the homeless families on the rivers in flatboats, in the coves and swamps, on barren hillsides, and on the roads. They were without homes, food, or work, half-clothed and sick of body and soul[53]— the "grapes of wrath" of a government which had not intended to harm them.

In Alabama, 809 landlords were asked why they evicted their tenants who were currently on relief. Twenty-six per cent said that acreage reduction reduced their need for tenants. Eighteen per cent blamed the uncertainty of crop acreage due to the government programs, and over half said they could not afford to "furnish" all their tenants.[54] In Texas, A. B. Cox, Director of the Texas Bureau of Business Research, charged that more than 450,000 people on relief rolls in Texas were there because of the agricultural adjustment programs. C. B. Baldwin, Assistant to the Secretary of Agriculture, challenged him to prove it, and few officials in the USDA or AAA took the charges seriously.[55]

Evictions were worst in the Delta country of Arkansas, Tennessee, and the Missouri "bootheel." A great wave of evictions came after settlement time in the winter of 1934–35. A reporter from the *Southeast Missourian* of Cape Girardeau made a tour of neighboring counties to check on conditions and found highways

---

[52] Hoover, *Hoover Report*, NA, RG 145; and Hoffsommer, "The AAA and the Sharecropper," *Social Forces*, XIII, 500–501.

[53] Kester, *Revolt Among the Sharecroppers*, p. 26.

[54] Hoffsommer, "The AAA and the Sharecropper," pp. 500–501.

[55] Baldwin to Cox, October 26, 1934, NA, RG 16.

"filled with families trying to get somewhere" and with large numbers of women and children who were "most pathetic." He talked to one planter who had laid off three of his five tenants because AAA trimmed his acreage more than he expected, and to another who had to evict sixty-four persons. The reporter was not one to pass judgment on AAA. He said he did not know who would take care of the homeless people, but he urged the citizens of Cape Girardeau "to lend a helping hand to the women and children stranded along the highway without thought of what caused their plight or who should by rights take care of them." [56]

By late 1934 there were several cases in state and federal courts involving tenants who were suing for their rights under the cotton contract.[57] A request from a group of such plaintiffs that AAA enter the case on their side led to a serious crisis inside AAA within a few months. In the meantime, the Cotton Section took the position that there were no more displaced tenants than usual and if there were it was not the fault of the cotton programs since every effort had been made to protect tenants.[58] When a reporter from the *Washington Post* went to the Cotton Section to check on reports of wholesale evictions of tenants because of AAA's programs, Charles Alvord, new Assistant Chief of the section, denied everything. He later reported to Cully Cobb that he had said nothing "other than satisfactory to the Administration." The reporter asked Alvord if complaints from tenants were given any consideration and was told they were when there was evidence of "any injustice." [59]

Another violation of the cotton contract which was common, although perhaps not so serious as evictions, was lowering the status of tenants from share-tenants to croppers or from croppers to day workers. According to Chester Davis, this was "another out" which the landowners had, against which AAA tried to furnish protection. Davis knew that the lot of a day hand on a cotton farm was "far worse than that of a share cropper." [60]

The motivations for landlords to downgrade their tenants were

[56] *Southeast Missourian*, Cape Girardeau, Missouri, undated, winter, 1934. Clipping in Mary Connor Myers File, NA, RG 145.
[57] W. I. Proffer to Mary Connor Myers, February 12, 1935, NA, RG 145.
[58] AAA, Cotton Section, "Resume of Tenant Problem," January 9, 1935, NA, RG 145.
[59] Alvord, Memo to Mr. Cobb, April 7, 1934, NA, RG 145.
[60] Chester Davis to author, June 15, 1959.

about the same as for evictions. They would not have to split rental payments or tax exemptions with share-tenants-made-croppers nor would they have to provide "furnish" or divide parity payments with croppers who had been forced to become day workers. To prevent this, AAA issued an administrative order early in 1934 providing that no contracts would be accepted if it appeared there was a "side agreement" between landlord and tenant which would cause the tenant to turn over his benefit payments to the landlord or would lower the status of the tenant for that purpose.[61]

Despite the efforts of AAA to prevent it, there were many instances where the status of tenants was lowered. The timing of benefit payments had something to do with it. By the end of spring, 1934, every landlord had received half of his rental payment, and by the end of summer the other half. All that remained then was the parity payment which amounted to only about 22 per cent of the total benefits. Thus, before the crop was harvested the landlord had received 78 per cent of what the government intended to pay him. He could violate the contract any way he wanted to and still lose only the remaining 22 per cent. Sometimes, landlords stood to gain more than they could lose by evicting tenants or lowering their status, even if AAA canceled their contracts.[62] In many instances, often in the middle of the growing season, croppers were converted to wage hands merely by the planter sending word that no further credit would be allowed them at the commissary. The tenants were then forced to accept work as day labor or leave the plantation.[63]

The variety of administrative problems which arose under the 1934–35 contract were almost unimaginable. For instance, such a simple matter as renting acres to the government could get extremely complicated. The contract provided that landlords were to allow tenants to use an adequate portion to grow food and feed for their own use. But could the landlord charge share-rent on the food and feed grown? Or conversely, could a tenant grow feed on government acres which he normally grew on the landlord's land, thus depriving the owner of the rental? The answer to both questions was no. Then the matter was raised of

[61] Administrative Rule No. 15, File 119, NA, RG 145.
[62] Richards, *Cotton Under AAA*, pp. 108–109.
[63] Raper, *Preface to Peasantry*, pp. 249–253.

who was to keep weeds out of the rented acres. Here the answer was the tenant who normally farmed it.[64] Next came a suggestion to use the rented acres to grow food for relief purposes. Alger Hiss was given the unenviable task of writing a legal opinion on this, and he decided the acres could not be used for relief purposes since the cotton contract did not specify it. However, he suggested ways around his ruling if the owner of the land were willing. The owner could shift feed crops for nonrented acres to rented acres thus freeing the nonrented acres for relief use, or he could name persons on relief as his tenants thus entitling them to use the rented acres.[65]

Even the most violent critics of AAA's cotton program were willing to admit that its problems were enormous in trying to enforce one million contracts. One such critic, Dr. William Amberson of the University of Tennessee, felt that the worst weakness of the program was the enforcement phase. He charged that the county agents, although technically qualified, were not trained in landlord-tenant affairs and were closely bound to the landlords. He also said AAA could not expect "harassed minor officials inspecting scattered cases on the run" to do a good job.[66]

The standard procedure for a tenant with a complaint was to take it to the county agent or the county committee, depending on which was functioning most effectively in the county. From there the tenant could appeal his case to the State Adjustment Board. If his complaint involved regulations, administrative rulings, or instructions issued by the Secretary, the decision of the State Board was final. If it concerned the provisions of the cotton contract, it could be appealed to the Cotton Section and eventually to the Secretary.[67] Complaints received directly by AAA in Washington were usually referred back to county agents or committees.[68]

However, county committees were notoriously pro-landlord. In fact, they generally consisted of landlords and planters. One group of eighteen tenants in Tennessee wrote the AAA that "the

[64] Jerome Frank, Memo to Mr. Campbell, May 15, 1934, NA, RG 145.

[65] Hiss, Memo to Mr. Frank, and accompanying Legal Opinion, April 18, 1934, NA, RG 145.

[66] William B. Amberson, "New Deal for the Sharecropper," *Nation*, CXL (February 13, 1935), 187.

[67] Cobb to Robinson, April 29, 1935, NA, RG 145.

[68] Cobb to Robinson, February 7, 1934, NA, RG 145.

small landowner and renter has no chance for a fair deal before the community committee, the county agent, or the county committee." [69] Gardner Jackson, an ousted AAA official touring the South in 1935, asked a county agent why no sharecroppers were put on county committees. The agent answered, "Hell! you wouldn't put a chicken on a poultry board, would you?" [70] Carroll Binder, a reporter for the *Chicago Daily News*, returned from the South to report that planters on county committees were "taking care" of themselves and their friends in a manner that would "smell to high heaven before the cotton reduction campaign is over." [71] Indications were rife that M. L. Wilson's and Henry Wallace's dream of enlightened democratic administration of the Adjustment Act at the local level had turned sour in the plantation South.

Criticism of AAA's tenant policies mounted steadily toward the end of 1934. The *Washington Post* carried an editorial in November entitled, "Where Planning has Failed," which was read in AAA offices with great consternation. It pointed out that farm employment was down in 1934 for the first time in twelve years and implied that AAA was to blame. "Officials must have realized," said the *Post*, "when they set out to curtail production that a large number of men would thereby be deprived of employment." The newspaper reported that the Administration had made no plans to provide jobs for the workers displaced by the acreage reduction and commented rather sadly that agricultural planning was evidently easier to discuss than achieve. [72]

A study made by Harold Hoffsommer in Alabama and reported in *Social Forces* concluded that AAA had failed miserably to help sharecroppers and low-class tenants. For instance, of 1,022 tenant families on relief, only 28 per cent had received AAA benefits in 1933. Among a group of sharecroppers questioned in one county, 43 per cent had received benefits; however, three-fourths of them had used the money to pay debts, and 60 per cent of these had been forced to do so by their landlord. [73]

[69] Bert Hodge, *et al.*, to Mary Connor Myers, February 8, 1935, NA, RG 145.

[70] Gardner Jackson, interview with author, July 28, 1959.

[71] *Chicago Daily News*, October 4, 1934.

[72] *Washington Post*, November 18, 1934. Clipping in AAA files, NA, RG 145.

[73] Hoffsommer, "The AAA and the Sharecropper," pp. 498–499.

Perhaps the most vocal critics of AAA were the Socialists. Norman Thomas carried on a personal crusade for Southern tenant farmers which lasted several years. He inspired the organization of a tenants' union in Arkansas, and at the 1934 Convention of the Socialist Party in Detroit, he reported to a special committee on tenancy and promised to raise money to study the problem.[74] Dr. William B. Amberson, a University of Tennessee physiologist, nationally known for his work in attempting to synthesize human blood, was appointed to head the study.[75]

Amberson and the Memphis Chapter of the League for Industrial Democracy together with the Tyronza, Arkansas, Socialist Party conducted a study of 500 Delta tenant families. They found that incomes and living standards were below the subsistence level and that landlords had cheated the tenants in numerous ways under the 1934–35 cotton contract. Their report charged that 15 to 20 per cent of the tenants studied had been driven from the land as a result of AAA's programs. It said that most of them were whites because the planters preferred to keep the more docile Negro tenants. Those tenants who were allowed to stay were being reduced to wage hands and the whole Southern sharecropping system was in danger of collapse. The Amberson Committee reported that relief administrators had been uniformly helpful to evicted tenants but added that county agents, committeemen, and planters were all "hostile." In summary, it charged that the farmers of AAA had been "exceedingly naive" in thinking they could prevent the displacement of tenants when cotton acreage was reduced.[76] Other criticism came from many quarters, and AAA was becoming more sensitive to it. But in the meantime, additional trouble for AAA and the Administration was brewing in eastern Arkansas.

[74] Thomas, *Plight of the Sharecroppers*, p. 13.
[75] *Time*, March 4, 1935, p. 14.
[76] William B. Amberson, "Report of Survey Made by Memphis Chapter, League for Industrial Democracy and the Tyronza Socialist Party," a part of Norman Thomas, *Plight of the Sharecropper*, pp. 19–25, 33.

chapter five

The Southern Tenant Farmers' Union

The cotton plantations in the Delta country of northeastern Arkansas were relatively new. The area was formerly swampland, having been drained only a few decades earlier, and the plantation owners there were new and more inclined to be profit-minded and less paternalistic than planters in the Old South.[1] Relations between the races were not the same as in a state like Georgia; some of the whites had come from the North or from mountain country in Tennessee or Kentucky, where the attitudes toward Negroes were more liberal. In addition, there was a relatively large and active group of Socialists in northeastern Arkansas. All of these factors furnished a favorable background for the formation of a biracial tenant farmers' organization.[2]

[1] Vance, *Human Factors in Cotton Culture*, pp. 21–22.
[2] H. L. Mitchell, Interview by Oral History Project of Columbia University during 1956 and 1957, p. 53. Hereinafter cited as Mitchell, Oral History Interview.

The people who worked in the cotton fields of northeastern Arkansas were mostly sharecroppers, usually assigned no more than twenty acres.[3] Their work was closely supervised by the planters. Although their living conditions were appalling, they were probably no worse off than thousands of croppers throughout the South. The thing which galvanized them to action was the injustice of one planter, Hiram Norcross. A St. Louis attorney, Norcross borrowed enough money from the bank at Tyronza, Arkansas, to buy Fairview Farms, a 4,500-acre plantation near Tyronza. He was determined to make it pay, which meant he had to exploit his tenants.

Ordinarily, the planters in Arkansas allowed their sharecroppers credit at the commissary on a basis of one dollar a month for each acre farmed. Norcross had his plantation surveyed and found that his commissary was allowing more credit than the plantation had acres. On other plantations it was the custom to grant additional credit to croppers with large families, but Norcross decided to end that practice at Fairview. He issued eviction notices to about forty families who had exceeded their allotted credit.[4] Even some of the other planters in Poinsett County condemned this action as not only harsh but in violation of paragraph 7 of the cotton contract.[5]

Later when the AAA began making parity payments to cotton farmers, Norcross decided that since his sharecroppers were farming less acreage under the cotton contract, they should get less of the parity payment than their rightful one-half.[6] This made his croppers extremely angry, and they began to hold meetings to discuss a means of relief. Other planters said Norcross was a fool to adopt this policy for he could raise prices at the commissary to get the additional money without his sharecroppers knowing it.[7]

Because of their resentment toward Norcross and what he represented, some of the sharecroppers turned for help to two Tyronza businessmen who had always treated them fairly. They

[3] U.S. Bureau of the Census, *Fifteenth Census of the U.S.: 1930, Agriculture*, II, Part 2, "The Southern States" (Washington: U.S. Government Printing Office, 1932), 1154–59, 1168–73. See statistics for Crittenden, St. Francis, Cross, Poinsett, and Mississippi Counties.
[4] C. T. Carpenter to Appleby, November 3, 1934, NA, RG 16.
[5] Mitchell, Oral History Interview, pp. 8, 9, and 12.
[6] C. T. Carpenter to Appleby, November 3, 1934, NA, RG 16.
[7] Mitchell, Oral History Interview, p. 21.

were Clay East, who operated a service station, and H. L. Mitchell, owner of a dry cleaning shop next door. Both were self-converted Socialists; they headed a Socialist-minded group in Tyronza and vicinity that numbered nearly a thousand and carried on extensive educational programs among the share-croppers. East and Mitchell at one time organized local unemployed people in a successful attempt to bring pressure on the Civil Works Administration to provide temporary jobs.[8] In early 1934, they invited Norman Thomas, oft-time candidate of the Socialist Party for President, to come to Tyronza and speak in the high school auditorium. Thomas came and talked with many sharecroppers in the county and later told a packed crowd in the auditorium how conditions among the cotton workers shocked him. He condemned the plantation system and the AAA for perpetuating it. He charged that the AAA was not enforcing its cotton contracts and had done nothing to aid tenants and sharecroppers. The audience, both planters and croppers, were astounded to hear anyone speak so bluntly about the plantation system.[9] Thomas later repeated his charges to reporters of the national press services, and the story appeared in newspapers throughout the country.[10]

While Thomas was having dinner at Clay East's house, Mitchell and East told him of their single venture in politics. They had attempted to run for local office as Socialists only to be ruled off the ballot on a trumped-up technicality. Thomas advised them politics was not in the cards for Arkansas Socialists and, according to Mitchell, said they should direct their efforts toward organizing a sharecroppers' labor union.[11] Later, Thomas denied being the sole originator of the idea. He wrote: "I was one of a group to whom the idea occurred practically simultaneously, and the most important figure in the group was the resident of Arkansas, H. L. Mitchell. . . ."[12]

In July, 1934, eighteen sharecroppers, eleven whites and seven Negroes, met at a dingy little schoolhouse called "Sunnyside" on Norcross' Fairview Plantation. They invited East and Mitchell to attend, but before the two arrived they began discussing what

[8] Kester, *Revolt Among the Sharecroppers*, pp. 56–57.
[9] Mitchell, Oral History Interview, pp. 20–21.
[10] *New York Times*, March 11, 1934, Sec. II, p. 2.
[11] Mitchell, Oral History Interview, pp. 20–21.
[12] Norman Thomas to author, June 6, 1960.

should be done about Norcross and other planters. There was wild talk of lynching, but Alvin Nunnally, who had been a member of the Farmers' Union, said if they committed any violence someone would go to the penitentiary or the electric chair. When East and Mitchell arrived, they suggested the group form a labor union. The eighteen approved the idea by a voice vote.

The next question was whether there would be two unions, one for blacks and one for whites, or one for both. An aged Negro was there who once had been a member of the Colored Tenants Union which was broken up by the Elaine Massacre in 1919. "There ain't but one way for us . . . and that's to get together and stay together," he observed. Others agreed that the planters had often been able to play white and Negro tenants against each other, and it was obvious that the Negroes would be in great danger from the planters if they attempted to form a union with no whites in it. It was decided to make the union for all races.[13]

The first chairman of the union was Alvin Nunnally. C. H. Smith, a Negro minister and sharecropper, was chosen vice-chairman. The secretary was an expatriated Englishman named H. J. Panes, who worked as bookkeeper and sharecropper on the Norcross Plantation.[14] No name was chosen for the organization at the first meeting. The one adopted later, "The Southern Tenant Farmers' Union," was the idea of Charles McCoy, an old-time Socialist who became a STFU organizer. He avoided the use of the word "sharecropper" because there was already a union by that name in Alabama.

"Uncle Charley" McCoy was typical of the leadership of the union, although he was about as atypical of Arkansas as a man could be. An Irish immigrant with no formal education, he became a skilled millwright in the Singer Sewing Machine Plant at Truman, Arkansas. His wife taught him to read because of his interest in the *Socialist Appeal*, a newspaper published in Girard, Kansas. Once he could read, McCoy became addicted to radical books, newspapers, and pamphlets.

During World War I, McCoy helped organize a union of Singer employees affiliated with the American Federation of

[13] Kester, *Revolt Among the Sharecroppers*, pp. 56–57.
[14] Mitchell, Oral History Interview, pp. 22–23.

Labor. He became leader of a long and bitter strike which the union lost. As a result, he was blacklisted and could never work again at his trade. The town of Truman had no sewage system, so "Uncle Charley" made a living cleaning outhouses and using the "night soil" for fertilizer on his five-acre farm, which became very productive. He organized a group of Socialists in Truman and helped many of his "comrades" through the lean years of the depression. Any Socialist candidate on the ballot at Truman was sure of at least 200 votes.[15]

One prime reason for the formation of the Southern Tenant Farmers' Union was to give the sharecroppers and tenants some bargaining power with the planters. But of equal importance was the desire to get AAA to stop evictions and guarantee tenants their rights under paragraph 7 of the cotton contract.[16] Howard Kester, who later became a key leader of the union, stated in 1936 that the rising consciousness of the sharecroppers was due in large measure to the "stupidity and viciousness" of AAA policies toward tenants. He wrote: "This was too much for even an humble sharecropper to understand and swallow without protest." [17]

At the end of the 1934 season, Hiram Norcross evicted more sharecroppers. On December 21, the STFU brought suit against Norcross on behalf of twenty-four tenants. The case, known as *West et al. vs. Norcross*, was heard in the Poinsett County Court and finally in the Supreme Court of Arkansas. The plaintiffs asked that Norcross be restrained from evicting them and that they be given access to woods for fuel and rented acres to grow food under the terms of paragraph 7 of the cotton contract.

In evicting the croppers, Norcross made the apparent mistake of giving notice in writing. One communication read:

Having no use for your services next year, we do hereby notify you to vacate and deliver possession of the house you now occupy to us together with all our property, real, personal and mixed, at the expiration of your present contract, to wit—not later than December 31, 1934.

Tyronza, Arkansas   FAIRVIEW FARMS
October 9, 1934   H. Norcross, President
                                     (signed)

[15] *Ibid.*, p. 28.
[16] H. L. Mitchell, interview with author, July 28, 1959.
[17] Kester, *Revolt Among the Sharecroppers,* p. 53.

In another written notice, Norcross told those evicted that their parity payments would be given to them on the day they vacated. If they did not leave by the appointed day, he warned that any expense incurred in bringing eviction would be deducted from their parity payments.[18]

In the trials, the evicted croppers claimed they had applied to the county committee and county agent for help, but to no avail. They said they were evicted because they were members of the STFU and asked that Norcross be restrained from discriminating against union members. They also asked that the landlord be enjoined from compelling tenants to sign any contract or stipulation whereby they waived their rights under paragraph 7.[19]

West vs. Norcross attracted considerable attention in the Delta country, and when he learned of it, AAA's Legal Counsel, Jerome Frank, seriously considered entering the case on the side of the tenants. This led to a series of important events in Washington which will be discussed later. In late December, Henry Wallace received a letter from Edward J. Meeman, Editor of the *Memphis Press-Scimitar,* which said that the case of Norcross' tenants was "additional evidence of the tragedy which has been the unintended result of the acreage reduction program." Meeman felt that planters who were willing to share the risks of growing cotton with sharecroppers did not want to share guaranteed income from the federal government.[20]

The union lost the case against Norcross. The Arkansas Supreme Court ruled that sharecroppers, not being parties to the cotton contract, had no rights to bring suit under its provisions.[21] This was a great disappointment to STFU leaders who had hoped for victory, especially if the federal government decided to intervene; however, the loss of the case tended to strengthen the union because the sharecroppers were forced to turn to it when they saw they could expect little from the courts.[22]

At first, Clay East and H. L. Mitchell felt that the sharecroppers could assume leadership in building the union, but they soon found themselves organizing new locals. They would load their cars with members and drive to some plantation school or

[18] C. T. Carpenter to Appleby, November 3, 1934, NA, RG 16.
[19] *Memphis Press-Scimitar,* December 21, 1934.
[20] Meeman to Wallace, December 24, 1934, NA, RG 16.
[21] 80 (2d) *Southwestern Reporter* (1935), pp. 67–70.
[22] Mitchell, Oral History Interview, p. 30.

church where a meeting had been called. The mere announcement of a meeting was enough to bring hundreds of sharecroppers, and most of them joined the union. The dues were only one dollar per year or ten cents per month, but those who could not pay were allowed to join also.[23]

To help organize the union, East ran for township constable at Tyronza and was elected. As constable, he was entitled to wear a badge and a gun. The sharecroppers, particularly the Negroes, now felt less fearful about joining the union because "Mr. Clay" was "the law." As the union gained membership, East and Mitchell decided to incorporate it under a state law which authorized charters to benevolent organizations. They wrote a rough draft and took it to Dr. William Amberson, a leading Socialist and friend of the union in Memphis. Amberson looked over the draft and said, according to Mitchell: "Why, boys, you're trying to have the Socialist revolution incorporated, and that can't be done." They toned down the document considerably, submitted it to the proper state authorities, and received a charter.[24]

East and Mitchell also wrote a constitution for the union, which provided that any farm worker over eighteen years of age could be a member, if he made his living from "rents, interest, or profits" derived from agriculture. The constitution required every local of the union to have a secretary, an executive committee, a defense committee, a president, and a vice-president. The entire union was to be governed by annual conventions and an executive committee elected by the annual conventions. The executive committee was to consist of seven to seventeen members and to meet every three months. The union officers were a president, a vice-president, and an executive secretary. Conventions were to be held each January after the crops were in, with locals sending delegations according to their size. The executive committee was also to set up a defense committee to lead the fight against the planters.[25]

The first annual convention was held in January, 1935, in front of "Uncle Charley" McCoy's house in Truman. At that time the

[23] *Ibid.*, p. 28.
[24] Mitchell, Oral History Interview, pp. 24–25.
[25] Southern Tenant Farmers' Union, *Proceedings, Third Annual Convention* (Muskogee, Oklahoma: n.p., 1937), pp. 82–84.

constitution authored by East and Mitchell was adopted and officers were elected. East became president of the union, E. B. McKinney, a Negro sharecropper, was chosen vice-president, and Mitchell got the job of executive secretary.[26] Soon after, East resigned, saying the president of a sharecroppers' union should be a sharecropper. He was in and out of the union for the next few years, but was usually available for the more dangerous missions into nearby counties. His successor as president was J. R. Butler, a white sharecropper who looked the part. He was tall, thin, with hair that stood straight up, and yet he could talk like a college professor. Butler had been a teacher during World War I and a conscientious objector, but he eventually entered the army rather than go to jail as a war resistor. He was also a doctrinaire Socialist and devoted to the union. E. B. McKinney, the Negro vice-president, was highly respected by union members and leaders, especially Mitchell, who backed him for the office.[27]

The man who did more than any other to hold the STFU together was H. L. Mitchell. As executive secretary, he ran the union from day to day. He was known around Tyronza as a radical and a "Red,"[28] and when he became secretary of the union the ladies of the Missionary Society of the Tyronza Methodist Church organized a boycott of his dry cleaning shop and drove him out of business.[29] He moved to Memphis, set up union headquarters, and lived for the next few years on his savings. For the first two years he received no pay from the union other than a few dollars occasionally to operate his car. In 1937 the annual convention voted him a salary of twenty-five dollars per week, but there was seldom money in the treasury to pay it.[30] The Socialist Party once furnished him a new automobile because Norman Thomas feared for Mitchell's life if his old car broke down some night in Arkansas after a meeting.[31]

[26] STFU, "Proccedings of 1st Annual Convention" (mimeographed copy on file with the Headquarters of the National Agricultural Workers Union, Washington, D. C.), 1935.

[27] Mitchell, Oral History Interview, p. 90.

[28] W. M. Landers (County Agent) to Cully Cobb (Telegram), n.d., NA, RG 145.

[29] Kester, *Revolt Among the Sharecroppers*, p. 66.

[30] STFU, *Proceedings, Third Annual Convention*, pp. 80–81.

[31] Mitchell, Oral History Interview, p. 45.

Mitchell was a sandy-haired young man in his early thirties
of Scotch-Irish descent. His father had been a sharecropper in
Tennessee, and Mitchell tried his hand at making a crop before
deciding to go into business. As a boy he saw a Negro burned
alive on the courthouse lawn at Dyersburg, Tennessee, for in-
sulting a white woman.[32] In his capacity as executive secretary
of the union, Mitchell provided a calm, determined courage
which inspired some and restrained others.[33] In 1936 Mitchell
broke with the Socialist Party because it was trying to run its
own candidates in the South and he felt this was politically fool-
ish. After that, Mitchell considered himself a Democrat.[34]

A surprising number of those who came to help organize and
work for the union were Protestant ministers, both black and
white. One of these was Ward Rodgers, a young Methodist who
was pastor of several rural churches in western Arkansas. He
was a native of Oklahoma and a graduate of Vanderbilt University and a seminary in Boston. When he heard of the STFU,
he left his churches to help in the organizational work. He lived
with Mitchell, but when Mitchell's business failed he was forced
to seek work elsewhere. He applied to the Workers Education
Bureau of the Federal Emergency Relief Administration in Washington and got a job teaching farmers around Tyronza.[35]

Another white preacher of great importance to the union was
Howard Kester. A Southerner, Kester graduated from Princeton
University and Vanderbilt Divinity School. He was an ordained
Methodist minister, but worked for a number of organizations,
including the Fellowship of Reconciliation, a pacifist group
which he served as Southern Secretary. He was once a special
investigator of lynchings for the National Association for the
Advancement of Colored People. Kester was a member of the
Executive Council of the National Socialist Party, and was
friendly with leading Socialists such as Norman Thomas and
Powers Hapgood. He had helped in relief work among striking
coal miners in Tennessee and had a deep understanding of
Southern problems. He knew many people in religious and
liberal organizations throughout the country, and a committee

[32] *Ibid.*, pp. 1–3; and Mitchell, interview with author, July 28, 1959.
[33] Kester, *Revolt Among the Sharecroppers*, p. 66.
[34] Mitchell, Oral History Interview, pp. 90–91.
[35] Kester, *Revolt Among the Sharecroppers*, p. 66.

of such people as Reinhold Niebuhr of Union Theological Seminary and Roger Baldwin, Secretary of the American Civil Liberties Union, supported and financed his activities in the South. Kester once offered to help the STFU if it got in trouble, and in an early crisis Mitchell sought his aid. Kester came and in the years that followed became one of the principal leaders of the union.[36]

A third white preacher and another graduate of Vanderbilt was Claude Williams, Director of Commonwealth College at Mena, Arkansas. He was an ordained Presbyterian minister and, according to H. L. Mitchell, a card-carrying Communist.[37] Williams had been active among the United Mine Workers in western Arkansas and with the unemployed there. In 1935 he was given a ninety-day jail sentence in Fort Smith, Arkansas, after addressing a meeting of striking relief workers. His trial lasted five minutes, and he was convicted of barratry (inciting litigation).[38] Williams started working with the STFU when the union first began to receive national publicity. He became a member of the executive council but was later tried by the council and expelled for taking part in a Communist plot to usurp control of the union.[39]

Many of the Negro organizers and officers of the union were preachers, but most of them were also sharecroppers. The Negro churches of the Cotton Belt could not afford fulltime preachers, so usually one of the members who had "the call" served as pastor. Few had any formal training. Typical of these was A. B. Brookins, the union chaplain and official song leader. Although past seventy, Brookins was once severely beaten by riding bosses and sheriffs' deputies. He told the 1937 convention: "They shot up my house with machine-guns, and they made me run away from where I lived at, but they couldn't make me run away from my Union. . . . When I lived at Marked Tree, Arkansas, the nightriders broke into my house, and they shot a bullet that

[36] Mitchell, Oral History Interview, pp. 40–41.
[37] Mitchell, interview with author, July 29, 1959. Mitchell claims he actually saw Williams' card in 1936 at a union convention.
[38] *New York Times*, February 24, 1935, p. 5.
[39] STFU, *Complete Proceedings, Trial of Claude Williams*, Records of the Headquarters, National Agricultural Workers Union, Washington, D.C. Hereinafter cited as STFU, *Trial of Williams*.

just went through my daughter's hair. But I am not afraid to go on being a union man." [40]

Because so many of the organizers were preachers and because of the nature of the people involved, union meetings took on heavy religious overtones. The songs of the union were much like those of the old camp meetings, and some were Negro spirituals with the words modified. The favorite was "We Shall Not Be Moved"; one refrain went, "Like a tree by the river side, We shall not be moved." This had special significance because of evictions by the planters. There was much praying at union meetings, and the speakers often quoted the Bible. When members were persecuted for being in the union, they often developed a martyrlike feeling. It took courage to join the union and more to stay in it.[41]

In the early days, there was no desire to build anything more than a tenant farmers' union, and there was no idea of spreading any farther than Arkansas. The leaders thought only in terms of dealing with the large planters and helping the sharecroppers get justice from AAA. Said H. L. Mitchell years later: "There were economic conditions that needed solution, but none of us were capable of thinking them through at the time." [42]

Within a few months after it was organized the STFU had around 1,400 members in four or five counties. It was impossible to get an accurate count because locals formed and operated for months before the union leaders learned of them. The Texas newspaper, *Ferguson's Forum,* took note of the formation of the union but held little hope for its success. An editorial expressed the belief that the union would either fall into the hands of labor racketeers or become a "cat's paw" for Communist and Socialist agitators.[43]

The charge was made often, even by AAA and USDA officials, that the STFU was dominated by Communists and Socialists, and there was no attempt by union officers to deny that both types of radicals were prominent in the movement. Howard Kester, himself a Socialist, wrote that the union was proud of the achievements of Socialists and Communists on its behalf, but he denied

[40] STFU, *Proceedings, Third Annual Convention,* p. 43.
[41] Mitchell, interview with author, July 26, 1959.
[42] Mitchell, Oral History Interview, pp. 27–28.
[43] *Ferguson's Forum* (Temple, Texas), August 13, 1934.

the union was "an adjunct or organ of either the Socialist or the Communist Party." Almost anyone who professed sympathy for the working class and volunteered to help organize the union was accepted. As a result, many of the key organizers were Socialists or Communists.[44] Mitchell has said: "For a long time I didn't know the difference between a Communist and a Socialist—just so they were on my side." In his years of working with the union, Mitchell learned that the Communists were on no one's side but their own.[45]

The Socialist Party willingly admitted its support for movements like the STFU. Powers Hapgood, member of the Executive Committee of the National Socialist Party, affirmed this while on a tour of eastern Arkansas addressing union meetings. He also said his party had "declined united action with the Communist Party." [46] Norman Thomas, in a letter to Henry Wallace in 1935, stated that the STFU was an "independent, bona fide union, not controlled by the Socialist Party." Most of its members, said Thomas, were Democrats who could not vote because of the poll tax.[47]

The Communist tactics were to infiltrate the STFU with CP organizers in an attempt to take over and use the union for their own subversive purposes. At first, the legitimate leaders of the union did not realize this, and later they could not rid the union of the influence of Communists and were drawn into two big convention fights with them for control.[48] On one occasion, Harold Ware, the alleged head of "Ware Cell" of Communists in AAA,[49] and his famous mother, "Mother Boor," visited union headquarters and talked to H. L. Mitchell for several hours. According to Mitchell, "the old lady gave all sorts of advice," but there is no indication he took any of it.[50]

At first, the planters of Poinsett County paid little attention to the STFU. Naturally, they wondered why East and Mitchell were organizing the sharecroppers. Some said the two "Reds"

[44] Kester, *Revolt Among the Sharecroppers,* pp. 54–55.
[45] Mitchell, Oral History Interview, p. 62.
[46] *Memphis Press-Scimitar,* February 9, 1935.
[47] Thomas to Wallace, April 16, 1935, NA, RG 145.
[48] STFU, *Trial of Williams.*
[49] Later, before a Congressional committee, Whitaker Chambers accused Alger Hiss of being a member of this group. Hiss was sent to jail by a federal court for perjury when he denied it.
[50] Mitchell, Oral History Interview, p. 64.

had political ambitions, but others pointed out that the Negro sharecroppers could not vote because of state laws and the white croppers had no money to pay the poll tax. As the size of the union meetings grew, the planters became more curious. One planter, H. F. Loan, entered a union meeting at Tyronza accompanied by four of his riding bosses with pistols swinging from their belts. When he was asked to leave, Loan became enraged at such unheard-of treatment. He later attempted unsuccessfully to get the union charter revoked.[51]

Because of its racial policy, the union was completely unacceptable to the planters and townspeople. Where the union tried to organize, the planters fought it by saying to their white tenants, "You don't want to belong to an organization that takes in 'niggers,' " and by telling the Negroes that the union was made up of "poor white trash." In the South, prejudice works both ways, and this was an effective stratagem. In some communities, the union found it necessary to set up two locals for the two races. But often the members of one local attended the meetings of the other, and the two locals eventually merged.

In some locals where the whites took the leadership, the Negroes dropped out. In others the opposite happened. H. L. Mitchell felt that if the union would limit its membership to whites, it could spread quickly throughout the South, but he also knew it would be "a flash in the pan." An exclusively white union, he reasoned, could do nothing for the sharecroppers; the planters would simply replace its members with Negroes and they would lose the fight. Mitchell and other union leaders [52] firmly believed that the hope of the STFU was based on its interracial policy. They knew that other organizations of white or black Southern farmers had flourished for a time and died.[53]

After the planters began to worry about the union, the activities of the organizers were bound to lead to trouble. On one organizing trip into Crittenden County, Ward Rodgers and C. H. Smith,

[51] Kester, *Revolt Among the Sharecroppers*, pp. 59–60.
[52] Claude Williams told the 1937 annual convention, "You must forget the lies that you were taught in school about five races in the world. . . . There is one race, and that is the human race. . . . You have been split in the past, but . . . [now] you must think about the great danger of drifting apart. Your union should be organized with all races." STFU, *Proceedings of the Third Annual Convention*, p. 16.
[53] Mitchell, Oral History Interview, pp. 80–84.

a Negro minister, were arrested near the town of Marion. Smith was put in jail and Rodgers escorted out of the county and told not to come back. Union leaders knew they would need a lawyer to get Smith out of jail, but no local lawyer would accept the case. Mitchell sent a wire to the American Civil Liberties Union in New York requesting the names of lawyers who might serve. The ACLU wired back the names of three Memphis lawyers, and Mitchell and East drove there to contact them. One had moved and another was ill. The only one available was Abe Waldauer, an assistant city attorney. When asked to help, Waldauer gave this memorable reply as quoted from memory by Mitchell: "I greatly admire you fellows; you are real Americans. It takes a lot of intestinal fortitude to undertake what you are trying to accomplish. No one needs help more than those Arkansas sharecroppers, but I served my country on the battlefields of France in the last war. I was with the Lost Battalion in the Argonne Forest, and I left all my courage over there. I'm one Jew who isn't going over in Crittenden County to get a Nigra out of jail because he is charged with organizing a union." The interview ended with Waldauer's explaining the single-tax theory to East and Mitchell and giving them a copy of *Progress and Poverty* by Henry George.[54]

East and Mitchell eventually found a lawyer. He was C. T. Carpenter, who practiced in Marked Tree, not far from Tyronza. Carpenter agreed to take the case without fee as he had a strong conscience on civil rights. He was also a capable lawyer with a distinguished appearance and more than normal courage. When he told East and Mitchell to have all of their sharecroppers gather at the Courthouse at Marion to back his attempts to free Smith, they gladly passed the word. Negro union members were told to stay at home to avoid trouble. At the appointed hour, hundreds of sharecroppers gathered on the courthouse lawn and moved silently behind Carpenter as he entered the building. They filled the halls and offices; and although they were orderly, it was obvious why they were there. Carpenter gained Smith's release, and that night a meeting was called at Sunnyside school to celebrate. Smith, who had been beaten while in jail, showed his battered body and said he was glad to bear this cross for the union.

[54] *Ibid.*, pp. 29–30.

After the freeing of Smith, the planters attempted to prevent further union meetings. They put padlocks on the doors of churches where croppers met and boarded over the windows. They packed schoolhouses with hay. Some union members received threatening letters and others were flogged or evicted from their homes.[55]

When the rumor spread that the planters were buying machine guns, many union members armed themselves with old shotguns. However, they found it difficult to buy shells at local stores. When the croppers began bringing their shotguns to union meetings, union leaders grew fearful that these people who had been oppressed all their lives might rise up in savage fury now that they were organized. The planters were already using brutality and terrorism to try to break the union, and they might go much further. Howard Kester, who attended many union meetings during this period, was convinced that the only reason the planters did not break up the meetings with violence was the presence of women and children.[56]

In the face of these dangers, the union leaders decided to adopt a policy of passive resistance. They asked members to leave their shotguns at home. At every meeting they emphasized that the union must proceed legally and peaceably.[57] Since the usual meeting places were closed, the leaders decided to gather in the open. At such meetings the riding bosses, planters, sheriffs, and deputies often gathered on the fringe of the crowd and amused themselves by shooting into the air. Union leaders had to learn to carry on while bullets whistled overhead and leaves and twigs fell from above. The intruders usually accompanied their fireworks with raucous laughter and profanity.[58]

In December of 1934, four organizers, two white and two colored, were working together in Cross County. One night near Parkin, the county sheriff and a large band of deputies, riding bosses, and planters broke into their meeting and arrested the four. They kicked A. B. Brookins in the face and stomach and kept him in jail until the next day without medical attention although he was permanently injured. Before Carpenter, the

[55] Kester, *Revolt Among the Sharecroppers*, pp. 61–62.
[56] *Ibid.*, p. 61.
[57] Mitchell, interview with author, July 25, 1959.
[58] Kester, *Revolt Among the Sharecroppers*, pp. 62–63.

union attorney, could get to them, the four were tried and convicted of "receiving money under false pretenses and disturbing
labor." Carpenter appealed the cases, bail was set at $500 each,
but the union could not pay. It was forty days before the money
could be raised; meantime, the four remained in jail.[59]

Meanwhile, the leaders of the STFU, working with the Amberson Committee, a group of Socialists in Memphis, compiled a
list of landlords who had violated the cotton contract. While
doing this, Amberson, Mitchell, and East kept up a steady
barrage of letters and telegrams to AAA officials citing violations
and warning of wholesale evictions in eastern Arkansas.[60] When
Cully Cobb received these, he called the county agent in Memphis to find out who the writers were. The agent reported that
Amberson was considered by the Memphis chief of police as a
"full-fledged Communist" who had already made a number of
efforts to start uprisings among the Negroes.[61] From another
county agent, Cobb learned that there was no indication of
wholesale evictions in Poinsett County.[62] Cobb's eventual reply to
Amberson and union leaders was that the government was
limited to enforcement of the cotton contract and that he had no
evidence of evictions in violation of the contract.[63] In the meantime, the *Washington Evening Star* carried a story describing the
letters and telegrams from the union warning of widespread evictions in eastern Arkansas and possible "open rebellion."[64]

Despite the reports from the county agents, Cully Cobb
decided to send his assistant, E. A. Miller, to Arkansas to investigate the charges made by Amberson and his group. After his
first day of investigation, Miller wired Cobb that every planter
should be required to compile a list of his 1933 and 1934 tenants
in order to protect the cotton program from "unfavorable criticism" and to remove the temptation to displace tenants.[65] Miller
toured the troubled area of eastern Arkansas accompanied always
by county agents and committeemen, planters, and reporters. He

[59] *Ibid.*, p. 65.
[60] Amberson, Mitchell, East, *et al.*, Letters and Telegrams, Landlord-
Tenant File, NA, RG 145.
[61] S. M. Landers to Cobb (Telegram), n.d., NA, RG 145.
[62] A. R. Sullivant (County Agent) to Cobb (Telegram), March 12, 1934,
NA, RG 145.
[63] Cobb to Amberson, March, 1934, NA, RG 145.
[64] *Washington Evening Star*, March 11, 1934.
[65] Miller to Cobb (Telegram), March 16, 1934, NA, RG 145.

told several planters the contract did not require them to retain undesirable tenants, just the usual number of tenants.

After concluding his investigations, Miller told a reporter of the *Memphis Commercial Appeal* that there was "absolutely no foundation" for the charges that the cotton program was causing wholesale evictions. The next day the newspaper carried a long story under the heading: "Wanton Evictions Charges Groundless; AAA Officials Say, Absolutely No Foundation for Attacks on Planters." The Poinsett County Committee and the Tyronza Community Committee were so pleased with Miller's investigation that they adopted a resolution in joint session thanking AAA for sending him and commending the entire acreage reduction program. The solution was proposed by the chairman of the Tyronza Community Committee, Hiram Norcross.[66]

The *Commercial Appeal* also carried an editorial which attributed the trouble in eastern Arkansas to "outside uplifters" and remarked that the South had never taken kindly to uplifters. The editorial said that Norman Thomas, "a man of integrity . . . despite his peculiar political views," had come to Arkansas in search of evidence to support his preconceived notions about peonage in the South. He had talked to a few "imaginative Negroes" and some "white trash" and upon their statements framed his indictment of the South. However, the Assistant Chief of AAA's Cotton Section, after a thorough investigation, had exonerated the planters, the AAA, and the South. The "complete vindication" by Miller, said the editorial, had made Thomas "somewhat ridiculous." [67]

Immediately, the cry went up from Amberson and the STFU leaders that Miller's mission had been a "whitewash." [68] H. L. Mitchell, who talked with Miller while he was in Arkansas, reported to Norman Thomas that Miller had shown no interest in a report concerning 100 evicted sharecroppers and had asked Mitchell to make no more complaints because "the landlords are all your friends and these share-croppers are a shiftless lot and there is no use of being concerned about them as they don't really count, you know—they are here today and gone tomorrow." Thomas was enraged by this and immediately wrote Paul

[66] *Memphis Commercial Appeal*, March 17, 1934.
[67] *Ibid.*, March 18, 1934.
[68] Mitchell to Editor of *The Arkansas Gazette*, March 20, 1934.

Appleby, Assistant Secretary of Agriculture, who demanded a report from Cully Cobb. Appleby said that if Miller had such an attitude, there should be "very strong disciplinary measures." [69]

When questioned by Cobb, Miller said he had instructions to investigate only matters around Tyronza while in Arkansas and was not authorized to receive other information offered. He emphatically denied having told Mitchell not to be concerned about the sharecroppers, but said he had told Mitchell and East that if they had any complaints in the future, it would be best to direct them to the county or community committee, of which Norcross was chairman. [70]

In his formal report, Miller described his mission to Arkansas. He had checked the records of the Tyronza Supply Company, which was the commissary for many of the plantations around Tyronza, and learned that there were actually more tenants in 1934 than in 1933. [71] Evidently, it never occurred to Miller to be suspicious of this information, even though the secretary of the supply company was John Emrich, the president of the bank from which Norcross made an excessively large loan to buy Fairview Farms. [72]

Miller found only three farms near Tyronza where there were fewer tenants than in 1933, and each owner agreed to increase his tenants to make the number as large as in 1933. [73] In a confidential report, Miller dealt with personalities. He said Mitchell and East were considered locally to be "very erratic." For instance, several years ago they announced they no longer believed in a Supreme Being and said that if one did exist, he was unjust. They even held meetings with people who believed similarly. East, Miller learned, came from a locally prominent family, but his relatives deplored the bad publicity he was causing the community. Miller felt that Norman Thomas, East, and Mitchell were trying to excite unrest in order to capitalize on it, but the "substantial people" in Tyronza saw them for what they were. [74]

[69] Paul Appleby, Memo to Mr. Cobb (Confidential), March 24, 1934, NA, RG 145.
[70] Miller, Memo to Mr. Cobb, March 26, NA, RG 145.
[71] Miller, Memo to Mr. Cobb, March 19, NA, RG 145.
[72] Mitchell, interview with author, August 2, 1959.
[73] Miller, Memo to Mr. Cobb, March 19, 1934, NA, RG 145.
[74] Miller, Memo to Mr. Cobb (Confidential), March 24, 1934, NA, RG 145.

Cully Cobb accepted Miller's findings and defended his assistant to his superiors. Cobb's view was that the clamor being raised by Amberson, Mitchell, East, and Thomas served a useful purpose: now the matter was out in the open "where we can get at it." Cobb felt this was better than a whisper campaign. He looked upon the activities of the STFU and its supporters as part of a "well-defined and very wide-spread political attack on our entire agricultural adjustment program and everybody connected with it." Events in Arkansas were only one phase of the attack, an attempt to create and capitalize on unrest. Trouble could be expected elsewhere, and the best way to meet it was to "keep our skirts clear and put our program over successfully." Cobb's idea was to be "most respectful and most guarded" in relations with "these people in Arkansas." [75]

Soon after the Miller mission, the Amberson Committee released the findings of its investigation of the effects of AAA's programs on tenant farmers.[76] Amberson took copies of the specific charges against individual planters to Washington and talked with J. Phil Campbell, Chief of the Agricultural Rehabilitation Section, who promised a full investigation.[77] Next, Amberson wrote a series of articles for *Nation* describing the activities of the STFU and charging that one-third of the rural unemployment in the South should be blamed on AAA. He said that AAA's programs aided owners and higher-type tenants but harmed sharecroppers and day laborers.[78]

Amberson also continued a steady stream of correspondence to AAA and to Paul Appleby, his friend from college days. In one telegram he pled with Appleby to act quickly: "We cannot control situation much longer," he warned.[79] To this, Appleby wired back that the difficulties in Arkansas seemed to be matters for state and local government and not for the Department of Agriculture. He promised, however, to give a "vigorous and impartial investigation" to specific complaints of violations of the cotton contract.[80] Amberson responded with a list of plantations

[75] Cobb, Memo to Mr. Appleby, March 28, 1934, NA, RG 145.

[76] See page 82 for a full treatment of the Amberson Report.

[77] Amberson to Eva Sams, Tennessee Transient Bureau, December 1, 1934, NA, RG 145.

[78] William Amberson, "New Deal for Sharecroppers," *Nation,* CXL (February 13, 1935), 186–187.

[79] Amberson to Appleby (Telegram), November 27, 1934, NA, RG, 145.

[80] Appleby to Amberson (Telegram), November 28, 1934, NA, RG 145.

and the violations which Appleby turned over to Cully Cobb. The violations were investigated by W. J. Green, a member of the committee in AAA which was assigned the task of handling landlord-tenant problems. Green found that on the plantations named by Amberson, evictions were no more than normal and small compared to the number of tenants kept. One of the cases cited by Amberson was that of Hiram Norcross. Green reported that Norcross had not violated the contract and actually had more tenants than in 1933. True, many of Norcross' new tenants were "cotton pickers" but Green did not choose to apply the rule prohibiting the lowering of tenant status by landlords. In every case investigated by Green except one, the landlord was cleared of breach of contract.[81] Green obtained all of his information from files in Washington, mostly from the reports of county committees. Cully Cobb reviewed Green's report and forwarded it to Chester Davis as evidence of the "nature of charges that have been made and facts developed upon investigation."[82]

And yet Amberson did not give up. He continued writing letters to Appleby, Jerome Frank, and Lawrence Westbrook of FERA. He felt that the sharecroppers were "burning with a sense of intolerable wrong," and he feared a serious uprising unless an administrative solution was found to their problem. One of his letters describing all of his efforts was sent to a relief official in Memphis.[83] It filtered eventually through government channels to the desk of Henry Wallace, who read it with interest and scribbled a note to Chester Davis asking if Campbell had made an investigation as promised, and what Davis knew about Hiram Norcross and "his compliance." He also wanted to know more about Amberson.[84] Evidently, it was the first Wallace had heard of these matters.

When it became evident to the leaders of the STFU that their letters and telegrams to Washington were accomplishing little, they decided to send a delegation to the Capitol to talk to Wallace and AAA officials. They chose H. L. Mitchell, Walter Maskop, and E. B. McKinney. The delegation arrived in Wash-

[81] W. J. Green to Amberson, December 12, 1934, NA, RG 145.

[82] Cobb, Memo to Chester Davis, January 5, 1933, NA, RG 145.

[83] Amberson to Eva Sams, Tennessee Transient Bureau, December 1, 1934, NA, RG 145.

[84] Elizabeth Scheiblich to Nels Anderson, December 17, 1934, and accompanying note by Wallace, NA, RG 145.

ington on January 10, 1935, after driving there in Mitchell's car. Having no idea they would need an appointment, they went to the office of the Secretary of Agriculture and asked to see Wallace. The receptionist told them the Secretary was busy, so they said they would sit in the outer office until he was free. Mitchell had a letter from Amberson to Paul Appleby, and he asked that it be delivered. When Appleby read the letter, he came out of his office immediately and talked to the four about conditions on the plantations. Appleby then went into the Secretary's office and brought out Wallace, who talked to the sharecropper delegation for half an hour and promised to send an investigator to Arkansas. He told them he would send Mary Connor Myers, who had just completed work with the Department of Justice on the Al Capone case in Chicago. According to Mitchell, Wallace advised the four to go back to Arkansas and tell their members that they had seen the Secretary of Agriculture, that he had said something was going to be done, and that he was "going to look into this matter and take action." [85]

While the STFU delegates were in Washington, Wallace set up a conference for them with Cully Cobb and his assistants, Campbell, Miller, and Green. Mitchell began the conference with a statement that the STFU delegation represented 4,500 to 5,000 sharecroppers, but the men of the Cotton Section tended to discount this because they had read the various unfavorable reports on Mitchell. Instead of accepting the four as representatives of a large group of sharecroppers, they tried to interview Mitchell and the others to find out what personal complaints each had against the cotton program. Naturally, Mitchell had no personal grievance since he was not a sharecropper, but he presented a list of 550 croppers and tenants who had been evicted at the end of the 1934 season in violation of paragraph 7 of the cotton contract. When he mentioned the Tschudy Land Company, an Arkansas plantation where the tenants were getting no rental payments, W. J. Green informed those present that he had investigated the case and nothing could be done because the tenants on the Tschudy plantation were not managing share-tenants. The general conclusion of the four AAA officials after the conference was that it accomplished nothing. The four did not take the STFU representatives seriously because they presented no griev-

[85] Mitchell, Oral History Interview, pp. 32–38.

ances of their own against the cotton program.[86] Later, in an article in *Nation,* Mitchell claimed that Cobb had called them "Reds" and refused to listen to their case.[87] Mitchell could not rightfully deny that they had been given a hearing, but perhaps he was right when he said Cobb had not listened.

[86] Report of Conference, STFU File, n.d., NA, RG 145.

[87] H. L. Mitchell and J. R. Butler, "The Cropper Learns His Fate," *Nation,* CXLI (September 18, 1935), 328–329.

chapter six

Agrarians *vs.* Liberals

The troubles in Arkansas had a catalytic effect on the troubles which were brewing inside the AAA. The two sides had been clearly drawn since the beginning. On one side were those who might be called traditional agrarians, men who had worked their way up through the ranks of the Department of Agriculture or the farm movements. They came from the triple alliance of Extension Service, Farm Bureau, and land-grant colleges.[1] Capable, well trained, and dedicated, they were the ones who made AAA work, and yet they were reconciled to the agricultural status quo and in general sympathetic with the larger and more successful farmers and landlords.[2] Although not all of them

[1] The connection between the Farm Bureau and the Extension Service has been studied by William J. Block in *The Separation of the Farm Bureau and the Extension Service: Political Issue in a Federal System* (Urbana: University of Illinois Press, 1960).
[2] Lord, *The Wallaces of Iowa,* pp. 380–383.

completely fit the description, the leaders of this group were George Peek, Charles Brand, Cully Cobb, and Oscar Johnston. Others included J. Phil Campell, E. A. Miller, and W. J. Green. The agrarians were in complete control of the various commodity sections, the Comptroller's Office, and most sections of AAA which dealt directly with farmers.

On the other extreme were the liberals; "Boys with their hair ablaze," Peek called them.[3] Led by Tugwell, their field commander in AAA was Jerome Frank because Tugwell's duties as Undersecretary did not extend to AAA. Many of the liberals were young lawyers, brought into the Legal Division by Frank at high salaries. There were Adlai Stevenson, Francis Shea, Alger Hiss, Nathan Witt, John Abt, Lee Pressman, Margaret Bennett, and Robert McConnaughey. In addition the Consumers Division contained two reformers, a generation apart, Frederick Howe as Consumers' Counsel and his assistant, Gardner Jackson.[4]

The liberals ranged from moderate to ultra, but generally they looked upon AAA as an opportunity for social reform. When Lee Pressman recruited Gardner Jackson for AAA, he told him, "Come on down to Washington with us; this is our chance to make the country over."[5] The ultras believed that capitalism was crumbling, that the profit motive was outdated, and that the place of the government in the economy must continually increase. Nearly all the liberals had accepted in part the precepts of a planned economy.

The agrarians looked upon the liberals as interlopers—idealistic, impractical, and inexperienced men who had never plowed a furrow or met a payroll. Occasionally, they called the liberals the worst name they could think of—"urbanites." Their favorite story was probably the one about Lee Pressman, who, when working on a macaroni code, was supposed to have asked: "Just tell me this; is this code fair to the macaroni growers?"[6]

For their part, the liberals saw the agrarians as representatives of the vested interests in agriculture. For instance, Tugwell identified the state Extension directors and their corps of county

[3] Russell Lord, *The Agrarian Revival* (New York: American Association for Adult Education, 1939), p. 155.

[4] Frank, Memo to Mr. Brand, August, 1935, NA, RG 145.

[5] Jackson, interview with author, July 27, 1959.

[6] Fite, *George N. Peek and the Fight for Farm Parity*, p. 51.

agents with the ruling casts of farmers, the most conservative Farm Bureau leaders, the cotton barons of the South, and the banker-farmers of the Middle West. Russell Lord, who was in the Department of Agriculture at the time and who was not unsympathetic to the agrarian group, states flatly that they were "extraordinarily landlord-minded, in the main." [7]

Outside of AAA, the liberals had some important allies in the Department. In addition to Tugwell, there was Paul Appleby, an assistant to the Secretary, Mordecai Ezekiel, an economic adviser, Louis Bean, a master statistician, and part of the time Wallace himself. The liberals often attempted to bypass the Administrator of AAA in a disagreement by going directly to Tugwell or Wallace. [8]

There are three excellent accounts of the struggle in AAA between the liberals and the agrarians. Arthur Schlesinger, Jr., tells the liberals' story largely through the eyes of Tugwell in Chapter I of his *Coming of the New Deal.* Gilbert C. Fite gives a balanced view with emphasis on the part played by Peek in Chapter XV of his *George N. Peek and the Fight for Farm Parity.* Much of the "inside" information and considerable insight are found in Russell Lord's *The Wallaces of Iowa,* which centers the story on Wallace. Yet none of these writers has given a full account of the conflict within the AAA.

The tenant farmer problem did not become an important part of the struggle within AAA until 1934. By that time, Administrator Peek had lost a showdown battle with the liberals and was eased out. Before leaving he warned his successor, Chester Davis, to get rid of "Jerome Frank and the rest of that bunch." [9]

To understand better the tenant farmer question as a phase of the split in AAA, it is necessary to know the principal players of the drama and the organizational framework in which they worked. The Legal Division at one time reached a strength of 130 men, most of them young lawyers. George Peek complained that one of them had been hired fresh out of law school at a yearly salary of $4,222 when $2,400 would have been more in line with pay in other government agencies. The average salary of lawyers in the Legal Division was a thousand dollars higher

[7] Lord, *The Wallaces of Iowa,* p. 359.
[8] Schlesinger, *The Coming of the New Deal,* p. 51.
[9] Fite, *George N. Peek and the Fight for Farm Parity,* pp. 264–266.

than in the Solicitor's Office of the Department or in the Department of Justice.[10]

Under Jerome Frank as General Counsel were three assistants: John P. Wenchel in charge of federal practice and procedure, Alger Hiss in charge of work on benefit contracts, processing and other taxes, appropriations and general matters requiring legal opinions, and Lee Pressman, who worked on agreements, codes, and licenses.[11] Under Hiss were three sections: the Benefit Contract Section which he headed with Robert McConnaughey as assistant, the Processing Tax Section directed by Prew Savoy, and the Opinions Section [12] with Francis Shea as chief. Arthur Bachrach served as Special Adviser to the General Counsel with supervision over the Litigations Section headed by John Abt and the Administrative Enforcement Section with John Lewin as chief.[13] Frank had constant difficulty keeping his section chiefs in line and issued several memoranda instructing them to make no important decisions without his approval. Co-Administrator Charles Brand once complained to Frank that his lawyers were expressing themselves too freely on policy matters.[14]

In the hectic years after World War II, it developed in the hearings before the House Un-American Activities Committee in the famous Chambers-Hiss case that there was a cell of Communists in AAA organized by Harold Ware. According to Whitaker Chambers, all the following were "incipient or registered Communists" brought into the Ware apparatus: Lee Pressman, Alger Hiss, John Abt, Charles Kramer of the Consumers' Counsel, and Nathan Witt.[15]

During the Hiss hearings in 1948, Pressman, Abt, Kramer, and Witt were called before the House Committee and asked if they knew Alger Hiss. Each took the Fifth Amendment and read a

[10] George N. Peek and Samuel Crowther, *Why Quit Our Own* (New York: D. Van Nostrand Company, 1936), pp. 141–143.

[11] Administrative Letter, October 18, 1934, Frank File, NA, RG 145.

[12] The purpose of this section was to prepare opinions on legal questions when requested by the Administrator.

[13] Adlai Stevenson was a Special Attorney under Pressman. He helped in negotiating several important marketing agreements. Frank, Memo to Mr. Brand, August 1, 1938, NA, RG 145.

[14] Frank, Memo to Mr. Brand, August 1, 1933, NA, RG 145.

[15] Whitaker Chambers, *Witness* (New York: Random House, 1952), pp. 334–335.

statement denying membership in any Communist group.[16] In 1950, the four were called again and repeated their refusal to answer questions, except Lee Pressman, who admitted he had joined a Communist group in 1934 and left it the following year. He said that Witt, Kramer, and Abt had also been members but not Hiss. The purpose of the group, said Pressman, was to receive Communist literature and to meet and discuss it.[17] Later, Nathaniel Weyl, who was economic adviser in the Department of Agriculture, testified before the McCarran Committee that he had been a member of the Ware Cell along with Hiss.[18]

Perhaps someday the full extent of Communist infiltration and influence in AAA will be known, but to date the evidence is too scattered and conflicting to allow a valid judgment. Henry Wallace felt in later years that "Communism was not an issue at that time." [19] Arthur Schlesinger, Jr., writes off Communists in the AAA by saying they were there because there were so many jobs to fill, but they influenced no course of action which the liberals would not have taken without them.[20] But this may not be the last word. The influence of Pressman and Hiss was strong in the Legal Division. Although the official correspondence of these two, plus that of Witt and Abt, seems to reflect no particular political viewpoints,[21] nonetheless, they played an important part in the decision in early 1935 to make a rash and dangerous move on behalf of the Southern tenant farmers. It was an action well calculated to disrupt the entire cotton program, cause trouble in the plantation areas, and tear AAA apart.

According to Russell Lord, Jerome Frank, leader of AAA's liberals, was "the most lovable and volatile of them all." [22]

[16] Earl Jowitt, *The Strange Case of Alger Hiss* (Garden City: Doubleday, 1953), pp. 122–123.

[17] U.S. Congress, House, Committee on Un-American Activities, *Hearings, Regarding Communism in the U.S. Government*, 81st Cong., 2nd Sess., 1950, pp. 2845, 2926.

[18] U.S. Congress, Senate, Judiciary Committee, *Hearings, Institute of Pacific Relations*, 82nd Cong., 2nd Sess., 1952, pp. 2799, 2800.

[19] Wallace, letter to author, June 13, 1959.

[20] Schlesinger, *Coming of the New Deal*, pp. 52–54.

[21] Representatives of the Republican National Committee have searched the records of AAA now in the National Archives for Communist implications but found nothing they could use. Interview with Dr. Harold T. Pinkett, Director of Agricultural Records Divisions, National Archives, August 1, 1959.

[22] Lord, *The Wallaces of Iowa*, p. 396.

Brilliant, hard-working, and seemingly possessed of endless driving energy, Frank built a successful law practice in Chicago after graduation from the University of Chicago Law School and then moved to greater success in New York. He became a friend of Felix Frankfurter, the Harvard professor suspected by some people of being the off-stage mastermind of the New Deal. When the AAA was being formed, Rexford Tugwell asked Frankfurter to recommend a capable and liberal lawyer for AAA, and he named Frank. This placed Frank among a select group in the New Deal known as "Frankfurter's Young Men," a group which included James Landis, Chairman of the Securities and Exchange Commission, and David Lilienthal, Director of the Tennessee Valley Authority.[23] Frank recruited many of the lawyers for his staff from Frankfurter's students, including Hiss, Pressman, Abt, and Witt.[24]

Even George Peek was willing to admit Frank was a "good lawyer," although he later claimed Frank was "more concerned with social theory than with law." [25] Part of Peek's objection to Frank may have gone back to the time in Chicago when Frank was a member of the law firm active in liquidating Peek's Moline Plow Company.[26] Frank's background and manner were strictly urban, a severe handicap in the eyes of AAA's agrarians. And, like many ardent liberals operating in new waters, he was inclined to leap before he looked. When Frank first had the intricacies of the system for milk distribution in large cities explained to him, he was shocked by the inefficiency, especially the duplication of competing milk routes. For an entire day he laid plans for reforming the whole system, until some of the agrarians who had studied the problem for years showed him what abolishing duplicated milk routes would do to the unemployment problem. After that, he acknowledged that the milk industry could probably not be reformed abruptly.[27]

The attitude of Frank and his lieutenants toward Southern tenant farmers was extremely sympathetic and protective, although it is doubtful that many of them had ever seen a share-

[23] Raymond Clapper, "Felix Frankfurter's Young Men," *Review of Reviews,* XCIII (January, 1936), 27–29.
[24] Schlesinger, *Coming of the New Deal,* p. 50.
[25] Peek, *Why Quit Our Own,* p. 21.
[26] Fite, *George N. Peek and the Fight for Farm Parity,* p. 260.
[27] Lord, *The Wallaces of Iowa,* p. 396.

cropper. Since the Legal Division made no policy, Frank and his lawyers had to fight for tenants' rights on a strictly legal basis. They did this through legal opinions on given questions, rulings made in individual cases, work on various landlord-tenant committees, opinions expressed at policy conferences which they attended as legal advisers and by "leaks" to the press. Most of their legal considerations revolved around the powers granted by the Adjustment Act and the provisions of the 1934–35 cotton contract, especially paragraph 7. Usually their opinions and rulings came out in favor of the tenants, but when the law or the provisions of the contract could simply not be stretched to fit their purposes, they accepted it.[28]

Perhaps in an effort to leave himself free to defend his lieutenants, Jerome Frank preferred not to express his views on policy officially.[29] Certainly the lawyers under Frank did not feel constrained to hold their tongues, especially Margaret Bennett, who squabbled so incessantly with members of the Cotton Section that they complained she was "difficult to get along with" and delayed the handling of complaints.[30] Miss Bennett's boss, Alger Hiss, served for a time on the landlord-tenant committee, where he fought for tenants' rights, but ordinarily he preferred, like Frank, to avoid policy matters in his official dealings. According to Hiss, the General Counsel's office considered it a lawyer's function to try to find lawful ways to carry out the Secretary's wishes. "We did not attempt," Hiss recalled years later, "to act or modify policy in our opinions." However, he and the other lawyers felt free as "informed members of the staff" to suggest policy while it was in the process of formulation.[31]

The philosophical leader of the liberal group was Rexford G. Tugwell. Often in the evenings, the liberals gathered at the house he shared with Jerome Frank for a heady fare of liquor and Tugwellian economics. A former professor at Columbia and a

[28] When Jerome Frank ordered his Opinion Section to look into the possibility of AAA entering the Norcross case on the side of the tenants, Francis Shea advised him that it would not be proper. Shea, Memo to Mr. Frank, NA, RG 145.

[29] For example, see Frank, Memo to the Secretary, January 12, 1935, NA, RG 145.

[30] Bennett, Memo to Mr. Hiss, July 7, 1934, NA, RG 145.

[31] Hiss to author, September 17, 1960.

member of Roosevelt's "Braintrust," Tugwell was highly intellectual and articulate. Early in his academic career, he decided to devote his study to the two classes of people who suffered most from industrial civilization—farmers and industrial workers. He wrote books and speeches in which he predicted the coming of an economic revolution in the United States, either orderly or violent, which would be similar to what had happened in Russia. In *The Industrial Discipline,* published in 1933, he advocated an enforced planned industrial economy, nationalization of certain industries, and abandonment of the laissez-faire principle. It was done with an oblique, pseudo-scholarly approach, but the message was there.[32] As Assistant Secretary of Agriculture, Tugwell had charge of the older agencies within the Department, leaving Wallace free to give direct supervision to AAA. In 1934 Roosevelt appointed him Undersecretary of Agriculture, but there was resistance to his confirmation in the Senate because he was considered the most radical of the "Braintrusters."[33] Tugwell, who was once voted "the handsomest New Dealer" by female readers of a Washington newspaper, appeared before the Senate Agriculture Committee in an immaculate white linen suit and two-toned shoes [34] to tell the senators that he was a farm boy who had once raised a prize-winning calf and that he was not the revolutionary they seemed to think. When some of his most volatile past statements were read to him by the senators, he said they were made before he had governmental responsibilities. He denied he was a "Braintruster" or a "Planner." One senator was led to remark, "Doctor, we are really shocked to learn that you are leaning so strongly toward ultra-conservatism." [35]

Another liberal who played an important part in tenant affairs was Gardner Jackson, Assistant Consumers' Counsel. Jackson took his job of looking after the interest of the consumer seriously, but then he had always taken worthwhile causes seriously. While in AAA he was not directly concerned with the tenant

[32] Rexford G. Tugwell, *The Industrial Discipline, and the Government Arts* (New York: Columbia University Press, 1933), pp. 189–219.

[33] U.S. Congress, Senate, Committee on Agriculture and Forestry, *Hearings, Confirmation of Rexford Tugwell,* 73rd Cong., 2nd Sess., pp. 1–20, 166–168.

[34] Gardner Jackson, interview with author, July 20, 1959.

[35] Senate Agriculture Committee, *Hearings, Confirmation of Tugwell,* pp. 1–173.

problem, but he was interested in it,[36] and later entered the thick of the fight on the tenants' side. Jackson's father was the builder of the Denver and Rio Grande Railroad and one of the biggest landowners in New Mexico and Colorado, but by the 1930's Jackson had spent most of his fortune fighting for lost causes.[37] It started with Sacco and Vanzetti, the two Italian radicals accused of murder and robbery in Massachusetts during the Red Scare of 1919–20. Jackson was a student at Harvard, but when he learned the details of the case he dropped out of class to work with the Sacco and Vanzetti Defense Committee. It was Jackson who put up much of the money to carry on the fight for an appeal or retrial, neither of which was ever granted. In the years that followed, Jackson championed so many such causes— the bonus army, Tom Mooney, the Spanish Loyalists—that he became well known in political circles. A friend once told him, "You're the only man I know who the underdog has on a leash." [38]

Jackson was a curious combination of charm, idealism, persistence, and brass. He once told Senator William E. Borah of Idaho, "Borah, I don't like you. You're not sincere, Borah. You're not a go-through guy." [39] But Jackson was a go-through guy: on one occasion when Wallace and Davis had gone to Chicago to sign a meat-packing code, he leaked a story to the press that the code permitted meat prices which would gouge the consumer. This caused so much unfavorable publicity that the code was canceled.[40] When Davis returned to Washington, he tried to find out who had released the story. Jackson proudly confessed, but Davis did not fire him, probably out of sheer admiration for his nerve.[41] Right or wrong, most people could not help liking Jackson. Years later, Henry Wallace recalled, "What Chester Davis understood a Pat Jackson could never learn. And yet strangely enough Pat Jackson is much more friendly with me today than Chester Davis." [42]

[36] Gardner Jackson, Memo to Mr. Hiss, March 17, 1934, NA, RG 145.
[37] Drew Pearson, "Washington Merry-Go Round," *Florida Times-Union* (Jacksonville), February 26, 1937.
[38] Jackson, interview with author, July 20, 1959.
[39] Pearson, "Washington Merry-Go-Round," February 26, 1937.
[40] Jackson to Senator Burton K. Wheeler, March 11, 1935, File 1737, NA, RG 145.
[41] Jackson, interview with author, July 20, 1959.
[42] Wallace to author, June 13, 1959.

The leader of the agrarians in tenancy matters was Cully Cobb. A land-grant college graduate, Cobb had come up through the Extension Service, first as Director of Boys' Agricultural Club Work and then as Assistant State Director. During the 1920's he was editor of the *Southern Ruralist* of Atlanta, Georgia. Cobb, who was born in a log cabin on a Tennessee farm, was intensely proud of having come "all the way up from the soil." [43]

As Chief of the Cotton Section, Cobb had a big job, and he did not intend to let anyone stand in the way. Much of the success of the cotton programs can be attributed to his administrative abilities. However, Cobb had a blind side: he tended to view anyone who threatened to interfere with the cotton programs as a personal enemy and definitely un-American. He was convinced there was a Communist and left-wing plot which "extended from one end of the Cotton Belt to the other" to discredit the Administration and thwart its efforts to save the cotton economy. He spoke often of the "incredible interference" of Communists and fellow travelers. [44]

Cobb looked upon the STFU as a pawn of the Socialist Party and Norman Thomas as a man whose opinions counted little because of his peculiar political beliefs. If a letter had to be written to STFU leaders or Thomas, Cobb delegated one of his assistants to write it; however, he usually gave correspondence with senators and farm leaders his personal attention and often found time to answer the letters of individual farmers himself. [45] Cobb looked upon most criticism as Communist-inspired and part of a "deliberate and continuous effort" by left-wingers to stir up trouble.

Cobb felt that every effort had been made to make the cotton programs completely fair to all types of tenants and landowners. He believed that, although some complaints from tenants were valid, most were not. To be as fair as possible, he brought several Negro employees into the Cotton Section to give counsel and assistance. The decision requiring landlords to keep the same number of tenants in 1933–34 as before, he said, was not based on "cold economics but upon humanitarian considerations." In 1933 and 1934 he used Negro ministers to explain AAA's pro-

[43] Cobb to author, June 13, 1961.
[44] Cobb to author, October 26, 1959.
[45] Cobb, correspondence file, NA, RG 145.

grams to tenant farmers in their churches because "those of us in charge of the program understood their situation and felt they were entitled to every fact that would help them. . . ."[46]

As for the liberals in AAA, Cobb claimed later that he knew most of them were Communists but could not prove it. He felt they could have given him much more trouble if they had known anything about agriculture. Fortunately, they did not. Cobb believed that he and the other agrarians were able to prevent the "social planners and fellow-travelers" in AAA from completely taking over the administration of the cotton programs only because Southern congressmen and senators backed the agrarians and because the control of the programs was decentralized.[47]

Cobb and his assistants in the Cotton Section had a theory that the great increase in the tenant population of the South since the beginning of the depression was caused by the return to the country of "destitute urbanites," farm families who had migrated to the cities in the 1920's and who were stranded there by the depression. Cobb believed that benevolent landlords had permitted these people to occupy abandoned shacks and cabins and to farm unused land, a condition which accounted for the swollen number of farmers in the South. Many of the "destitute urbanites" became tenants, and in order to protect them AAA required landlords to allow them to stay on the farm in 1934 and 1935. But many of them no longer wanted to stay. They wished to return to the cities so that they could get on relief. This created the "wholesale evictions" which certain left-wing groups charged were taking place. The leaders of the Cotton Section knew there was a considerable amount of shifting among tenants each year, and they believed it was unfair to blame AAA for this or the accompanying back-to-the-city migration. Cobb and his lieutenants believed fervently that there had been no great displacement of tenants due to AAA's acreage reduction; they reasoned that, although cotton acreage was less,[48] profits were higher and there was less land to cultivate. This situation, they hoped, would allow women and children to stop working in the fields and allow more time to tend cows and chickens. The

[46] Cobb to author, October 26, 1959, pp. 1–5.
[47] *Ibid.*, pp. 5–8.
[48] Cobb to J. J. Miller, March 26, 1934, NA, RG 145.

standard of living throughout the South would thus be immeasurably improved.

Above all, Cobb and the leaders of the Cotton Section feared the attempt by the liberals to make the cotton program into one of social reform because it might ruin good relations between landlords and tenants. They felt that they alone understood tenancy because most of them were from the South and had lived with the problem all their lives. They were not opposed to social reform, but they were convinced that the best way to achieve it was by the economic rehabilitation of the South through crop control. To try to do more than that, they were sure, would be a grave mistake. In one of its studies of the problem, the Cotton Section warned that "to trust the future to those who are more or less unfamiliar with the [South] and its problems" would lead only to new problems and no solutions for the old ones.[49]

Oscar Johnston shared most of the views held by members of the Cotton Section. In addition to being AAA's Comptroller, Director of the Cotton Pool, and Assistant Director of the Commodity Credit Corporation, he was also President of the British-owned Delta and Pine Land Company of Scott, Mississippi. With 38,000 acres of cotton land, Delta and Pine was the biggest plantation in the South. It had 1,000 Negro sharecropper families, 1,000 mules, and a net income in 1936 of $153,600. Johnston was a native Mississippian who had taken legal training at Cumberland University. He ran for governor of Mississippi in 1919 representing the wealthier classes of the state.[50] According to the Amberson Report, the Delta and Pine organization was the fairest plantation studied in dealing with its tenants.[51] Like the Cotton Section, Johnston felt that the interest of tenants could best be looked after by their landlords and that AAA had neither the authorization nor the capability to reform Southern tenancy.[52]

Caught between warring factions in AAA were their two bosses, Chester Davis and Henry Wallace. George Peek once de-

[49] Cotton Section, "Resume of Tenant Problem," January 9, 1935, NA, RG 145.

[50] "Best Cotton Plantation," *Fortune*, XV (March, 1937), pp. 125–132.

[51] William R. Amberson, "Report of Survey Made by Memphis Chapter, League for Industrial Democracy and the Tyronza Socialist Party," in Thomas, *Plight of the Sharecropper*, p. 34.

[52] Johnston, Memo to Chester Davis, January 26, 1935, NA, RG 145.

scribed Wallace as mystical, religious, dreamy, honest-minded, and rather likeable.[53] Russell Lord added that he was shy and folksy and had "corn country" still written all over him.[54] Wallace characteristically spoke and wrote in terms of high idealism but his actions were strictly middle of the road. He detested extremes, either political or economic. As Secretary he learned to resist what he called "newspaper drives" and pressure groups. He felt it was his duty to look after the interests of the nation as a whole and not give in to the powerful and well-represented minorities.[55] These qualities, in many ways desirable in a cabinet member, also make it possible for him to turn a deaf ear to what he probably considered a very small minority—the tenants and croppers who had been wronged under AAA's cotton programs.

By 1938, Wallace came to the conclusion that although AAA had attempted to prevent the displacement of tenants in the South, it was "impossible to write iron-clad rules with respect to these matters." He said the Department of Agriculture would continue its efforts to protect the interests of tenants, but that trends in agricultural practice must be considered. One-third of all American farmers lived on cotton farms, and with the reduced world market, it was obvious to Wallace that all of them would not be able to make a living indefinitely from cotton.[56]

Chester Davis was not unlike Wallace in many ways. He had a broad social outlook and avoided extremes, but he was essentially a much more practical man. If anyone could have successfully refereed between the agrarians and the liberals, it was Davis. Like Wallace, he was an Iowan. Educated in Grinnell, he became editor of the *Montana Farmer* and later Commissioner of Agriculture in Montana. During the 1920's he was Director of Grain Marketing for the Illinois Agricultural Association and Washington Representative of the American Council of Agriculture, of which George Peek was President. He had been Peek's righthand man in the McNary-Haugen fight.

Russell Lord remembered Davis as being "kind and intelligent, humorously self-deprecatory, cordially open-minded, and capable

[53] Peek, *Why Quit Our Own*, pp. 59–60.
[54] Lord, *Wallaces of Iowa*, p. 246.
[55] Wallace, *New Frontiers*, pp. 65–66.
[56] Wallace to Congressman George Mahon, December 30, 1938, Landlord-Tenant File, NA, RG 145.

of continuing learning. . . ." Davis was a capable and patient administrator who had developed negotiation and conciliation to a fine art. According to Lord, it was Davis who kept AAA running while Wallace "plugged on ahead at the top, keeping more and more to himself." [57]

In all of AAA there was only one man in high position who was equipped by experience and attitude to achieve a compromise between the agrarians and the liberals. D. P. Trent was a Southerner who understood tenancy intimately, and yet he wanted to take positive action to help tenants. Thus, his background was agrarian, but his ideas were liberal. Trent, whose full name was Dover Parham Trent, was born in Arkansas and raised on an Oklahoma farm. For a time he operated his own farm, but at the age of twenty-two he entered Oklahoma Agricultural and Mechanical College, now Oklahoma State University. After receiving a degree in agriculture, he became a school teacher and eventually a school superintendent. In 1919 he entered the government service as a county agent in eastern Oklahoma. Showing great administrative ability, he rose to District Agent and finally State Director in 1927.[58] According to one of his subordinates, Trent was ambitious, perhaps egocentric, and did not make friends easily.[59]

Trent was brought to Washington by Chester Davis as an expert on tenancy, and Davis consulted him often on such matters. As Assistant Director of the Commodities Division, Trent was Cully Cobb's immediate superior, and certainly the men of the Cotton Section could not accuse him of being an urbanite who had never seen a tenant farmer. Yet Trent had deep compassion for the sharecroppers. He was determined that their rights be protected, and he was full of new ideas about how to reform the system. He soon became suspect among the agrarians, and the Cotton Section refused to cooperate with him. On the other hand, Trent did little better with the Legal Division. He feared the young lawyers were too radical and impractical, while they

[57] Lord, *Wallaces of Iowa*, pp. 400–402.
[58] Ed Lemons, Head of Oklahoma State University Agricultural Information Services, to author, July 20, 1961; and D. P. Trent, Application for Position, Oklahoma A. and M. College Extension Division, December 2, 1924, on file in the State Extension Service offices, Stillwater, Oklahoma.
[59] Dan Diehl to author, August 5, 1961.

did not completely trust him because of his agrarian background.[60]

Perhaps there was something in Trent's personality that prevented him from finding a middle ground for AAA on tenancy. Maybe he was not given enough authority. Or it could well be that compromise was impossible. Whatever the reason, Trent was unable to accomplish his mission in Washington.

With the characters thus drawn and the issues set, it is now time to describe the great fight as it developed between the agrarians and the liberals in AAA.

[60] D. P. Trent, correspondence file, NA, RG 145.

chapter seven

The AAA's Landlord-Tenant Committees

Despite the Cotton Section's repeated denials that wholesale evictions of tenant farmers were taking place in the South, evidence to the contrary continued to mount during the winter of 1934–35. The number of tenant families moving to towns to get on relief rolls grew so great that the Federal Emergency Relief Administration became concerned. Colonel Lawrence Westbrook, Assistant Administrator of FERA, sent to AAA a proposal that his agency provide relief for evicted tenants and loans on the 1935 crop for those who remained on the land. However, he wanted AAA to give assurance that it would force landlords to retain the normal number of tenants. The Cotton Section thought it wise to accept Westbrook's offer since the requested provisions were already in the 1935 cotton contract.[1]

[1] J. Phil Campbell, Memo to Mr. H. R. Tolley, December 24, 1934, NA, RG 145.

However, the position of the Cotton Section concerning evictions remained largely unchanged. Cully Cobb continued to believe that a certain number of tenant complaints were to be expected and to attribute displacement to the nature of tenancy. He took comfort from the fact that in eastern Arkansas, where many complaints originated, the vote of farmers, including tenants, had been overwhelmingly in favor of more controls in the Bankhead referendum. Cobb pointed out that the total value of the cotton crop in Arkansas had risen from $48,860,000 in 1932 to $75,039,922 in 1933 and $79,669,435 in 1934, including government benefits. In addition, Arkansas producers received $1,220,994 through the sale of surplus tax exemptions.[2]

Cobb was never impressed with the complaints of tenant leaders. When J. O. Green of the STFU wrote AAA requesting that the contracts of several landlords be suspended while it was determined whether their tenants were managing sharetenants, Cobb had him investigated. Later, Cobb sent instructions to county agents and committeemen in two eastern Arkansas counties to ignore Green because he was "fanatic and possibly . . . slightly unbalanced."[3]

But in the Legal Division, several key figures were working on behalf of what they considered to be the tenants' interests. Alger Hiss continually urged Jerome Frank to get an expert on landlord-tenant relations appointed to the staff of AAA.[4] John Abt, obviously disappointed when Frank made arrangements to have Department of Justice lawyers try AAA's cases, attempted to arrange with the Attorney General for AAA lawyers to handle them. He was willing to let the Department of Justice have veto power over cases and plan the strategy, but this was unacceptable to the Attorney General. Finally, they agreed that AAA lawyers would take part only in the preparation and briefing of cases, which was a blow to the Litigations Section, which Abt headed.[5]

Francis Shea and others in the Legal Division corresponded frequently with H. C. Malcom, Deputy Commissioner of Labor in Arkansas, who in his own words was "fighting the battle of the sharecropper." Malcom gathered data on violations of the cotton

[2] Cobb to Robinson, August 26, 1935, NA, RG 145.
[3] Cobb, Memo to Mr. Frank, July 24, 1934, NA, RG 145.
[4] Hiss, Memo to Mr. Frank, January 4, 1934, NA, RG 145.
[5] Abt, Memo to Mr. Frank, July 14, 1934, NA, RG 145.

contract by landlords and forwarded them to AAA.[6] He claimed
to have records of 3,000 violations,[7] and his department was
trying in a "feeble way to right some of the wrongs of the cotton
program." In one day, Malcom and his assistants recovered $700
which landlords had wrongfully withheld from their tenants.[8]
Eventually, Assistant Secretary Paul Appleby became interested
in Malcom as a "means for getting a more representative view of
the situation than we have yet had."[9]

Even the top administrators of AAA became more concerned
about tenancy as a result of events in Arkansas. But when
Chester Davis inquired of the chiefs of all commodity sections
if they had encountered any difficulties concerning tenants, most
responded they had not. Claude Wickard of the Corn-Hog Section, for instance, reported receiving only a few complaints,
mostly from landlords. These were handled by a letter stating
flatly that tenants should share in rental payments as well as
parity payments.[10]

Assistant Administrator W. E. Byrd, whose sympathies were
more with the liberals than the agrarians, received a letter from
a Mississippi planter who styled himself "one of those vicious
landlords." He asked if there was not some way to "get rid of
that swarm of pests headed by Socialist Thomas who seem[ed]
to consider it their special duty to rescue the most fortunate class
of people on earth, the plantation sharecropper." Byrd passed
the letter to Paul Porter, Executive Assistant to the Administrator, with the suggestion that "because of this gent's reference to
sharecroppers, I thought you might be able to hand him a
bouquet with a bumble bee in it."[11]

In December, 1934, Frank Tannenbaum of the Rosenwald
Foundation and the Brookings Institution came to AAA with the
preliminary findings of a study conducted by the Committee
on Minority Groups in the Economic Recovery.[12] The project,

[6] Malcom to Shea, August 21, 1934, and other letters in Malcom correspondence file, NA, RG 145.
[7] *Arkansas Gazette*, November 15, 1934.
[8] Malcom to W. J. Green, January 2, 1935, NA, RG 145.
[9] Appleby, Memo to Mr. Boyd, January 7, 1935, NA, RG 145.
[10] Wickard, Memo to Chester Davis, May 4, 1934, NA, RG 145.
[11] John C. Stephens to Chester Davis, March 13, 1935, and attached note
from W. E. Byrd, NA, RG 145.
[12] Tannenbaum to Appleby, December 29, 1934, NA, RG 145.

sponsored by the Rosenwald Foundation at a cost of $50,000, had taken one year to complete.[13] The report concluded that tenancy, especially white tenancy, was growing rapidly and that only government relief had prevented wholesale starvation and rioting among tenant farmers. It strongly advocated adopting a system of "peasant proprietorship" whereby the government would purchase land rather than rent it to keep it out of production. The land would be sold to landless farmers on easy terms. This would create a class of peasants in the South, which the authors of the report thought desirable.[14] The Rosenwald report was read by Wallace, Davis, and other high officials, and, although they were probably sympathetic to tenants' becoming landowners, they could see nothing AAA or the Department of Agriculture could do to accomplish this goal.[15]

Also toward the end of 1934, AAA began considering making its own studies of the effects of its programs on tenancy. Such studies were strongly recommended by Professor John D. Black, a Harvard economist and trusted adviser to the Administration on agriculture. Black resented the "very false statements that are appearing in certain types of allegedly liberal journals" about AAA and felt that the South was furnishing the most fruitful field for criticism. Black understood the feeling of the Cotton Section that its problems were its own and should be handled without help of outsiders, yet he realized that this attitude could lead to "unfortunate circumstances." He therefore suggested that AAA begin studies of Southern problems, make the results public, and be guided in its policies by the conclusion.[16]

As a result of Black's recommendations, Secretary Wallace and Administrator Davis asked Professor Calvin B. Hoover, an economic adviser to AAA on leave from the faculty of Duke University, to make a study of the effects of cotton acreage reduction on Southern tenant farmers. Hoover was an expert on

[13] *New York Times*, March 21, 1935.
[14] Committee on Minority Groups in the Economic Recovery, "Foreword and Conclusion of a Study of Agricultural, Economic and Social Conditions in the South," NA, RG 145. The full report of this committee was later published by Charles Johnson, Edwin Embree, and Will Alexander, *The Collapse of Cotton Tenancy* (Chapel Hill: University of North Carolina Press, 1935).
[15] Tannenbaum to Appleby, December 29, 1934, and attached routing slip, NA, RG 145.
[16] Black to Chester Davis, November 15, 1934, NA, RG 145.

tenancy, so rather than make extensive field studies he simply applied his knowledge to an analysis of the cotton program. In the internal politics of AAA, Hoover was more sympathetic to the liberals than to the agrarians. His final report, which was released to the public, was surprisingly outspoken on some points, but was guarded and noticeably vague on others. For instance, Hoover concluded that it was inevitable from the first that acreage reduction would lead to widespread tenant displacement and he confirmed that it had done so in 1933 and 1934, but he was careful not to blame this situation on AAA. The causes of displacement, he said, were normal movement, evictions by landlords before signing contracts, and tenants moving to town to get relief.

Having denied the validity of one charge against AAA, Hoover confirmed others. He said that tenants were not receiving the full amount specified in the cotton contract and that the acreage reduction program had created a motive for reducing the number of tenants. He recognized that paragraph 7 of the cotton contract was designed to prevent evictions, but he concluded that enforcement was "inadequate." The professor found that the share of rental payments received by sharecroppers and non-managing tenants under the cotton contract was unfair when compared to tobacco or corn-hog contracts. He further concluded that the wording of the 1934 contract produced confusion in the classification of types of tenants with the division of benefit payments hinging on the interpretation.

Hoover reviewed the reasoning which had gone into the decision to give cotton tenants less than other tenants. He recognized that favoring the landlords had been necessary in order to induce them to sign the contract; however, he could not escape the conclusion that it had been unjust to bargain for landlord support at the expense of tenants. He added that the decision had been influenced by the fact that cotton tenants would be allowed to use the rented acres to grow food and feed, and he felt that if the tenants were to receive any real benefit from the existing cotton program, it would have to be through the "free use" of the rented acres.

Hoover concluded that the cotton programs had greatly improved economic conditions in the South and that these advantages "far outweigh[ed] any unfortunate results and individual injustices." [17] He went about as far as he could go in his public report in condemning the cotton program: he denied it caused evictions but said it created a motive to evict. He courageously pointed out the inequitable division of benefits between landlords and tenants but took the edge off his criticism by saying, with some justice, that the cotton program had been of general benefit to the South.

Hoover's report provided ammunition for both critics and supporters of the cotton program. William Amberson charged in *Nation* that many officials in the Department of Agriculture ignored the report although it said the cotton program created a motive for evictions and that enforcement of the contract was inadequate.[18] H. C. Malcom, the pro-tenant labor commissioner in Arkansas, called the report "propaganda pure and simple" and offered to make his records available to prove mass evictions caused by AAA.[19] On the other hand, the Cotton Section took comfort from Hoover's general conclusion about the improvement of economic conditions in the South.[20]

In recommendations to Secretary Wallace, which were not made public, Hoover went much further. He reversed his position on tenant displacement and said there was "strong and definite" evidence that the acreage reduction program was causing evictions, at least in the Southeastern states. He recommended that landlords be required to sign a statement of the number of tenants on their land before receiving rental checks and also that they be forced to make an accounting of their distribution of rental and parity payments. However, Hoover despaired of ever forcing landlords to retain tenants which they did not need, and he foresaw continued evictions. He felt that this situation created a major problem of helping the thousands of farm families set adrift with no training other than farming and little hope of finding jobs. A possible solution would be to place evicted tenants on small subsistence farms where they could

[17] Calvin Hoover, "Human Problems in Acreage Reduction in the South," 1935, NA, RG 145.

[18] Amberson, "The New Deal for Sharecroppers," *Nation*, CXL (February 13, 1935), 185–186.

[19] *Arkansas Gazette*, November 15, 1934.

[20] Cotton Section, "Resume of Tenant Problem," January 9, 1935, NA, RG 145.

grow most of their own food and feed. Hoover reasoned that it would be best to use former cotton and tobacco land for this purpose. He pointed out that the government could have bought considerable amounts of such land in 1933 for what it paid in rentals. He recognized that the former tenants on such land would not be ready to operate their own farms without a period of supervision and commented that experimentation with collective farming communities might be worthwhile. Hoover also recommended that the rented acres be used in 1934 and 1935 to provide land for a "very limited number" of displaced families, and that surplus dairy cows be "transferred" to the South to be distributed to tenants through local relief agencies.[21]

Calvin Hoover's recommendations to Wallace represented sentiments which were becoming more widely accepted throughout the country. Eventually, the Resettlement Administration, headed by Rexford Tugwell, attempted to place homeless tenants on small subsistence farms and even experimented with collective farms.[22] However, such ideas gained little vogue in AAA or in the Department of Agriculture, and one can easily imagine the reaction to them in the Cotton Division.

Secretary Wallace, Administrator Davis, and other key figures contended that AAA was not an agency of reform; therefore the liberals in AAA were forced to carry on their fight with very limited objectives and within the existing framework of AAA. A major battleground was the various landlord-tenant committees created by AAA. The history of these committees began in August, 1933, when the "Legal Advisory Committee" was set up to handle tenant complaints. When this arrangement proved inadequate in January, 1934, the Committee on Violations of Rental and Benefit Contracts was created, consisting of representatives from the Cotton Section, the Legal Division, and the Comptroller. E. A. Miller usually represented the Cotton Section and Alger Hiss or Margaret Bennett spoke for the Legal Division.

The Committee on Violations was to hear all complaints and adjudicate them,[23] but it experienced considerable difficulty. In February, 1935, it had a backlog of 1,655 cases under considera-

[21] Hoover, Memo to the Secretary, March 7, 1934, NA, RG 16.
[22] Resettlement Administration, *What the Resettlement Administration Has Done*, R. A. Misc. Pub. (Washington: U.S. Government Printing Office, 1936), *passim*.
[23] Margaret Bennett, Memo to Mr. Frank, February 4, 1935, NA, RG 145.

tion, 1,419 of which involved 1933 contracts and 158 from 1934. In a representative week the committee received 124 cases, 99 of which involved cotton. However, it was able to settle only 65 cases in a four-month period. Cases came in much faster than they were adjudicated and the committee quickly found itself more than a year behind in its work.[24] The principal reason, according to the committee, was "lack of adequate personnel to handle the great mass of complaints received." [25]

Despite its limitations the Committee on Violations made some important decisions. One was the case of the Tchula Plantation of Jefferson County, Arkansas, first reported by H. C. Malcom of the Arkansas Labor Bureau and later included in the Amberson Report. An investigation of the Tchula Plantation by Francis Shea revealed that the landlords had paid their tenants for the 1933 plow-up in the form of canceled debts including usurous interest. The Committee on Violations ruled that usury was a matter between landlord and tenant and had no bearing on the cotton contract. When it ordered payment on the Tchula contract, the Secretary approved the action.[26]

In another case the circumstances were almost identical, except investigators established that the landlord had not distributed or credited his sharecroppers with the full amount due them. The committee recommended that the landlord be requested to allow the Cotton Pool to pay his tenants directly out of money due the plantation. If he refused, his pooled cotton would be sold by the government and the proceeds given to the croppers.[27] The committee was also responsible for suspending payments to the Twist brothers of Cross County, Arkansas. The Twists were stubborn landlords who felt that the customary 50–50 arrangement was more than sharecroppers deserved. They steadfastly refused to make any division of payments to their tenants until forced to do so by the committee.[28]

In the spring of 1934, after Chester Davis became alarmed

[24] Report of the Committee on Violations, February 4, 1935, NA, RG 145.
[25] Committee on Violations, Memo to Administrator, Re: Contract of Twist Brothers, February 15, 1935, NA, RG 145.
[26] Memo of the Committee on Violations, December 4, 1935, NA, RG 145.
[27] Memo to the Secretary, Re: Contract of J. G. and Jesse Myar, October 11, 1935, NA, RG 145.
[28] Memo to Administrator, Re: Contract of Twist Brothers, February 15, 1935, NA, RG 145.

about enforcement of the tenant provision of the 1934 contract, he ordered D. P. Trent to have extension directors in the Cotton Belt set up three-man committees at the district level. These committees would settle or make recommendations concerning landlord-tenant disputes appealed from county committees. The members of the committees were to travel from county to county, giving advance notice of their arrival to "all interested parties," and hold hearings similar to court trials. Each case handled would be reported to Washington. In his instructions to the committeemen, Trent told them not to interfere with the normal agreements between landlords and tenants but to ensure "as far as possible" that those who grow and harvest cotton, particularly tenant farmers, received their just share of benefit payments.[29]

A rumor was circulating through AAA about this time that a "Compliance Committee" would also be set up in Washington. This story, combined with the order to organize the three-man committees in the districts, caused the Committee on Violations to ask Chester Davis for a clearer definition of its jurisdiction. However, the memo from the committee never reached Davis and the Legal Division suspected it had been sidetracked by the Cotton Section.[30] Their suspicion seemed confirmed on May 9 when Chester Davis announced to the press that eight district agents from the Extension Service had been named as field men to investigate complaints arising from the cotton contracts. Trent had supervisor responsibility over the new organization, and J. Phil Campbell, Chief of the Agricultural Rehabilitation Section and Former Director of Extension in Georgia, was to head this work. A committee in Washington consisting of Campbell, E. A. Miller, and W. J. Green would review the reports from the field adjustors.[31]

The Legal Division first knew of this new Adjustment Committee when members read about it in the newspaper. The lawyers assumed it was the work of the Cotton Section because there were no more steadfast supporters of Cully Cobb in all of AAA than Campbell, Miller, and Green.[32]

Chester Davis' instructions to the field adjustors were to

[29] "Procedure for Conducting Hearings," n.d., Landlord-Tenant File, NA, RG 145.
[30] Margaret Bennett, Memo to Mr. Frank, February 4, 1935, NA, RG 145.
[31] USDA, Press Release, May 19, 1934, NA, RG 145.
[32] Margaret Bennett, Memo to Mr. Frank, February 4, 1935, NA, RG 145.

familiarize themselves with the case files in Washington for three days before going to their assigned districts. Then, they were to go to the counties where cases were pending, get the tenants and landlords together, review their cases, and try to settle differences by conciliation. Davis warned the adjustors to work closely with local and state AAA officials and be careful not to offend them. Where the adjustors found willful violations they were authorized to cancel contracts or tell violators what must be done to keep the contract in force. They would also recommend substitute contracts if, for example, a managing share-tenant had been refused his proper status. Davis, recognizing that tenants might be reluctant to speak frankly before their landlords, suggested that adjustors interview tenants privately when the situation warranted. He told adjustors to make weekly reports to Campbell and to file full information of their actions with the county committees concerned.[33]

During the next four months, the field adjustors investigated 2,098 complaints of tenants in 320 counties. They were able to adjust 215 cases, they assisted county committees in settling 347 more, and they found 1,512 cases in which the complaint was unjustified. The investigators canceled twenty-four contracts, including eleven in Arkansas, but only after landlords refused to make the suggested adjustments.[34]

Having reviewed the investigations of the adjustors, the Adjustment Committee of Campbell, Miller, and Green made a general report to Davis. They concluded there had been no "wholesale displacement" of tenants and that in practically every case of eviction, the landlord had "some good reason for doing so." The committee found landlords cooperative "as a class" and said the charges that landlords were shifting from croppers to day labor were "overdrawn." The committee felt that most tenants entitled to the status of managing share-tenant had received it and, although there were probably some tenants who had been wrongfully denied the status, there were many tenants who attempted to defraud their landlords. To the allegation that county committees were landlord dominated, the committee answered that on the whole county committeemen were "very honest . . . and fair."

The committee also answered charges in the Amberson Report

[33] Chester Davis to District Agents and others, May 5, 1934, NA, RG 145.
[34] D. P. Trent, Memo to Chester Davis, December 28, 1934, NA, RG 145.

which specified eleven cases of contract violation. They found the charges in seven of these cases to be unfounded, canceled one contract, and adjusted the others. E. A. Miller personally investigated the Norcross Plantation, one of those mentioned, and spent "a good part of one day talking to riders and tenants." He found that Norcross had more tenants in 1934 than in 1933, which exonerated him of not keeping the normal number.[35]

The Adjustment Committee was not intended to be a permanent fixture. Its purpose to clear up accumulated tenant complaints while a new method was being found to handle them on a continuing basis. This was part of what Chester Davis had in mind when he created the Compliance Section in AAA at this time. The section was responsible for "development of compliance methods" and coordinating them with all commodity sections, but according to Margaret Bennett, no one ever quite understood this setup, and it never functioned effectively with regard to cotton contracts.[36]

In the meantime the Legal Division was unhappy with the Adjustment Committee, and Margaret Bennett, still serving on the Committee on Violations, began building a case against it. She found some strong evidence of pro-landlord sentiment on the part of the adjustors. One example involved hearings at Truman, Arkansas, at which J. O. Green, the STFU leader, appeared on behalf of a tenant who claimed the status of managing sharetenant. The landlord involved had agreed to grant the status and all that was needed was action by the county committee; however, when a hearing was held a county committeeman produced a signed statement in which the tenant retracted all his claims. The adjustor ruled that the tenant was not a managing share-tenant and recommended that Green be prosecuted for using the mails for extortion. The Adjustment Committee upheld the decision, but Margaret Bennett was convinced the action was pro-landlord because of the hasty withdrawal of the tenant's claim and the recommendation to prosecute Green when no evidence was given to show that he benefited personally from the case.[37]

[35] "Report of the Adjustment Committee," September 1, 1934, NA, RG 145.
[36] Bennett, Memo to Mr. Frank, February 4, 1935, NA, RG 145.
[37] Bennett, Exhibit "D," Memo to Mr. Frank, February 4, 1935, NA, RG 145.

In a case in Poinsett County, Arkansas, Miss Bennett found that fourteen tenants, who had complained to Secretary Wallace that they had not been allowed to use rented acres, were called in by the adjustor and told their claim was denied. In reporting this case, the adjustor wrote the word "none" in the space provided for evidence, and the Adjustment Committee accepted the decision.[38] The same adjustor accepted a list of tenants supplied by the manager of the Twist Plantation as conclusive evidence that there had been no wholesale evictions there.[39]

Meanwhile, Miss Bennett feuded openly with the representatives of the Cotton Section in the Committee on Violations. R. H. Polk of Helena, Arkansas, had withheld 1933 benefits from his tenants,[40] and when his case came before the committee, all but Miss Bennett were willing to allow final payment on Polk's contract. Miss Bennett kept the case open until the other members of the committee finally agreed that Polk had violated the contract and that half the money due him from the Cotton Pool should be given to his tenants. Polk was also forced to resign as chairman of his community committee.[41] Later, both Senator Hattie Carraway and Senate Majority Leader Joe Robinson of Arkansas wrote Secretary Wallace on behalf of Polk.[42] Despite this pressure, Wallace upheld the decision of the committee;[43] however, he penciled a note on the final report stating that Polk's tenants should not receive more than they were entitled to under the contract.[44] Finally, in August, 1935, Oscar Johnston of the Cotton Pool was ordered to sell Polk's options and distribute payments to thirty-six of his sharecroppers. It had taken AAA a year and a half and a tremendous effort through hearings, correspondence, special investigations, and consideration by high ranking officials to make final disposition of the Polk case.[45]

[38] Bennett, Exhibit "E," Memo to Mr. Frank, February 4, 1935, NA, RG 145.

[39] "Report of the Adjustment Committee," September 1, 1934, pp. 66–69, NA, RG 145.

[40] Dell, Memo to Mr. Frank, July 19, 1934, NA, RG 145.

[41] Bennett, Memo to Mr. Hiss, July 7, 1934, NA, RG 145; and Chester Davis, Memo to the Secretary, September 27, 1934, NA, RG 145.

[42] Robinson to Wallace, December 19, 1934, NA, RG 145; and Tugwell to Carraway, November 21, 1934, NA, RG 145.

[43] Wallace to Robinson, January 15, 1935, NA, RG 145; and Payne to Frank, January 7, 1935, NA, RG 145.

[44] Chester Davis, Memo to the Secretary, September 27, 1934, NA, RG 145.

[45] Tugwell, Memo to Oscar Johnston, August 30, 1935, NA, RG 145.

Because of such delays, the Legal Division sought a clear statement of policy regarding the handling of tenant complaints and creation of a landlord-tenant committee in AAA which could decide such disputes with finality. Meanwhile, Margaret Bennett reached the conclusion that "investigation will not be adequate if left to the local authorities." [46] Jerome Frank agreed, since he believed that local committees were "frequently composed of landlords," [47] and he applied enough pressure on Chester Davis to force him to call a conference in D. P. Trent's office on July 3, 1934. Davis put Trent in charge of considering Frank's proposal for a landlord-tenant committee. Present at the conference in Trent's office besides Trent were Commodities Division Chief Victor Christgau, Frank, Comptroller John B. Payne, E. A. Miller, W. J. Green, Margaret Bennett, and Alger Hiss. They agreed that a definite landlord-tenant policy was needed and that a policy committee should be created to make recommendations. Trent, Calvin Hoover, Frank, Payne, and Cully Cobb would constitute the new committee. Alger Hiss suggested that once they determined a policy, a subcommittee should be created to make investigations and adjudicate cases. This idea was accepted. It was further agreed that the Violations Committee should be abolished and its records taken over by the new subcommittee.[48]

Plans progressed for a new committee until Cully Cobb changed his mind about it and addressed a memorandum to Christgau opposing its creation.[49] He said his Division had primary responsibility for the cotton program and that the people in it understood cotton problems better than anyone else in AAA. He felt that if the cotton producers and local committees were made to feel they had lost responsibility for enforcement of the contracts to some agency in Washington, the results would be "disastrous to the program." [50] The Legal Division pointed out in rebuttal that no clearly stated policy for settling tenant claims had been made, that there was no reason why such matters should be left solely to the Cotton Section since one policy could apply to all commodities, and that a landlord-tenant committee

[46] Bennett, Memo to Mr. Appleby, January 14, 1935, NA, RG 145.
[47] Frank, Memo to Mr. McConnaughey, January 25, 1935, NA, RG 145.
[48] Hiss, Memo of Conference, July 3, 1934, NA, RG 145.
[49] Bennett, Memo to Mr. Frank, February 4, 1935, NA, RG 145.
[50] Cobb, Memo to Mr. Christgau, September 8, 1934, NA, RG 145.

could make such a policy.[51] But Cobb nevertheless remained adamant.

Trent's stand on the proposed landlord-tenant committee was, as usual, eminently reasonable. Although he recognized that Cully Cobb and the Cotton Section were "entirely conscientious in their point of view," he knew that if the proposed committee were pushed through it would be over their objections. "I would like to say frankly," he wrote to Jerome Frank, "that there has been a rather systematic effort [by the Cotton Section] to delay or forestall most of the efforts which we have made to deal with this problem." Trent was genuinely concerned about the large numbers of complaints being received by AAA, and he observed that "we have been inclined to pussy-foot and dodge responsibility" by telling claimants to see their county agent or committee. Trent did not seek the job of handling the landlord-tenant committee, but he would take it because of his interest in protecting the rights of tenants.[52]

The Legal Division continued to press for the Landlord-Tenant Committee, but their efforts were fruitless as Cobb successfully blocked formation of the committee. Hopes for a compromise between the agrarians and the liberals suffered a major setback when Trent became convinced that the situation was hopeless and decided to return to his post as Director of Extension in Oklahoma. Acceptance of Trent's position was probably the only chance that AAA had to avoid a great battle over tenancy.

Trent's recommendations, first expressed in the spring of 1934, contained the nucleus of almost everything accomplished by the New Deal for tenants as well as some things that were never done. He proposed a thorough government study of tenancy, better means for adjudication of landlord-tenant disputes outside the influence of county agents, the inclusion of all tenants in cotton contracts, the founding of farming colonies for stranded farm workers, efforts to get greater cooperation from the states in solving tenant problems especially in Negro education, a careful study of the possibility of using the minimum wage set by NRA for farm labor, and help for capable tenants in securing their own land. Trent felt the goal of making tenant farmers an

[51] R. K. McConnaughey, Memo to Mr. Frank, September 24, 1934, NA, RG 145.
[52] Trent to Frank, September 18, 1934, NA, RG 145.

independent and productive class should be "administratively recognized" and that the full force of the federal government including all agencies concerned should be put behind the task.[53] If there is one man in the fight in AAA who stands out for his wisdom and compassion, it is D. P. Trent. His departure removed the middle ground of the battle in AAA.

Before Trent left, he made one last effort to solve immediate problems. Having just learned of FERA's plans to provide relief for evicted tenants, he expressed his misgivings to Chester Davis. Though he approved of the plan, he feared it implied that AAA did not intend to stand firm against landlords who took unfair advantage of their tenants. He wondered if AAA was perhaps passing its own responsibility to FERA. Once they learned that FERA would take care of their tenants, Trent warned Davis, the landlords would cease their own efforts to do so.

Trent also told Davis that, although the Adjustment Committee had done a good job, there was a flood of new complaints concerning landlords converting from tenants to day labor. "Information which I have," he wrote, "indicates this practice is rather general throughout the cotton belt." He also indicated landlords were setting up new financial charges against their tenants and making side agreements to deprive them of government benefits. Trent warned Davis that great difficulties lay ahead for AAA in protecting tenant farmers, and he called for a "very definite and positive stand" on the problem of landlord-tenant relations.[54]

Meanwhile, the situation in which the Violations Committee found itself had become impossible. The Cotton Section refused to make summaries of the cases so that the committee could consider them expeditiously. It prevented Margaret Bennett from seeing complaints until the day before they were presented to the committee and occasionally delayed claims as much as eight months. Miss Bennett notified her immediate superior, Alger Hiss, that matters had reached the basic issue of whether complaints were to be investigated to see that government money was distributed fairly or whether they were to be ignored and money paid just as if no complaints had been received.[55]

[53] Trent to Extension Directors in Southern States, April 12, 1934, NA, RG 145.
[54] Trent, Memo to Chester Davis, December 28, 1934, NA, RG 145.
[55] Bennett, Memo to Mr. Hiss, July 7, 1934, NA, RG 145.

In early February, 1935, Miss Bennett grew so exasperated that she wrote a memorandum to Chester Davis and Jerome Frank declaring bluntly that there was "growing and justifiable public dissatisfaction" with the handling of landlord-tenant disputes and that if something were not done, the reduction program would be "seriously discredited." She complained that there were six different sections in AAA handling tenant complaints with no clear jurisdiction or policy to guide them.

The outspoken lady lawyer indicated four major tenancy questions which needed immediate policy decisions. They included whether judgments withholding the status of managing share-tenant could be appealed beyond county committees, the procedure to be used in handling claims in 1935, the extent to which paragraph 7 should be enforced, and the question of what section of AAA had final responsibility for enforcement. The solution offered by Miss Bennett was a landlord-tenant committee. Her plan was to abolish all functions of local committees in tenant disputes and let the new committee handle them in Washington. If necessary, field representatives could be sent out to investigate and make recommendations.[56] The chiefs of AAA took no action on Miss Bennett's suggestions, and the problems continued.

[56] Bennett, Memo to Mr. Frank, February 4, 1935, NA, RG 145.

chapter eight

Purge in AAA

The situation in AAA had now reached the breaking point. All that was needed to goad the two sides into full combat was an issue which was clearly defined. With almost unbelievable irony, such an issue was provided by the case of Hiram Norcross, whose evictions led to the formation of the Southern Tenant Farmers' Union. Norcross' case was currently pending before the Committee on Violations.

The first complaints concerning Norcross reached the Cotton Section in the spring of 1934. As mentioned earlier, E. A. Miller gave Norcross a clean bill of health on his tour through eastern Arkansas. J. Phil Campbell's survey came to the same conclusion, both men exonerating Norcross of any contract violation because he had more tenants in 1934 than in 1933. But the Amberson Report charged that Norcross had not reduced acreage ratably and was replacing white tenants with black ones. When the Cotton Section investigated, it found these charges false. No further action was taken until Amberson wrote his friend Paul Appleby that Norcross was evicting tenants solely for membership in the tenants' union and had threatened to withhold their payments if they caused trouble. Appleby turned the matter over to Jerome Frank, who gave it to Margaret Bennett, his representative on the Committee on Violations. Miss Bennett, knowing E. A. Miller had previously investigated the case, asked him to prepare a memorandum to Appleby for the committee.[1]

In his memorandum, Miller took the view that, since the contract required landlords to maintain only the normal number of tenants, and since his own investigations revealed that Norcross had done this, he had not violated the contract. Miller felt that if Norcross actually withheld parity payments from tenants, it would be a violation of the contract, but to threaten to do so was not a violation. Since there was no concrete evidence that Norcross had withheld payments, Miller recommended that parity payments be made on Norcross' contract. He also said that Norcross should be advised of the situation, and then, if he failed to distribute the parity money, he should be forced to do so by legal action.[2]

When Miller's memorandum reached Appleby, he wrote a scorching message to Cully Cobb saying Miller's attitude was "clearly loaded on the side of the landlords," as it seemed to him an effort "to find out how not to do something for the tenants." He pointed out that it would be much simpler for AAA to withhold Norcross' parity check and pay his tenants separately than to take legal action to recover from Norcross if he did not distribute the money properly.

Appleby told Cobb that the Cotton Section seemed biased in favor of the landlords and that the complete file of the Norcross Case was being turned over to Secretary Wallace. Appleby wrote: ". . . no single problem before the Department [is] more difficult or more important to the continuing success of our program than this one of landlord-tenant equities in the cotton belt." He told Cobb that solution of the problem would require extraordinary effort and positive plans by the Cotton Section, rather

---

[1] Bennett, Memo to Mr. Frank, January 10, 1935, NA, RG 145.
[2] Miller, Memo to Mr. Cobb, December 26, 1934, NA, RG 145.

than attempts "to evade responsibility." [3] Before sending the
memorandum, Appleby asked Assistant Administrator Byrd if he
thought it would help any "to jar Cobb a little bit with a statement of this kind from me." Byrd felt it would.[4]

About this time, Jerome Frank received an urgent plea from
C. T. Carpenter, attorney for a group of tenants evicted by Norcross who were suing in an Arkansas court for their rights under
paragraph 7. Carpenter wanted AAA to enter the dispute on the
side of the tenants to ensure that the paragraph was enforced.
Frank wired him for more details [5] and ordered his Litigations
Section to look into the possibilities of intervening in order to
remove the case to federal court.[6] Cully Cobb learned of this action and assured Chester Davis that his section would not allow
Norcross to withhold parity payments from his tenants for making trouble as he had threatened. He also said that the government could not intervene between Norcross and his tenants in
court because the cotton contracts gave the government a concern only in matters between itself and landlords or tenants, not
in landlord-tenant disputes.[7] Strangely enough, after some painful legal machinations, the Litigations Section reached much
the same conclusion.[8]

Also about this time, the delegation from the STFU arrived
in Washington. Members talked to Henry Wallace, who promised
to investigate conditions in Arkansas. A mass meeting of sharecroppers in Marked Tree gathered to hear the report of the
delegation when it returned to Arkansas, and after a near-riot
Ward Rodgers was arrested for anarchy and blasphemy.[9]

Union members in eastern Arkansas were in an ugly mood
over the arrest of Rodgers; H. L. Mitchell and William Amberson
wired collect to AAA that it was imperative for a government
investigator to come to Arkansas immediately if bloodshed and

[3] Appleby, Memo to Mr. Cobb, December 27, 1934, NA, RG 145.
[4] Appleby, Memo to Mr. Byrd, December 28, 1934; and accompanying
endorsement, NA, RG 145.
[5] Carpenter to Frank, January 11, 1935, NA, RG 145.
[6] A. M. Wilding-White, Memo to Mr. Abt, January 17, 1935, NA, RG
145.
[7] Cobb, Memo to Chester Davis, January 5, 1935, NA, RG 145.
[8] A. M. Wilding-White, Memo to Mr. Abt, January 17, 1935, NA, RG
145.
[9] For a full account of these events, see Chapter 9.

class war were to be avoided.[10] Since sentiment was already growing in the AAA for an impartial investigation of matters in Arkansas, Assistant Administrator Byrd recommended that an unbiased report be made immediately by someone "other than the Cotton Section." Byrd felt that if a lawyer from the Legal Division were sent it would do much to stop evictions by landlords.[11] In addition, Harry Hopkins, Administrator of FERA, requested Jerome Frank to send a lawyer to look into the arrest of Ward Rodgers since he was an FERA employee and the agency had no legal staff.[12]

When Wallace and Davis had approved sending an investigator to Arkansas, Byrd recommended red-haired Mary Connor Myers, a Boston lawyer who had just come to AAA at the request of Henry Wallace.[13] Mrs. Myers had an excellent record as an attorney and was one of the few lawyers in the Legal Division with a truly conservative background. Perhaps both these factors played a part in Byrd's choice. Jerome Frank instructed Mrs. Myers to go to Arkansas "for the purpose of making an investigation concerning the eviction of sharecroppers from the Fairview Farms Company farms at Tyronza, and to determine whether suit should be brought in the Federal court under paragraph 7. . . ." Frank also told her to look into the case being brought against Norcross by his former tenants in state court, and the case of Ward Rodgers. Frank said there should be no publicity and Mrs. Myers was to make no statements to the press.[14]

Before leaving, Mrs. Myers called on Cully Cobb to see if he had any instructions. Cobb knew little about Mrs. Myers, only that "she knew nothing about agriculture." He suspected she was one of the radicals of the Legal Division; so he told her that he was not sending her to Arkansas and therefore had no instructions.[15]

Chester Davis ordered Mrs. Myers to find out how many tenants Hiram Norcross had in 1933 and 1934, how much acreage

[10] Mitchell and Amberson to AAA (Telegram), January 16, 1935, NA, RG 145.

[11] Byrd, Memo to Mr. Appleby, January 9, 1935, NA, RG 145.

[12] Mary Connor Myers to author, October 6, 1959, p. 2.

[13] *Time*, March 5, 1935.

[14] Mary Connor Myers to author, October 6, 1959, p. 2.

[15] Cobb to author, October 6, 1959, p. 6.

in cotton there was each year, how many new houses there were, how many nonunion members had been evicted, how many members of the tenants' union were left.[16]

When Mary Connor Myers arrived in Arkansas she found it impossible to avoid publicity. The trial of Ward Rodgers had attracted reporters from all over the country, and they found her presence in Arkansas made good copy. She wired Frank that she was going to explain her mission because the reporters were talking to "union and Socialist" officers and she felt it better for her to explain what she was doing in Arkansas than for them to.[17] Accordingly, the next day the *Memphis Press-Scimitar* announced that Mrs. Myers had come to Arkansas to investigate charges of violations of cotton contracts. It called her a "fearless and most thorough investigator" and said if she found any fire where there was so much smoke, Secretary Henry Wallace would "put it out." [18]

For several days Mrs. Myers talked to hundreds of share-croppers, took eighty or ninety affidavits, and was constantly amazed that so many croppers came to see her despite the icy weather. It apparently never occurred to her that H. L. Mitchell, her guide on her tour of the plantation area, was responsible for the sharecroppers' gathering.[19]

On January 18, Mrs. Myers wired Jerome Frank that she was hearing "one long story [of] human greed" and that paragraph 7 was only one part of the cotton contract which was being "openly and generally violated." She confided to Frank that the share-croppers she talked to were of a "much higher class" than she had expected and that all of them were "pathetically pleased" that the government sent someone to listen to them.[20] Reports hinting at Mrs. Myers' findings began to appear in newspapers, and this caused great worry to Frank, Byrd, and Appleby, who did not want such matters publicized.[21]

When she checked the Norcross plantation according to Chester Davis' instructions, Mrs. Myers confirmed the earlier

[16] Myers, Memo to Chester Davis, February 13, 1935, NA, RG 145.
[17] Myers to Frank (Telegram), January 20, 1935, NA, RG 145.
[18] *Memphis Press-Scimitar*, January 21, 1935.
[19] Mary Connor Myers to author, October 6, 1959, p. 2.
[20] Myers to Frank (Telegram), January 18, 1935, NA, RG 145.
[21] Frank, Memo to Paul Porter, February 2, 1935, NA, RG 145; and Frank, Memo to Alfred Stedman, January 30, 1935, NA, RG 145.

reports that Norcross had more tenants in 1934 than a year before, even though his acreage was considerably less. She saw three new tenant houses but was told there were ten. She asked Mitchell how many union members were still on the plantation and, although he said about forty, she could find only five or six who would admit it. And they were reluctant to talk. Mrs. Myers found that no nonunion members had been evicted.[22]

Mrs. Myers did not report her findings concerning Norcross until she returned to Washington. Before then, however, a letter arrived in the AAA offices from Norcross explaining his side of things. Norcross claimed that he told E. A. Miller during the investigation of his plantation that he would withdraw his contract if it infringed on his power to evict tenants. According to Norcross, Miller told him that paragraph 7 required a planter to keep only the same number of tenants, not the identical tenants. Norcross also claimed he expressed concern to Miller that the paragraph required landlords to allow tenants to live in their houses rent-free. By Norcross' account, Miller explained this meant only those houses which the landlord could not fill with working tenants. Later, because of the agitation of his share-croppers by the STFU, Norcross wrote to Poinsett County Agent R. L. McGill to ask if he could evict certain undesirable tenants for union activities. McGill told him the government's only concern was that he keep the same number of tenants. In his letter to AAA, Norcross pointed out that every house on his plantation was occupied and he had built eleven new ones. He claimed he had paid all evicted croppers their part of the parity payment although he had not yet received his, and he said he was willing to abide by all AAA rulings and would welcome an investigation of his plantation.[23]

When Norcross' letter reached the desk of Jerome Frank, it caused a major explosion, for it was from reading the letter that Frank first learned that the Cotton Section was telling landlords they did not have to maintain the same tenants, only the same number.[24] Frank talked to E. A. Miller to determine if Miller had actually given Norcross that interpretation. Miller said he could

[22] Myers, Memo to Chester Davis, February 13, 1935, NA, RG 145.
[23] Norcross to Appleby, January 5, 1935, NA, RG 145.
[24] Frank, Memo to Mr. Byrd, January 12, 1935, NA, RG 145.

not remember what he told Norcross, but it was entirely possible he had given the interpretation because it was the one being used by the Cotton Section.[25]

Frank now went into high gear. Chester Davis was out of town, so he notified Assistant Administrator Byrd that the Cotton Section had apparently been making legal opinions and that his Opinions Section was preparing a new interpretation of paragraph 7. He also persuaded Byrd to send out a telegram to AAA officials in Arkansas saying that the Norcross case was now before the Secretary and instructing them to make no statements and take no action which might be considered as interpretation of the paragraph.[26] Then Frank drafted a memorandum to Cully Cobb for Acting Administrator Christgau's signature ordering Cobb in the future to submit all legal questions to the Legal Division before sending out information on them to the public, or to county agents.[27] Frank next put his Opinions Section to work on the question of whether the Cotton Section's interpretation was legally binding.[28] The Opinions Section ruled it was not. Meanwhile, Alger Hiss had worked up an opinion, concurred in by Frank, that membership in the tenants' union did not make tenants a menace or nuisance within the meaning of paragraph 7. Consequently, the Legal Division prepared to take legal action against Norcross.[29]

At the same time, the Opinions Section was busy on the most important opinion, the reinterpretation of paragraph 7. Telford Taylor, a lawyer in the section, had charge of the research and drafting of the opinion, with Francis Shea, the Chief of the section, and his immediate superior, Alger Hiss, participating in the substance and even the language of the draft.[30] The opinion, when it was finally finished in early February, was thirty-six pages long; it attempted by the use of strictly legal devices to settle the outstanding questions concerning tenancy. The most important of these was, of course, evictions. The opinion came to the conclusion that a landlord was required to keep the

[25] Frank, Memo to Mr. Byrd, January 14, 1935, NA, RG 145.
[26] Frank, Memo to Mr. Byrd, and attached telegram, January 14, 1935, NA, RG 145.
[27] Christgau, Memo to Mr. Cobb, January 14, 1935, NA, RG 145.
[28] Frank, Memo to Mr. Shea, January 14, 1935, NA, RG 145.
[29] Frank, Memo to Mr. Byrd, January 12, 1935, NA, RG 145.
[30] Hiss to author, September 17, 1960.

identical tenants, provided they were willing to remain and did not become nuisances or menaces. If a tenant left or was rightfully replaced, the landlord was required to replace him with a person of equal status "if possible." The opinion declared that the Cotton Section's interpretation had not been a "sound construction of paragraph 7." It readily admitted that the phrase in paragraph 7 requiring the landlord to maintain "the normal number of tenants and other employees" contained no express requirement of identity or continuity of personnel from year to year; however, these words should be read in context. Landlords were required elsewhere in the paragraph to permit *all* tenants to occupy their houses rent-free and to carry out the acreage reduction with the "least possible amount of labor, economic, and social disturbance." Discharging tenants at the end of 1934, according to the opinion, violated both these requirements.

Another argument offered by the Opinions Section was that landlords needed to keep the same tenants in order to have a prior standard to use in making the acreage reduction among tenants "as nearly ratable as practicable" as the contract specified. Also, since landlords were forbidden to reduce the status of a tenant or deprive him of any right to which his status before the signing of the contract would entitle him, the opinion reasoned that the same tenant must be retained after the signing of the contract; otherwise, a landlord could reduce the status of a tenant, hire another to take his place, and not have to divide parity payments with either tenant. Nor would this procedure violate the requirement to keep the same number of tenants.

One feature of paragraph 7 posed a threat to reinterpretation. Certain rights in the paragraph were granted to tenants "and other workers"; other privileges were given only to tenants. Only tenants had the right to occupy houses rent-free during the contract period. Obviously, it was imperative that sharecroppers be considered as tenants, or else the strongest argument for their tenure on an individual basis would be destroyed. The opinion went to great lengths with legal arguments to establish that croppers were tenants. Finally, it stated flatly, ". . . the status of a share-tenant and a sharecropper is precisely the same, except that the tenant receives a larger percentage of the crop and must provide his own work stock and equipment." [31]

[31] Shea to McConnaughey, February 4, 1935, NA, RG 145.

While all the feverish activity was taking place in the Legal Division concerning Norcross, Margaret Bennett called a special meeting of the Committee on Violations to consider a complaint received from eleven of Norcross' tenants who, they said, had been evicted solely for union membership.[32] When Miss Bennett presented a proposal that landlords should be allowed to evict tenants only if they were nuisances or menaces, Miller and W. C. Hudson voted it down.[33] The two then wrote a committee report to the Secretary saying that if the Legal Division attempted to reinterpret paragraph 7 to require landlords to keep the same tenants, it would constitute an "interference with the contractural relationship existing between landlords and tenants." They argued that the purpose of paragraph 7 was to require landlords to provide houses and fuel for tenants without charge as an offset to the fact that landlords got the lion's share of government benefits. They said the paragraph was not intended to force landlords to take care of tenants for whom they had no use. Miller and Hudson recommended that the Secretary not attempt to enforce the Legal Division's reinterpretation of paragraph 7 because it would be "inadvisable administratively" and not in keeping with "public policy." Margaret Bennett did not sign the report, saying she would write a dissenting opinion. Cully Cobb and the Comptroller John Payne approved the report, but Jerome Frank would not sign it.[34]

In her separate report, Miss Bennett argued that if the majority position were sustained, AAA would have no legal power to prevent evictions. She boiled the problem down to an administrative question of whether AAA should assert its legal rights or make no effort to obtain compliance with the contract. She said that Norcross' tenants had organized merely to protect their rights, pointing out that the National Industrial Recovery Act and other recent legislation guaranteed the right of workers to organize. She recommended that Norcross be forced to restore his tenants, saying no action would do more to stop the "rising tide of criticism" against AAA.[35]

[32] Petition of Eleven Sharecroppers to H. A. Wallace, December 12, 1934, NA, RG 145.

[33] Bennett, Memo to Mr. Frank, January 10, 1935, NA, RG 145.

[34] Committee on Violations, Memo to the Secretary, January 10, 1935, NA, RG 145.

[35] Bennett, Memo to the Secretary, January 12, 1935, NA, RG 145.

In explaining why he had not approved the majority report of the Violations Committee, Jerome Frank told Secretary Wallace that Miller and Hudson based their arguments on the intent of those who wrote paragraph 7. The established principle of law, he said, was to ignore the subjective intent of those writing a law or contract and judge it solely on the wording. He complained that the Cotton Section, through Miller, had made a legal opinion in the majority report of the Violations Committee and that legal opinions were the job of the Legal Division. Frank acknowledged Margaret Bennett's recommendation but said he preferred not to suggest a policy in this matter. Final decision, he felt, would have to come from Administrator Davis and Secretary Wallace.[36]

When Chester Davis returned from his Western field trip, he found his agency split down the middle over the Norcross Case and the fundamental issues involved. He was also greeted with hundreds of wires and letters from landlords, chambers of commerce, cotton growers' associations, and county agents clamoring for him to stop the threatened reinterpretation of paragraph 7.[37] One such letter, from nineteen county agents in northeastern Arkansas, pointed out that all the committeemen in their area had told the landlords that they need keep only the normal number of tenants and that to change now would cause "the greatest embarrassment," possible withdrawal of many contracts, and "endless litigation."[38]

On February 5, Frank forwarded the legal opinion reinterpreting paragraph 7 to Davis. It was signed by Francis Shea and approved by Frank and Alger Hiss.[39] Along with it, Frank sent a memorandum from Hiss which affirmed that paragraph 7 required landlords to keep the same tenants but suggested it would be "difficult in most instances" to enforce. He foresaw that the government would have trouble proving unwarranted evictions in court because landlords could claim the evicted tenants had become menaces or nuisances.[40]

[36] Frank, Memo to the Secretary, January 12, 1935, NA, RG 145.
[37] Calvin B. Hoover, Memo to the Secretary, Febrauary 5, 1935, NA, RG 145.
[38] Nineteen County Agents to Chester Davis, January 26, 1935, NA, RG 145.
[39] Frank, Memo to Chester Davis, February 4, 1935, NA, RG 145.
[40] Hiss, Memo to Mr. Frank, January 26, 1935, NA, RG 145.

Davis decided to go to Wallace with the matter. He asked the Secretary to secure from "whatever agencies you deem appropriate" a legal opinion on the question of whether paragraph 7 required landlords to keep the same tenants or the normal number in 1935. He asserted that this question had been discussed at length during the writing and approval of the 1934–35 contract and that all concerned agreed that the purpose of paragraph 7 was to prevent the acreage reduction from cutting loose large numbers of tenants in 1934. Also, if normal arrangements were not renewed in 1935, it was agreed that the paragraph would allow former tenants to remain in their houses rent-free and to have the use of the rented acres for subsistence purposes. Davis stated that the Legal Division gave no "intimation" at the time of an interpretation contrary to this. He pointed out to Wallace that since that time both he and the Secretary had declared in official publications that landlords were required to keep only the normal number of tenants and that the same interpretation was found in the report of Calvin Hoover.[41]

The chips were now down. Wallace knew that if he upheld the new interpretation of paragraph 7, Davis, Johnston, most of the Cotton Section including Cobb, and many other agrarians in AAA would probably resign, thus leaving AAA with a void of experienced men to administer the cotton program. Nor were the urban liberals qualified to take their places. Also, Wallace realized the outcry from the powerful landlords of the South would be unparalleled. Oscar Johnston warned that if the Secretary attempted to intervene in "private labor disputes" between landlords and tenants, it would be "absolutely fatal to the success of the cotton program" and "a serious political blunder." [42] He was probably right.

On the other hand, if Wallace backed Davis and the agrarians, one of the major functions of the Legal Division, that of giving legal opinions, would be undercut and some of the liberals might resign in order to make the matter public. If that happened, it might add weight to the charges that AAA was unfair to tenants. Wallace's natural inclinations were probably to back Jerome

[41] Chester Davis, Memo to the Secretary, February 7, 1935, NA, RG 145. Davis was correct in citing these instances. However, Jerome Frank managed to convince Hoover that he had been wrong in the interpretation, Hoover, Memo to the Secretary, January 9, 1935, NA, RG 145.
[42] Johnston, Memo to Chester Davis, January 26, 1935, NA, RG 145.

Frank and the liberals but his fear of repercussions among the Southerners in Congress was overriding. "Of course," he wrote years later, "[the liberals] presented a strong case for the tenants but the reforms they wanted would have blown the department out of the water at that time." Wallace felt that if he stood by Frank, he would have to resign as Secretary and "make way for someone else who could get along better with the men from the South in Congress." But he knew this would be no solution since the next Secretary would only have to face the same problem. Therefore, Wallace decided to side with Chester Davis because he thought the reinterpretation of paragraph 7 was "bad law and would endanger the whole agricultural program." [43]

Davis saw the efforts of the Legal Division to guarantee the tenure of tenants as only part of "deep and long-continued" differences which went "far beyond the questions of cotton tenancy." The thing that angered Davis most was that the liberals, "with some help from the outside office of the Secretary [Appleby], sought to put over, during my absence from the office, a dishonest legal opinion radically changing the interpretation . . . of the 1934–35 cotton contract . . . midway during its two year term." He felt the opinion was dishonest because the same men who prepared and approved the reinterpretation sat through the tough week-after-week sessions of preparing the contract in 1933 and approved it then with "full understanding of the agreed meaning of the tenancy clauses." [44]

After Wallace disapproved the proposed interpretation of paragraph 7, Davis dismissed Jerome Frank, Francis Shea, Lee Pressman, and Gardner Jackson on February 5, 1935. He forced Frederick Howe to resign as Consumers' Counsel but let him accept a position of less responsibility in the section. Davis would have fired Paul Appleby if Appleby had been working in AAA rather than in the Secretary's office.[45] Those fired were the ones who had a part in writing the reinterpretation of paragraph 7, plus Gardner Jackson, who had crossed Davis and Wallace before as Assistant Consumers' Counsel. Davis also wanted to purge Hiss, but Wallace would not agree. The reasons for this refusal remain something of a mystery. Perhaps Hiss's memoran-

[43] Wallace to author, June 13, 1959.
[44] Chester Davis to author, June 15, 1959.
[45] Lord, *The Wallaces of Iowa*, p. 405.

dum which accompanied the fatal legal opinion saved him. He resigned several weeks later, along with Victor Christgau, but it was not clear whether they resigned voluntarily or were forced out.[46] Years later Hiss stated that his resignation was neither "asked for or suggested" and was based solely on an inability to continue his duties with AAA because of his work with the Senate Munitions Committee. Hiss had been on loan to the Committee for several months and had been dividing his time between the Committee and AAA.[47] Jerome Frank and Gardner Jackson thought Hiss should have resigned the day they were fired, and years later they refused to come to his aid for this reason when he was accused of espionage.[48] According to Hiss, he offered his resignation orally to Davis shortly before the purge when Davis told him the reinterpretation of paragraph 7 was not intellectually honest. When Davis apologized for this remark, Hiss withdrew his resignation.[49] The only explanation for the absence of Margaret Bennett from the list of those purged is that, although she was probably the most outspoken champion of tenants' rights, she had no part in writing the reinterpretation of paragraph 7 and was not influential in policy matters.

Late in the day of the dismissals, Wallace sent word that he would see two of the liberals. Frank and Hiss went to the Secretary's office. Wallace greeted them as "the best fighters in a good cause" with whom he had ever worked, but added that he would have to confirm the dismissals. Frank asked Wallace why he had not talked it over with the liberals beforehand, rather than letting Chester Davis swing the axe. Wallace replied that he just could not face them.[50]

Within a few days, Wallace sent a telegram to the Memphis Chamber of Commerce, one of the groups which had protested the reinterpretation of paragraph 7. It said: "Section seven of cotton contract does not bind landowners to keep the *same* tenants. That is the official and final interpretation of the Solicitor of the Department of Agriculture and no other interpretation will be given." Wallace explained that landowners would be

[46] *New York Times,* February 7, 1935, p. 2, and February 21, 1935, p. 1.
[47] Hiss to author, December 28, 1961.
[48] Gardner Jackson, interview with author, July 28, 1959.
[49] Hiss to author, December 28, 1961.
[50] Gardner Jackson, "Henry Wallace: A Divided Mind," *Atlantic Monthly,* CLXXXII (August, 1948), 28.

expected not to reduce the number of their tenants but individual tenants would be no more secure in their tenure than they would be without the cotton contract. No attempt would be made to supervise the customary arrangements between landowners and tenants, he said, but compliance with the spirit of paragraph 7 would be expected. The contents of the telegram were released to the press.[51]

On the day after the dismissals, Chester Davis and Henry Wallace stood shoulder-to-shoulder at a press conference before a hundred reporters, some of them openly hostile. The questions of the newsmen were barbed, a few of them planted. Was Hiss to go? No, said both Davis and Wallace. What about Tugwell? He would continue his duties.[52] One reporter reminded Wallace that "right winger" George Peek had walked the plank last year and now the left wingers were being ousted. Which way was AAA going, he asked. Wallace, indulging in his weakness for mixed metaphors, replied, "You can't have the ship listing right and then left. It must go straight along. Straight down the middle of the road."

Wallace said the liberals were being dismissed "for the greatest possible harmony" in AAA, and that he and Davis had first discussed the matter in December. He also expressed the view that it was important to have the key positions in AAA filled with men who had an agricultural background. For his part, Davis attributed the shake-up to "mounting difficulty in getting things done." The executives also announced that Calvin Hoover would take over as Consumers' Counsel and that the agencies would become chiefly a statistical service.[53]

The reinterpretation of paragraph 7 was not mentioned at the press conference. Naturally, Wallace and Davis did not want the purge put in that light, since it would make them look prolandlord. And certainly, there was much more involved than this one issue. Some of the liberals, however, chose to raise it. Gardner Jackson, now fighting mad, arranged to have a *March of Time* film made of tenant union activities in Arkansas, and when he appeared in the film he stated in a booming voice that

[51] Wallace to Memphis Chamber of Commerce (Telegram), February 12, 1935, NA, RG 145.

[52] Lord, *Wallaces of Iowa*, p. 407.

[53] *New York Times*, February 7, 1935, p. 2.

Jerome Frank and the others were purged because they tried to help the sharecroppers.[54]

Jackson's friend, Marquis Childs, reported in the *St. Louis Post-Dispatch* that the blowup in AAA was the result of a dispute over paragraph 7 and quoted Jackson as saying, "I don't blame Chester Davis . . . for what he did. He was under great pressure from the planters." [55]

During the weeks that followed the purge, rumors persisted that Tugwell would resign. On February 22 he announced he would stay, and reporters assumed it was out of loyalty to the President.[56] Jerome Frank accepted a position as Assistant Railroad Counsel for the Reconstruction Finance Corporation,[57] and most of the other purgees moved into good jobs with other government agencies. This turn of events may explain Tugwell's failure to resign. However, there were also rumors that some of the purgees felt Tugwell had not given them the support they deserved or expected.[58]

The press reaction to the purge in AAA was mixed. The *New York Times* wondered why such a peaceful pursuit as agriculture was so plagued by discord. It saw the purge as the beginning of the end of the Brain Trust. "The millennium-rushers have been rushed," it commented. The *Times* felt that what had happened in AAA was victory of the bureaucrats over the idealists, and now all would go smoothly in the agency—until the next reorganization.[59]

Raymond Gram Swing in *Nation* viewed the dismissals as the defeat of the social outlook in agricultural policy. He said Chester Davis was a man dealing with realities, feeling his way between the interests of the agricultural producers and distributors, making concessions here and there to get things done, and satisfied with half-measures because they seemed aimed in the right direction. But Davis had found the Consumers' Counsel and Legal Division telling him that he was giving away fundamental principles. They fought with him, delayed his actions, and

[54] *March of Time*, "Trouble in the Cotton Country," 1936, National Archives Film Library.
[55] *St. Louis Post-Dispatch*, January 31, 1936.
[56] *New York Times*, February 21, 1935, p. 1.
[57] *Ibid.*
[58] *Ibid.*
[59] *New York Times*, February 7, 1935, p. 18.

went past him to the Secretary until he would tolerate it no longer. Wallace, Swing said, sided with Davis because of the Administrator's powerful friends in agriculture. Swing saw the appointment of Calvin Hoover as Consumers' Counsel and the fact that Tugwell had been put on the AAA advisory board as evidence that "some of the damage of the purge" had been repaired, but generally he felt the cause of the small farmers and consumers in AAA had been sacrificed for the sake of the special interests.[60]

Newsweek thought the purge was an attempt by Davis and Wallace to achieve a frictionless, smooth-running operation. The obstreperous liberals in the AAA had balked at coordinated action, affronted powerful middlemen, and agitated for strict Federal control of processors' and wholesalers' profits.[61] Thus, they had to go. *Time* cited the firings in AAA as the most striking of several signs that the New Deal had taken a turn away from reform and toward recovery. The magazine remarked that "with Franklin Roosevelt's consent the biggest single bevy of Brain Trusters in the administration had been quietly but firmly turned out as trouble makers." [62]

Years later, Henry Wallace, recalling the purge, remarked, "The fake liberals have always criticised me for what I did in February of 1935. I have never regretted it although I had considerable personal affection for both Jerome Frank and Pat Jackson." Wallace felt that the liberals had been too much concerned with "social reform by publicity" when social reform through Congress had to be approached another way. He admitted that he admired Rexford Tugwell and believed in his ideals, but Tugwell had "moved too far too fast." It was up to Wallace to be around to "pick up the pieces" when Tugwell left the government later. "Every man has to fight for social justice in his own way," said Wallace. "I do not criticise either Chester or Frank but between them they surely loaded a gun which went off with a bang." [63]

It is difficult to separate the heroes and the villains of the purge in AAA. It would be easy enough to side with the liberals,

[60] Raymond Gram Swing, "The Purge at the AAA," *Nation*, CXL (February 20, 1935), 216–217.

[61] *Newsweek*, January 16, 1935, p. 7.

[62] *Time*, February 18, 1935, p. 14.

[63] Wallace to author, June 13, 1959.

whose intentions were undeniably worthy, but this would mean disregarding the legitimate arguments of the agrarians. Cully Cobb and the men of the Cotton Section were primarily concerned with getting the job done. They had to deal directly with over a million cotton farmers, and they wanted no changes which would further complicate matters. Their attitude was that tenants should receive the rightful share of government benefits, but it was not worth endangering the entire cotton program to accomplish this goal. Cobb and the others were pro-landlord but not anti-tenant unless there was a conflict of interest between the two. Their position sustaining the right of landlords to evict tenants may have been cruel, but it was practical. Few Southern landlords were ready to let the government dictate to them about the firing of unwanted tenants.

In early 1935, after the cotton contract had been in force for a year, it would have been disastrous to AAA's program to reverse the existing policy and require landlords to keep the identical tenants, and yet to continue the existing policy meant more evictions and hardships for thousands of sharecroppers. How had matters reached this unpleasant dilemma? The tenant policies of the cotton program had been ill-conceived in the first place, but once they were in effect it was next to impossible to change them materially. The time for the Legal Division to protect tenant rights was in the writing of the cotton contract, but the liberals missed that opportunity because of their ignorance of tenant problems.

When the complaints of tenants first began to reach AAA, the agrarians of the Cotton Section took refuge in the cotton contract, saying all they could do was enforce it and thus placing a great importance on the exact wording of the agreement. For nearly a year, the Legal Division attempted to obtain justice for tenants through the various tenant committees within AAA, by the creation of a new committee outside the control of the Cotton Section, and by getting a clear statement of tenant policy. When all of these efforts were blocked by the Cotton Section, Frank and the others decided to fight on the ground chosen by their enemies—the actual wording of the contract. Frank ordered a legal reinterpretation of paragraph 7, and the document prepared by the Opinions Section was no more than a brief designed to justify the General Counsel's previous decision to guarantee tenants' rights to stay on the land. But Frank's strategy was unwise and impractical in view of the fact that a different policy had been in effect for a year. If he had not known about it before, it was his own fault for not keeping up with what the Cotton Section, the Administrator, and the Secretary had been saying in official publications throughout 1934.

Chester Davis and Henry Wallace cannot be blamed for their actions in the purge. No other course was open to them except their own resignations. They had to achieve peace in AAA, and the only way to do it was to remove the disturbing element— the liberals. In the final analysis, there were no real heroes in the battle, not even D. P. Trent, who threw in the towel while there was still hope. However, it is much easier to excuse the liberals for their brashness, ignorance of agriculture, delay in acting, faulty strategy, and compassion for suffering tenant farmers than it is to forgive the agrarians for their close-mindedness, refusal to tolerate interference with their programs, pro-landlord bias, and hard-heartedness toward tenants.

chapter nine

The Reign of Terror

There is a reign of terror in the cotton country of eastern Arkansas. It will end either in the establishment of complete and slavish submission to the vilest exploitation in America or in bloodshed, or in both. For the sake of peace, liberty and common human decency I appeal to you who listen to my voice to bring immediate pressure upon the Federal Government to act.

— Norman Thomas on the NBC Radio Network

The weeks of the upheaval and purge in AAA were also the weeks of a reign of terror in eastern Arkansas. It started when the delegation of the Southern Tenant Farmers' Union returned from Washington in mid-January, 1935. The desperate sharecroppers had high hopes that the mission would cause the government to recognize their plight and do something about it. Many of the croppers had contributed their last few pennies to send the four delegates to the capitol, and they waited anxiously for their return. When the day came, Ward Rodgers called a meeting of the entire union at Marked Tree to hear their report. Sharecroppers began arriving soon after dawn. They came from all over northeastern Arkansas and crowded into the small town. They climbed on roof tops and perched in trees and on the tops of trucks, boxcars, and wagons. There were almost five thousand of them. They waited for hours, but the delegation did not arrive. Several times the people on the speakers' stand asked the crowd if Mr. Mitchell or Mr. McKinney, Negro vice-president of the union, had arrived yet. For most of the people present it was the first time they had ever heard a Negro addressed as "mister."[1]

When the crowd grew restless, Ward Rodgers decided to make a speech to kill time. Rodgers was a forceful speaker, and now he was just plain angry. The night before he had been questioned by a group of planters who resented his teaching sharecroppers to read and "figure" in his capacity as an FERA instructor. Perhaps the planters also objected to Rodgers' explaining the advantages of the union and Marxism, since he was doing that also.[2] The planters told Rodgers to report to the Marked Tree Superintendent of Schools the next day. Rodgers went, and the Superintendent advised him to go back to western Arkansas or he might be found dead some morning. When Rodgers asked if that was a Ku Klux Klan order, the Superintendent told him he could call it what he wanted to.

As Rodgers addressed the crowd of sharecroppers, his big voice boomed out through the sunny January air. He spoke at length of the many injustices to sharecroppers. The crowd moved in closer; this was the kind of talk they had come to hear. Rodgers warmed to his subject,[3] and while he orated, the four delegates arrived from Washington. They mounted the platform but the young preacher did not stop. He told of threats against the lives of union organizers. Then he roared, "Well, that is a game two can play. If necessary, I could lead the sharecroppers to lynch every planter in Poinsett County!"[4] The audience, which had grown more and more excited as Rodgers spoke, became suddenly still. Then with a great shout they threw their

[1] Kester, *Revolt Among the Sharecroppers*, p. 69.
[2] *Time*, March 4, 1935, p. 14.
[3] Kester, *Revolt Among the Sharecroppers*, pp. 67–68.
[4] *Time*, March 4, 1935, p. 14.

hats into the air and began to dance around embracing each other.[5] Some of the men began to yell, "Let's go get 'em!"

This was much too unruly to suit H. L. Mitchell, who told Rodgers to sit down while he tried to pacify the crowd. Mitchell attempted to explain why Rodgers was so agitated, but as he spoke the thought of what had happened to Rodgers made him more and more angry. Finally, he said, "Now Ward Rodgers is staying at my house. If anybody wants to chase him out of the country, that's where he is. And the first man that comes around my house with a pillow case over his head is just going to get hell shot out of him."[6]

The report of the delegation, made by McKinney, was something of an anticlimax. Fred Stafford, Poinsett County Attorney, witnessed the whole affair from the edge of the crowd. When the meeting broke up, he arrested Rodgers as he left the platform for "anarchy, attempting to overthrow and usurp the Government of Arkansas, and blasphemy."[7] After a long interrogation, Rodgers was jailed in Marked Tree. It was a small, brick building, and soon hundreds of sharecroppers surrounded it. They were in an ugly mood, and they talked about tearing the jail apart, brick by brick. Through the barred windows, Rodgers assured them he was safer in jail than outside where the aroused planters could get to him.[8] Next day, Rodgers was moved from Marked Tree to the Poinsett County jail at Harrisburg. Then local officials shifted him again to Jonesboro because they feared the sharecroppers would attempt to free him. At Jonesboro, a new charge was brought against him—"interfering with labor," but he was freed on bail.

Rodgers received a preliminary hearing in justice of the peace court at Marked Tree. County Attorney Fred Stafford brought the charges. By this time, the case was attracting national attention. It was news that a Methodist minister was charged with anarchy, barratry, and even blasphemy. Rodgers' picture appeared in newspapers as far away as New York. Soon, the justice of the peace court ruled that Rodgers should go to trial in circuit court.[9]

[5] Kester, *Revolt Among the Sharecroppers,* p. 69.
[6] Mitchell, Oral History Interview, pp. 36–37.
[7] Kester, *Revolt Among the Sharecroppers,* p. 69.
[8] *Ibid.,* pp. 70–71.
[9] *New York Times,* January 27, 1935, p. 12.

Immediately after Rodgers' arrest, Mitchell and Amberson wired collect to AAA telling of the case and stating it was imperative that a government investigator come to Arkansas immediately if the situation was to be controlled.[10] Mary Connor Myers was already on her way to Arkansas, in keeping with Wallace's promise to the STFU leaders. She attended the daylong trial of Ward Rodgers and, according to a planter named W. R. Frazier, seemed "very interested in Mr. Rodgers' welfare."[11]

The trial of Rodgers at Marked Tree was little more than a farce, and reporters from the metropolitan newspapers and national magazines reported it as such. Fred Stafford, the prosecuting attorney, said Rodgers was a "foreign agitator" who had attempted to form a lynch mob and was teaching the "niggers" to read and write. He charged that Rodgers called Negroes "mister" and was from a Yankee school, Vanderbilt University. Evidently, he did not know that Vanderbilt was in the neighboring state of Tennessee.[12] Rodgers denied that he offered to lead a lynch mob, but admitted that he called a Negro "mister."[13] A jury, described by one planter as "twelve good citizens, including two Sharecroppers, three renters, one Undertaker, four merchants, and only two landlords,"[14] convicted Rodgers of anarchy. The judge sentenced him to six months in jail and a $500 fine. C. T. Carpenter, STFU attorney, got him freed on bond pending an appeal which Norman Thomas and the League for Industrial Democracy promised to finance.[15]

After the trial, Mary Connor Myers told Tyronza planter W. R. Frazier that she was not surprised at any verdict rendered in Marked Tree with the feeling running like it was.[16] *Nation* magazine commented that the issue in the Rodgers case was not anarchy but his activities in organizing the STFU. The magazine blamed the "eruption" on "what the AAA has done—and left undone—in connection with its reduction program." It sug-

[10] Mitchell and Amberson to AAA (Telegram), January 16, 1935, NA, RG 145.
[11] W. R. Frazier to Chester Davis, February 16, 1935, NA, RG 145.
[12] Mitchell, Oral History Interview, pp. 37–41; *Time*, March 4, 1935, p. 14; and *New York Times*, January 22, 1935, p. 12.
[13] *Memphis Commercial Appeal*, January 17, 1935.
[14] W. R. Frazier to Chester Davis, February 16, 1935, NA, RG 145.
[15] *New York Times*, January 22, 1935, p. 12.
[16] W. R. Frazier to Chester Davis, February 16, 1935, NA, RG 145.

gested that newspapers "in search of good dramatic American copy" dispatch a few reporters to Marked Tree.[17] The *New York Times* said the case might well become "another Scopes affair." However, the newspaper attributed part of Rodgers' difficulties to his public utterances and the fact he was "an admitted adherent of communism."[18] The editor later received a letter saying that Rodgers was a Socialist and not a "communist."[19]

Ward Rodgers' appeal was held over for three terms of court and never tried. Meanwhile, he remained free on bond. He lost his job with FERA after conviction, but he was never forced to serve his term. The conviction of Rodgers marked a turning point in the history of the STFU. This court action, and the suppression of Mary Connor Myers' report, brought national publicity to the sharecroppers' plight which was followed by a nationwide surge of indignation. As a result of the publicity, new organizers and workers, including a group from Commonwealth College at Mena, Arkansas, came to help the union. The League for Industrial Democracy offered aid, and money and clothing began to arrive from sympathetic people throughout the nation.[20]

With the conviction of Rodgers the planters began a reign of terror in northeastern Arkansas which became a national disgrace. Perhaps they feared the union would benefit from the publicity the case received, and probably the planters were angered at the interference of "outside agitators," including Northern journalists and government investigators. In any event, they formed a Klan-like organization called the "nightriders," and began systematically terrorizing members of the STFU.[21]

The threat was so great to union officers that Mitchell and others fled across the Mississippi River to Memphis, where they set up union headquarters.[22] Those who ventured into the Delta counties of Arkansas ran great risks. Lucien Koch, Director of

[17] *Nation*, CXL (February 6, 1935), 143.
[18] *New York Times*, January 27, 1935, sec. IV, p. 6.
[19] *Ibid.*, February 4, 1935, p. 18.
[20] Mitchell, Oral History Interview, pp. 37 and 41; *Sharecropper's Voice*, May, 1935.
[21] "Terror in Arkansas," *Nation*, CXL (February 13, 1935), 174.
[22] John Herling, "Field Notes From Arkansas," *Nation*, CXL (April 10, 1935), 419–420.

Commonwealth College, and Bob Reed, a young radical student at the college, while holding a meeting near Gilmore, were attacked by a band of planters and deputies. Koch later wrote, "They brandished their revolvers and dragged me from the seat, and kicked me from the room." Outside, the violence continued: "They poked guns into our faces and bellies, they kicked us, punched us. . . . We were both bloody about the face and head. . . . Drunken deputies stood around and allowed it to go on." [23] The assailants took Koch and Reed away in cars, and the sharecroppers in the meeting formed a rescue party. On the road, they found a rope with a neatly tied hangman's knot; however, the mob released Koch and Reed later without hanging them. [24]

The next day the indefatigable Koch, with three other organizers including Rodgers, went to Lepanto to meet with sharecroppers. Constable Jay May arrested them for "obstructing the public streets, disturbing the peace, and barratry." The Constable later told a reporter, "They are liable to from $10.00 to $50.00 and as much as six months in jail. They'll probably get the jail sentence because we are going to put all we can on 'em." For the next few days, eighteen men guarded the jail and adjacent streets at Lepanto for fear the sharecroppers would try to break in. [25] After three days, the organizers were tried, fined fifty dollars each, and released. They reported later they were kept in cells without adequate food or heat and with floors flooded with sewage and refuse. [26]

Howard Kester and H. L. Mitchell also found it difficult to travel in the planter-dominated counties. Kester wrote Alfred Baker Lewis, Secretary of the Socialist Party in Boston, asking for aid, and Lewis offered to furnish an armored car so that they could drive to meetings. Mitchell thought an armored car would be open invitation for the planters to use dynamite, so he vetoed the idea. [27] Even the union lawyer, C. T. Carpenter, was terrorized. By his own description, ". . . the landowners and their agents in an armed body came to my house the other night and probably would have taken me out and killed me had it not

---

[23] *Nation*, CXL (March 13, 1935), 294.
[24] Kester, *Revolt Among the Sharecroppers*, pp. 75–77.
[25] *Memphis Press-Scimitar*, February 4, 1935.
[26] Kester, *Revolt Among the Sharecroppers*, pp. 77–78.
[27] Mitchell, Oral History Interview, p. 45.

been for my good gun." When Carpenter came out of his house ready to fight, the mob fled into the night. One of them shot out the porch light to avoid identification. The lawyer, having heard that Rexford Tugwell was "close" to the President, wrote Tugwell describing the reign of terror and saying FDR should be told of it.[28] Two months later Tugwell replied, asking for specific suggestions as to what the Administration could do. Before he sent the letter he deleted a paragraph saying the federal government had no right to interfere in police matters within a state.[29]

The reign of terror lasted two and one-half months. There is no complete record of all the brutality, but during a ten-day period in late March the following incidents occurred. A mob of about forty planters and riding bosses, led by the manager of a big plantation, a constable, and a deputy sheriff, attempted to lynch Reverend A. B. Brookins and then shot into his home with machine guns.[30] W. H. Stultz, President of the STFU, received a letter signed with ten X's giving him twenty-four hours to get out of his home county. Next day, the nightriders abducted him to provoke him to some action which would give them an excuse to kill him. They told him to leave the county or they would shoot his brains out. Later, after the nightriders attempted to blow up his home, Stultz moved to Memphis.[31] T. A. Allen, a Negro preacher and organizer of the union, was found shot through the heart and weighted with chains in the Coldwater River near Hernando, Mississippi. Sheriff Sid Campbell of Hernando admitted that Allen was "probably killed by some plantation owner." [32] Mary Green, wife of an organizer of the STFU in Mississippi County, died of heart failure when nightriders came to her home to lynch her husband.[33] An angry mob drove Clay East and Mary Hillyer, a union worker from New York, into the office of C. T. Carpenter in Marked Tree. The Mayor saved them and had them escorted out of the county by armed men. One of them told East if he ever returned he

[28] Carpenter to Tugwell, April 5, 1935, NA, RG 145.
[29] Tugwell to Carpenter, June 7, 1935, NA, RG 145.
[30] Herling, "Field Notes From Arkansas," *Nation,* CXL (April 10, 1935), 419–420.
[31] *Dallas Morning News,* March 23, 1935, p. 1.
[32] *San Antonio Express* (Texas), March 30, 1935, p. 2.
[33] *New York Times,* March 22, 1935.

would be shot on sight.[34] John Allen, a union member, escaped a mob of riding bosses and deputies who were trying to lynch him. During the search for him, the mob beat up several Negroes who would not tell where he was. One woman received a blow which cut off her ear.[35] A band of nightriders mobbed a group of Negro families returning from church near Marked Tree. They beat the men and women with pistols and flashlights, trampling the children underfoot as they attacked.[36] At Holly Grove, the nightriders burned the Colored Baptist Church to the ground. The church was being used as a meeting place for the Holly Grove local of the STFU.[37]

The planters also used less violent but equally effective means of combatting the union. On many plantations, they canceled the contracts of their sharecroppers and offered them work by the hour at less than subsistence wages. To the planters this had the double advantage of punishing union members and avoiding the division of parity payments with sharecroppers. However, lowering the status of tenants was not confined to Arkansas; planters were doing it all over the South.[38]

During the height of the reign of terror, H. L. Mitchell wrote AAA, "We are on the edge of bloodshed, and these people [the croppers] will defend themselves if attacked. When that blood flows it will drip down over your Department, from the Secretary at the top to the cotton Section at the bottom." Mitchell said AAA would be responsible for the "incredible folly of the whole reduction program . . . the absolutely inequitable contract which has borne so heavily upon these people. . . ." Mitchell claimed that for nearly a year he had been sending AAA cases of contract violations, but the agency usually did not even acknowledge receipt.[39]

In response to a demand that he take action to guarantee the rights to assemble and organize in Arkansas, Henry Wallace stated flatly that he had no jurisdiction in matters of that sort.[40]

[34] *Memphis Press-Scimitar*, March 22, 1935.
[35] *Ibid.*, March 27, 1935.
[36] *New York Times*, April 16, 1935, p. 18.
[37] *Sharecropper's Voice*, May, 1935.
[38] Kester, *Revolt Among the Sharecroppers*, p. 35.
[39] Mitchell to Paul Porter, March 27, 1935, NA, RG 145.
[40] Wallace to Prof. Paul Brissenden (Telegram), March 29, 1935, NA, RG 145.

When the union asked if the rented acres could be used temporarily to house evicted tenants, Wallace said no.[41] The Second Annual Convention of the STFU condemned the "insane policy of economic scarcity" and demanded the repeal of the Adjustment Act, but AAA took little notice.[42]

So much correspondence was received by the AAA from the STFU that Paul Porter was given the unenviable task of corresponding with union officials and making recommendations to the Secretary. When the STFU learned of this, Mitchell wrote Porter to warn him that the Cotton Division, especially Cully Cobb, was prejudiced against the union, that Chester Davis was weak and would not back him, and that county agents in the plantation areas could not be trusted because they were "absolutely controlled by the planters."[43] Porter was puzzled by this completely negative attitude, and he wrote asking what the union hoped to accomplish if they were sure the government would do nothing for them and the local administration was dominated by the landlords.[44] When Mitchell sent a list of 500 evicted tenants, Porter wired back asking if the evicted tenants' houses had been filled by other tenants. Professor Amberson wrote him angrily that this was a matter for AAA to determine.[45]

When Mitchell wired Mary Connor Myers asking for information on what she had learned in Arkansas,[46] Porter advised her not to answer. A suggestion by Mrs. Myers that she turn over some information to Senator Edward Costigan of Colorado so alarmed Assistant Solicitor J. P. Wenchel that he quashed the whole matter.[47]

To the sharecropper, the most feared action by the planter, outside of violence, was eviction. Once he was cast off the plantation and his credit stopped at the commissary, the cropper had no means of support except federal relief, or the STFU. Very few sharecroppers could find a new landlord or any other sort of work. Howard Kester had charge of the union's relief work. He and his helpers distributed medical supplies and services, cloth-

[41] Wallace to Mitchell (Telegram), February 7, 1935, NA, RG 145.
[42] STFU, *Proceedings, Second Annual Convention*, Resolution 19, 1936.
[43] Mitchell to Porter, March 27, 1935, NA, RG 145.
[44] Porter to Amberson, April 2, 1935, NA, RG, 145.
[45] Amberson to Porter, April 4, 1935, NA, RG 145.
[46] Mitchell to Myers (Telegram), February 10, 1935, NA, RG 145.
[47] Porter, Memo to Mr. Wenchel, February 11, 1935, NA, RG 145.

ing and food to union members who had been evicted or were in dire need. Sympathetic donors sent the union tons of used clothing and considerable amounts of money for the needy.[48]

When a union family was evicted, the union staged demonstrations which were in keeping with the policy of passive resistance. When the sheriff and his deputies came to carry the family's possessions out of their shack, dozens of union members would stand watching and singing "We Shall Not Be Moved." When the sheriff left, they would carry the possessions back into the shack.[49]

In a move to stop union meetings, many towns in northeastern Arkansas passed ordinances prohibiting public gatherings. The one in Marked Tree was typical: ". . . it has been declared unlawful for any person to make or deliver a public speech, on any street, alley, park or other public place within the corporate limits of Marked Tree." [50] In most towns, the ordinances gave mayors the right to waive the ban. The Mayor of Marked Tree told a *New York Times* reporter, "Anyone can speak except the radicals. I'd give permission to 'most anybody to hold a meeting so long as they haven't been mixed up with the union and have not been listed in the Red Net-Work Book." [51]

While terror reigned in the eastern part of the state, the Arkansas Legislature passed a bill which was obviously aimed at the STFU. The law made it a felony to possess five or more copies of any labor union literature which was "seditious," or which "attacked" a state official. The penalty was five to twenty

[48] Mitchell, Oral History Interview, p. 45, and Kester, *Revolt Among the Sharecroppers,* p. 35.

[49] Mitchell, Oral History Interview, pp. 39–40.

[50] *New York Times,* April 21, 1935, sec. II, p. 5.

[51] *Ibid.* The "Red Net-Work Book" referred to by the Mayor was *Red Network: A Who's Who and Handbook of Radicalism for Patriots,* by Mrs. Elizabeth Dilling (Milwaukee, 1934). It contained a list of 460 organizations and 1,300 people who were suspected by Mrs. Dilling. Along with a few real radicals, it listed some extremely prominent people who had worked at one time or another with various humanitarian groups. *New Republic* recommended it to readers as a good guide to worthwhile organizations. *New Republic,* LXXIX (July 4, 1934), 218. It was not unusual for Southerners to think that any person who favored fair treatment for Negroes was a Communist or Red agent. *The Georgia Woman's World* once told its readers that President and Mrs. Roosevelt were Communists because they were courteous to Negroes. Arthur Raper, "The South Strains Toward Decency," *North American Review,* CCXLIII (Spring, 1937), 112.

years imprisonment. The *Memphis Commercial Appeal* commented that this would make it a worse crime to expose a grafter than to be one.[52]

In March, 1935, the planters decided on a new strategy—they would form a union of their own and lure away STFU members with promises of jobs. Reverend Abner Sage, the Methodist minister at Marked Tree, was the spokesman and executive secretary of the organization which was called the "Marked Tree Cooperative Association." Sage once told a *New York Times* reporter, ". . . it would have been better to have a few no-account, shiftless people killed at the start than to have all this fuss raised up. We have had a pretty serious situation here, what with the mistering of the niggers and stirring them up to think the Government is going to give them forty acres." [53]

Even at the height of the troubles in Arkansas, two intrepid British ladies came to speak to the sharecroppers. They were sponsored by the Socialist-dominated League for Industrial Democracy. One was Jennie Lee, a former member of Parliament and later the wife of Aneurin Bevin, leader of the British Labour Party. When the Mayor of Marked Tree forbade the union to assemble in town to hear Miss Lee, a crowd of more than 2,000 gathered two miles away on property owned by a member. After she spoke, Miss Lee and Howard Kester led the entire crowd marching to town singing "We Shall Not Be Moved." They paraded past the Mayor's office and into the union hall to continue their meeting.[54] The Association headed by Sage soon collapsed because the STFU was able to keep its members from joining.[55]

Naomi Mitchison, a well-known British writer and globe-trotter, also addressed a meeting in Marked Tree. She wrote in a British magazine that about 300 people were there in the "drafty, dimly lit hall." She was struck by the beauty of the union singing, especially by the Negroes. The chairman, a man with a "terribly bashed face" and "most of his teeth missing," led earnestly in the Lord's Prayer. When she spoke, Miss Mitchison noted that if she used the word "slavery," the audience "shivered

[52] *Memphis Commercial Appeal*, February 20, 1935.
[53] *New York Times*, April 16, 1935, p. 18.
[54] Kester, *Revolt Among the Sharecroppers*, pp. 78–79.
[55] Mitchell, Oral History Interview, p. 44.

and shifted." [56] Later, after seeing some of the shacks of the sharecroppers, she told a Memphis reporter, "We in England woudn't let animals live like these people are forced to live." [57]

Perhaps the peak of the reign of terror was the famous "Birdsong Incident." Norman Thomas' return to northeastern Arkansas was certain to bring trouble. The planters knew of his role in founding the STFU and were aware of his more recent activities. For instance, in February, 1935, he had sent telegrams to President Roosevelt and Governor J. Marion Futrell of Arkansas, the texts of which he released to the news services. The telegrams told of violations of civil rights in Arkansas and asked for remedial action. The wire to Roosevelt requested the President to provide tents and food for evicted tenants, and hold up further AAA payments until the situation was adjusted.[58] Early in March, in an address over the NBC Radio Network, he said the exploitation of sharecroppers in the cotton country was leading to "the most wretched conditions" in America. He charged, "These sharecroppers and casual day laborers . . . are the Forgotten Men of the New Deal. AAA has practically washed its hands of their problems." [59]

In mid-March, Thomas came to Arkansas. After a long and fruitless interview with Governor Futrell, he began a tour of the cotton counties. He saw much suffering and many displaced tenants on the roads. STFU officials had invited him to speak at the small town of Birdsong, near Tyronza in Mississippi County. Thomas must have known of the personal dangers involved in speaking at a union meeting in the toughest of all the planter-dominated counties, but he accepted.[60]

In a Memphis hotel the day before he was scheduled to speak at Birdsong, Thomas was asked by a reporter if he was not dramatizing the situation in Arkansas. The Socialist leader jumped angrily to his feet and said, "Emphatically not! In the cotton fields are to be found the most stark lack of decent culture . . . anywhere." In answer to a charge by the pro-planter *Memphis Commercial Appeal* that he was an outsider, Thomas

[56] Naomi Mitchison, "White House and Marked Tree," *New Statesman and Nation*, LX (April 27, 1935), 585–586.

[57] *Memphis Press-Scimitar*, February 19, 1935.

[58] *New York Herald Tribune*, February 11, 1935.

[59] *Time*, March 4, 1935, p. 14.

[60] Kester, *Revolt Among the Sharecroppers*, p. 80.

said some of the worst plantations were owned by "outside" corporations, and he added, "Whenever there is an evil so gross that it poisons and pollutes the body politic, nobody is an outside agitator." [61]

On March 15, about 500 union members assembled to hear Thomas at Birdsong. Howard Kester was to introduce him, but as he began, "Ladies and Gentlemen, ———" he was interrupted by a rough voice which said, "There ain't no ladies in the audience and there ain't no gentlemen on the platform." About forty armed planters and riding bosses came forward and dragged Kester away. Thomas held up a copy of the Arkansas Constitution, which had an excellent bill of rights, and asked by whose authority the meeting was being broken up. One of the planters told him, "We are the citizens of this county, and we run it to suit ourselves. We don't need no Gawd-damn Yankee bastard to tell us what to do with our niggers. . . ." [62]

Thomas spoke only a few words before being attacked from behind and dragged from the platform. During the scuffle, a riding boss clubbed a union official over the head. The county sheriff intervened and told Thomas to leave immediately or he could not be responsible for his safety. Thomas and his party allowed themselves to be shoved into their cars and then drove away. Several carloads of men followed them to make sure they left the county.[63]

No small factor in the reign of terror was the national publicity concerning it which called attention to tenant problems not only in Arkansas but throughout the South. Magazines such as *Nation, New Republic,* and *Survey Graphic* carried running accounts of the events in Arkansas and other parts of the South. Almost every issue of *Nation* mentioned some new incident, and the magazine openly solicited financial aid for the STFU. Probably more significant was the coverage given by the *New York Times, Time* magazine, the Scripps-Howard newspaper chain, and the national press services. When such diverse media took notice of tenant troubles, the general public began to learn something of the situation and the matter became an embarrassment to the Administration.

Time magazine reported in March, 1935, that the plight of

[61] *Memphis Commercial Appeal,* March 15, 1935.
[62] Kester, *Revolt Among the Sharecroppers,* pp. 80–81.
[63] *Ibid.;* and Thomas to author, June 6, 1960.

the sharecroppers "weighed heaviest" on the minds of Department of Agriculture and AAA officials. The AAA, said *Time,* had received some 7,000 painfully scrawled letters from sharecroppers protesting the policies, and even as impartial an observer as the Federal Drought Relief Director in Arkansas reported "wholesale unloading" of tenants by landlords onto the relief rolls.[64]

Hugh Russell Fraser, a feature writer for the Scripps-Howard chain, did a lengthy series on the sharecropper problem after a tour through the South. Having seen "thousands" of displaced croppers, he wrote, "Along the highways and byways of Dixie they straggle—lonely figures without money, without homes, and without hope." He called the problem "one of the greatest and most far-reaching challenges to the whole New Deal program." [65]

When three members of the STFU visited Norman Thomas in New York City in February, 1935, it caused quite a stir in the metropolitan newspapers. One of the three was Walter Maskop, who provided some dramatic copy for reporters with his stories of privation and injustice among sharecroppers. One reporter suggested that New Yorkers paying good money to see tenant farmers like Jeeter Lester in the Caldwell-Kirkland play *Tobacco Road* on Broadway, should see Walter Maskop if they wanted a look at the real thing.[66]

AAA officials were sensitive to such publicity, and clippings of these stories circulated from desk to desk within the huge agency —not always with favorable reactions. When the clippings about Walter Maskop in New York reached W. J. Green of the Adjustment Committee of the Cotton Division, he wrote a long memorandum to Cully Cobb. Green pointed out that Maskop was one of the men who once represented the STFU in a conference in Cobb's office, and that, although the newspapers quoted Maskop as saying he was an evicted sharecropper, he was not one. "He owned a farm," wrote Green, "but lost it in 1932 before the Agricultural Adjustment program got started. Since that time he has been living in a small town and working as a day laborer when he could get work." Apparently, this information discredited Maskop as a representative of the share-

[64] *Time,* March 5, 1935, p. 14.
[65] *Memphis Press-Scimitar,* February 26, 1935.
[66] *New York Sun,* February 28, 1935; and *New York World-Telegram,* February 28, 1935.

croppers. In the memorandum, Green admitted that "many of the conditions mentioned [by Maskop] are no doubt true," but he was positive the AAA reduction program was not responsible. Cully Cobb was so pleased with Green's comments that he forwarded them to Chester Davis.[67]

The thousands of complaints about evictions and lowering of status reaching Cobb also fell on deaf ears. In 1937 he wrote, "Every year at this season since 1934, a few letters of this nature have been received by [the Cotton] Division." Cobb issued orders that year for county committees to look into such cases with the idea of withholding the landlords' parity payments if they were guilty. This had been his policy since the beginning. Stopping the parity check was the maximum penalty the Cotton Division felt it could assess against a landlord, and obviously this provided little comfort to tenants evicted long before. It might even be a hardship, since their checks would be delayed also.[68] Cobb felt also that events in Arkansas should not influence Administration policies. He wrote a Massachusetts clergyman: ". . . some persons, instead of availing themselves of the State and Federal Courts, have been disposed to relate their stories to well-meaning people in other parts of the United States with the hope of arousing bitterness and adverse feeling toward the present National Administration." Cobb reasoned that the very fact that "isolated cases" were given so much publicity was evidence of the infrequency with which they occurred.[69]

The official attitude in AAA toward tenant complaints was that nothing could be done about them unless there was some definite violation of the cotton contract. An example of this was the reaction to a wire in March, 1935, from STFU leaders who claimed that at mass meetings in Gilmore, Marked Tree, and Lepanto, 409 out of 1,766 people raised their hands when asked if they had no work or crop to make.[70] Paul A. Porter, Executive Assistant to Davis, wired back that if the union could provide the names of sharecroppers who had been evicted and not replaced, AAA would begin immediate action against the landlords.[71]

[67] Memo to C. A. Cobb, March 5, 1965, STFU File, NA, RG 145.
[68] Cobb to Scholl, January 19, 1937, NA, RG 145.
[69] Cobb to James Hiller, November 14, 1936, Landlord-Tenant File, NA, RG 145.
[70] Stultz, Mitchell, and Thomas to Wallace (Telegram), March 21, 1935, NA, RG 145.
[71] Porter to Stultz (Telegram), March 21, 1935, NA, RG 145.

H. L. Mitchell sent Porter a list of evicted croppers and described two plantations that warranted investigation. One was the Delta and Pine Land Company of Mississippi, managed by Oscar Johnston, AAA's Director of Finance. Mitchell charged that Johnston had failed to replace tenants who left voluntarily and that there were more than 127 vacant cabins on the plantation. Mitchell added that the STFU had nothing against Johnston personally, since he was one of the more enlightened planters, but still he had violated the contract which he helped write.

A worse case was that of the Twist Brothers of Twist, Arkansas. Mitchell charged the brothers had kept all parity payments due their tenants, denied tenants access to rented acres, and reduced almost every sharecropper on their plantation to the status of a wage hand. In addition, he said the Twists allowed such cruelty to their workers that even one of their riding bosses could no longer stand it and was willing to testify against them. Mitchell told Porter, "Your failure to take proper action has strengthened the farm owners in the continuance of the most brutal regime in this territory." [72]

As long as the complaints concerning AAA's cotton program came from tenants and tenant union organizers, AAA was able to keep the problem confined within its own house, but the Birdsong incident gave Norman Thomas an excellent opportunity to go all the way to Roosevelt with a dramatic complaint. As soon as he reached the safety of Memphis, after being driven out of Arkansas, Thomas sent a wire to the President describing the Birdsong incident and called it the "most arrogant tyranny" in the country. He told the President, "Nothing less than action by you . . . will avail to save tragedy from arising out of potentially the most dangerous situation I have seen in America." [73]

The President was much too wise a politician to become personally involved in the sticky Arkansas troubles. He referred Norman Thomas' telegram to Chester Davis for an answer. Davis' letter to Thomas was conciliatory. It referred to "definite steps" being taken by AAA to prevent aggravation of the conditions Thomas described. Davis declared that once these steps were explained to him, Thomas would be convinced of the "genuine concern" of AAA for the sharecropper problem. Davis pointed

[72] Mitchell to Porter, March 28, 1935, STFU File, NA, RG 145.
[73] Thomas to Roosevelt (Telegram), March 15, 1935, NA, RG 145.

out that the denial of free speech and assembly in Arkansas was obviously a state matter.[74]

There was some legal basis for Davis' position,[75] but in reality he was attempting to pass the buck. The Constitution of the United States means nothing if it can be violated with impunity as it was at Birdsong. Davis' stand was the easy way out, but of course he may have had no support from Wallace or Roosevelt for any other action.

Norman Thomas answered Davis' soothing letter with a blistering reply which must have raised the Administrator's blood pressure considerably. He stated that the "wholesale evictions" were the most important facts in the cotton country, and he had sweeping criticisms to make of AAA's policies toward tenants.[76] Davis did not answer.

A few weeks later, Thomas wrote Henry Wallace. The Socialist leader had learned that Wallace suspected him of championing the sharecroppers for political reasons. Thomas denied this; he said that as a Socialist, he found enough wrong with AAA that he did not have to "rejoice" at the reign of terror in Arkansas. He asked: "Does not the situation demand at least open investigation with power to protect witnesses? Does it not demand legislative protection of the right of workers to organize?"

Then Thomas spoke with a frankness foreign to most politicians. He granted that Wallace and the Administration held "most of the cards" and they had more to fear from the "Republican reactionaries" and the courts than from himself and the Socialist party—"at the present juncture." But Thomas felt that Wallace and the President had a sense of history. He told Wallace that history would acquit the New Deal of inventing the "damnable"

[74] Chester Davis to Thomas, March 19, 1935, NA, RG 145.

[75] The Bill of Rights in Article I forbids Congress (not the states) from abridging free speech and assembly; however, the Fourteenth Amendment to the U.S. Constitution prohibits the states to deny citizens the "privileges and immunities of citizenship." Since the Supreme Court in the Slaughter House cases in 1873 defined the right to assemble as one of the "privileges and immunities," and since county and local governments were defined as "creatures" of the state in *Atkin vs. Kansas* in 1903 and in *Hunter vs. City of Pittsburgh* in 1907, it is clear that county and local officials cannot allow denial of the right of assembly without violating the Constitution. U.S. Senate, *The Constitution of the United States, Analysis and Interpretation*, 82nd Cong., 2nd Sess., Doc. No. 170 (Washington: U.S. Government Printing Office, 1953), p. 967.

[76] Thomas to Chester Davis, March 22, 1935, NA, RG 145.

plantation system, but it would not acquit Wallace and FDR of their "failure to act adequately and promptly in this Arkansas matter." "This," wrote Thomas, "I have sought to bring to your attention for the sake of humanity rather than for any sort of political advantage." He argued that it was not too late to act.[77]

Henry Wallace was a man of deep conscience, and Thomas' letter angered him, perhaps most because he felt unable to do anything about the conditions described. He dictated a reply to Thomas which must have been close to his real thoughts, but after consulting with Rexford Tugwell, he decided not to send it. Wallace first wrote: "The effort on the part of some of your socialistic brethren to make it appear that the situation has resulted from the Agricultural Adjustment Act appears to me to be totally unwarranted." If there was to be bloodshed in eastern Arkansas, in Wallace's opinion, "the socialists and others who have come in from the North will be largely responsible." Wallace noted that it was very interesting how "right wing northerners and left wing northerners" cooperated in going to a "sore spot of long standing" to gain the maximum publicity for their respective dogmas.[78]

Twenty-five years later, when he read the contents of Wallace's unsent letter for the first time, Norman Thomas commented, "I rather think Wallace today is glad he never sent the letter. . . ." Thomas recalled that Wallace had not tried to defend his handling of the sharecropper situation when he ran for President in 1948. He felt that Wallace had "behaved very badly" over the issue and probably was a "little ashamed." Thomas remembered that Roosevelt would at least talk to him about the sharecroppers; Wallace would not.[79]

By mid-April, 1935, the fury of the planters was spent and the reign of terror had ended. Certainly, without the policy of passive resistance enforced on the croppers by the leaders of the STFU, there would have been much more bloodshed.[80] The major achievement of the union in the reign of terror was to survive. The planters were the real victors. They were able to get rid of their surplus tenants and continue receiving rental and

[77] Thomas to Wallace, April 16, 1935, NA, RG 145.
[78] Wallace to Thomas (not sent), n.d., NA, RG 145.
[79] Thomas to author, June, 6, 1960.
[80] *New York Times,* April 21, 1935, pp. 1 and 8.

parity payments. Moreover, the efforts of the STFU to bring the AAA into the struggle were largely unsuccessful. True, the national publicity made the AAA, the Administration, Congress, and the entire nation more aware of the sharecropper problem, but this had no immediate effect on the plight of the sharecropper.

The steadfast refusal of the AAA to side with the embattled sharecropper in the reign of terror and the purge of the liberals in AAA caused a growing resentment toward the agency by the leaders and members of the STFU. Therefore, they decided to send another delegation to Washington. The idea, and probably the money, came from the recently purged Gardner Jackson, who was now the union's official but unpaid representative in Washington.[81]

Nine members of the STFU, including Mitchell, Brookins, and McKinney, began to picket the main building of the Department of Agriculture on May 18, 1935. Their pickets stood directly outside the offices of Henry Wallace and carried printed signs demanding fair treatment for sharecroppers.[82] Gardner Jackson was present but did not take part in the demonstration except to talk a policeman out of trying to break it up.[83] Secretary Wallace watched the picketers from his window, consulted with Cully Cobb, and then summoned Gardner Jackson to his office. He told Jackson that Cobb was "frothing at the mouth" and personally he felt "awfully uncomfortable," but he confessed he was glad the sharecroppers were picketing because it would help him do what he had to do.[84]

The *Washington Post* carried pictures and an article about the pickets. It happened that the picketing occurred on the same day that 3,000 county agents arrived in Washington to review the accomplishments of the agricultural programs. The *Post* published an editorial called "The Nine Versus the 3,000," which emphasized the difference between what the county agents were told AAA was accomplishing and what the sharecroppers thought about the program.[85]

[81] Mitchell, Oral History Interview, pp. 48–49.
[82] *Washington Post*, May 19, 1935.
[83] Mitchell, Oral History Interview, pp. 48–49.
[84] Gardner Jackson, interview with author, July 20, 1959.
[85] *Washington Post*, May 19, 1935.

Throughout the remaining months of 1935, the STFU carried on its fight with the planters in northeastern Arkansas. In late September the union organized a strike of cotton pickers which led to much violence but was eventually successful in raising the pay of pickers to better than seventy-five cents per hundred pounds—still inadequate wages but a considerable improvement.[86]

After the success of the cotton pickers' strike, union membership shot skyward. By the end of 1935 it had reached 30,000 and spread into several states. The executive secretary had difficulty keeping track of new locals, several of which were organized and in operation for months before he learned of their existence. In Oklahoma a Cherokee Indian named Odis Sweeden had great success in organizing. He volunteered his services to the STFU after reading of the strike in Arkansas, and within a year he had more than eighty locals in Oklahoma. Later, the migration of the "Okies" to California virtually wiped out the membership in that state.[87]

But as the union grew, so did planter opposition. During the last week of 1935 the powerful eastern Arkansas plantations began an all-out campaign against the STFU. They evicted nearly two hundred families for union activities. With no place to go, the evicted croppers camped along the roadsides, huddled around open fires in the bitter cold, and wondered where their next meal would come from.[88] The planters openly circulated blacklists of union members who were not to be hired. When union leaders wired relief agencies in Washington for aid for the dispossessed, officials were sympathetic and ordered help, but local functionaries in Arkansas refused to act.[89]

The plight of the evicted was publicized throughout the country, and the result was a deluge of wires and letters on the Administration in Washington. Even the White House was

[86] STFU, "The Voice of the Disinherited, A Brief History of the Agricultural Workers Union, 1934–1959," Files of the Agricultural Workers Union, Washington, D.C.; and John Herling, "The Sharecropper Fights for His Life," *New Republic*, LXXXV (January 29, 1936), 336.

[87] Mitchell, Oral History Interview, pp. 54–55; and STFU, *Proceedings, Third Annual Convention*, p. 4.

[88] John Herling, "The Sharecropper Fights for His Life," *New Republic*, LXXXV (January 29, 1936), 336.

[89] STFU, *Proceedings, Third Annual Convention*, Speech by Gardner Jackson, pp. 56–58.

swamped with messages. Drew Pearson and Robert S. Allen reported in their "Washington Merry-Go-Round" column that the matter came up in cabinet meeting. Secretary of Labor Frances Perkins, they said, proposed sending an abritrator to Arkansas to settle the differences between the planters and the union, and members of the cabinet agreed, as did the President. But Vice-President Garner objected, saying, "It would embarrass Joe Robinson, [and] we ought not do anything without taking it up with him. He's up for re-election this fall, and that's a very delicate situation in Arkansas." Robinson had been so cooperative with the Administration that this argument evidently carried great weight. The cabinet and FDR, according to Pearson and Allen, yielded to Garner and decided to do nothing.[90]

Throughout 1935, the sharecropper problem was one of the sore spots of the New Deal. And the man who kept it sore was the STFU's official but unpaid representative in Washington, Gardner Jackson. When FDR sent a message to Congress in February, 1937, calling for tenancy legislation, Washington correspondent Drew Pearson reported it was the climax of one of the most important behind-the-scenes controversies of the New Deal, and the center of the controversy was Gardner Jackson. Pearson wrote that Jackson "probably more than any other man . . . [was] the indefatigable and belligerent instigator of the President's message."

According to Pearson, Jackson caused the AAA officials who ousted him far more trouble outside of AAA than when he was under their roof. Also, "Jackson made life miserable for Miss Perkins and Secretary Wallace. He raised unmitigated hell with Attorney General Cummings. He had the ear of Mrs. Roosevelt. He got a newsreel to film the strikers. He raised thousands of dollars to finance them. He got Harry Hopkins to feed them." [91]

Pearson identified Jackson as the "godfather, the chief financial angel" of the STFU, a union which, he said, was not large, but which made up for its size by its vociferousness. Pearson said Jackson supplied the megaphone. He referred to Jackson's handling of events in Arkansas as "stage-managing" and said: "When striking Negroes were jailed in Arkansas, when a preacher and a

[90] *Florida Times-Union* (Jacksonville), March 17, 1936.
[91] *Ibid.*, February 26, 1937.

woman were horsewhipped, when union organizers were run out of the strike area, he made the most of it every time." [92]

It was Gardner Jackson who made arrangements for H. L. Mitchell to appear before the Resolutions Committee of the Democratic National Convention in Philadelphia in 1936. He also set up a meeting with the committee chairman, Senator Joe Robinson. The way Jackson accomplished this was typical. A rumor, perhaps started by Jackson, circulated at the convention that the sharecroppers' union might picket the convention. Ed McGrady, Undersecretary of Labor, apparently had the job of preventing such unfavorable publicity, so Jackson contacted him. He promised there would be no picketing if McGrady would arrange for Mitchell to see Robinson and appear before the Resolutions Committee. This was done and at the meeting with Robinson, both Mitchell and Jackson told the senator they wanted the convention to adopt a resolution saying the Democrats would protect the civil rights of sharecroppers in Arkansas and ensure their right to organize. Robinson agreed, but McGrady suggested the wording of the resolution be changed to apply to all workers in the country. He pointed out this would be more acceptable to the Southerners in the convention.[93] The resolution passed the convention,[94] but it was so general in application that it did the STFU little good.[95]

Jackson was once invited to a dinner in Washington at which several important senators were to be present. Howard Kester was visiting him and Jackson wangled an invitation for Kester. At the dinner Kester became the center of attraction with descriptions of his experiences in Arkansas including a beating he had recently received while holding a union meeting. Senator Robert M. LaFollette, Jr., listened carefully, and within a few days he introduced a motion in the Senate to create a committee on civil liberties. The LaFollette committee investigated violations of civil liberties all over the country and received wide

[92] *Ibid.*, February 26, 1937.
[93] Mitchell, Oral History Interview, pp. 69–73.
[94] Democratic Platform, 1936, *New York Times*, June 26, 1936, p. 13.
[95] During the conference, Robinson turned to Mitchell and said, "They tell me you are a foreign agitator." Mitchell became angry and said he had lived in Tennessee and Arkansas all of his life and had as much right to go any place in Arkansas as Robinson did. The Senator apologized. Mitchell, Oral History Interview, p. 72.

publicity; however, it never looked into the sharecropper situation in Arkansas. Years later, Mitchell asked LaFollette about this, and the senator indicated he had found too much opposition from Southern senators to tackle the problem.[96]

During a cotton croppers' strike in 1936, Jackson went to officials of the Resettlement Administration to ask for aid for evicted families. According to him, they said, "This is awful; we will certainly help you." But when they ordered aid to displaced families, RA administrators in Arkansas refused to act.[97] Drew Pearson reported the reason for the refusal was fear of reprisal by Senator Joe Robinson if they interfered in the strike.[98] When Jackson demanded that RA officials in Washington enforce their own orders, they refused because they feared the wrath of the Southern Bloc in Congress. Robinson later relented and allowed the families to receive aid.[99]

Jackson was a power in Washington, and he had a well-earned reputation as a champion of the underdog. He sought no personal gain and few doubted his sincerity. His personal friends included several cabinet members and Supreme Court justices. Franklin Roosevelt was aware of his work. In fact, Jackson's incessant campaign on behalf of the sharecroppers had an important bearing on the President's decision in 1936 to appoint a special committee on farm tenancy.[100]

The clamor raised by the Southern Tenant Farmers' Union and the constant agitation of Norman Thomas and Gardner Jackson eventually had some effect on AAA. The troubles in Arkansas had served the purpose of dramatizing the plight of sharecroppers throughout the South, and AAA could not ignore them. The attention which the agency gave to tenant problems during the last year of its existence will be the subject of the next chapter.

[96] Mitchell, Oral History Interview, pp. 64–65.
[97] STFU, *Proceedings, Third Annual Convention,* Speech by Gardner Jackson, p. 40.
[98] "Starvation in Arkansas," *New Republic,* XXXVI (April 1, 1936), 209.
[99] STFU, *Proceedings, Third Annual Convention,* Speech by Gardner Jackson, p. 40.
[100] *Florida Times-Union* (Jacksonville), February 26, 1937.

chapter ten

The Last Year of the First AAA

When Mary Connor Myers returned to Washington on February 7, 1935, she found AAA in a turmoil. Most of those who had sent her to Arkansas had been fired, and no one in AAA was interested in hearing her report or recommendations. One day a reporter from the United Press was in her office and saw on her desk some pictures which she had taken of poverty-stricken sharecroppers in Arkansas. Using the snapshots and his own deductions,[1] he wrote a story stating that Mrs. Myers had uncovered contract violations which caused "cruel hardships to part of the farm population," and that she had seen sharecroppers straggling along the highways, homeless and unable to obtain relief.[2]

[1] Mary Connor Myers to author, October 6, 1959.
[2] *Time*, March 5, 1935, p. 12.

Chester Davis was greatly annoyed by the appearance of this story in the nation's newspapers, and when Mrs. Myers tried to explain, even the Acting General Counsel, Seth Thomas, refused to discuss the matter. Disturbed that her superiors seemed to think her expedition to Arkansas was her own idea and that she had behaved dishonorably, Mrs. Myers wrote a long memorandum to Chester Davis, demanded an appointment, handed him the memo, and insisted he read it. Davis received her icily, but being a fairminded man, he read the memo and then talked with her for several hours.

The Myers memorandum, entitled "Tenants on Cotton Plantations in Northeastern Arkansas," contained information on living conditions, the absentee ownership of many Arkansas plantations, the organization and development of the STFU, the Ward Rodgers case, and specific reports on the cases she was instructed to investigate, especially that of Hiram Norcross. It also described dozens of affidavits she had taken from tenants in Arkansas. Mrs. Myers' conclusions were that she had found enough evidence of contract violation and evasion with hardship to tenants to warrant a full-scale investigation.

Davis called in several advisers to consider what to do about Mrs. Myers' findings. They decided to order an investigation, but when the question was raised of making the Myers memorandum public they balked because it was in many ways unfavorable to AAA. Mrs. Myers suggested that her memorandum, like an FBI report, should be kept secret because it contained names of possible witnesses and defendants, and some particulars of prospective court cases. In addition, it quoted the controversial private views of several well-known people. Davis and his advisers agreed not to publish the report, and they instructed Mrs. Myers not to give copies of her memorandum to anyone and to discuss the matter with no one.[3]

Mrs. Myers left the original copy of her memorandum with Davis, and after hearing "some weird reports of desks being rifled" in an attempt to find the other copies she took them all home. When Chester Davis learned of this, he sent word that she had no right to take the copies from AAA. Mrs. Myers then sent Davis all copies but one, which she kept for self-protection, saying the whole "sharecropper situation" had been the "most

[3] Myers to author, October 6, 1959.

humiliating professional experience" of her career and that she was delighted to see the last of the memorandum.[4]

In the weeks that followed, a great clamor was raised throughout the country for publication of the "Mary Connor Myers Report." The AAA received literally thousands of requests and demands, some of them evidently inspired by Socialist groups in large Northern cities.[5] Letters came from the American Civil Liberties Union, the Methodist Federation for Social Service in New York, the Women's International League for Peace and Freedom in Minneapolis, the Business and Professional Women's Department of the YWCA in New Orleans, the Cleveland Junior Division of the NAACP, and others. There was evidence that fictitious names were used on some of the letters.[6]

Most of the letters urging publication of the Myers report were similar, but the ones from the STFU contained a desperate note since the union had counted so heavily on Mrs. Myers' investigation to help its cause. Professor Amberson charged that "by supporting the Myers report you have given [the planters] aid and comfort. They consider that the Union has failed in its efforts to get federal intervention, and that they may now, with impunity, adopt any illegal methods which they wish to employ." [7] H. L. Mitchell wrote that the suppression of the report encouraged the planters to begin the reign of terror.[8]

On the other hand, planters wrote that Mrs. Myers spent most of her time in Arkansas in the company of Mitchell and other Socialists[9] and that she "paid practically no attention to anyone except the disgruntled tenant." When Hiram Norcross offered to furnish her with a sharecropper to show her around, she refused, saying she had employed H. L. Mitchell to drive her. J. A. Emrich, a relative of Norcross' banker and store manager, charged that Mrs. Myers was "already prejudiced against the landlords and made no effort to understand their side of the situation." [10]

[4] Myers to Chester Davis, March 8, 1935, File 467, NA, RG 145. No copy of the original Myers memorandum is in the records of the AAA now in the National Archives.
[5] C. B. Baldwin to Darwin Neserole, April 18, 1935, NA, RG 145.
[6] AAA, "Study on Myers Report Correspondence," n.d., NA, RG 145.
[7] Amberson to Porter, April 4, 1935, STFU File, NA, RG 145.
[8] Mitchell to Porter, March 27, 1935, STFU File, NA, RG 145.
[9] W. W. Barton to Chester Davis, February 13, 1934, MCM File, NA, RG 145.
[10] Emrich to W. I. Driver, February 26, 1935, NA, RG 145.

Officials of AAA answered all the letters and telegrams. The tone of these replies was set by Chester Davis in his response to Roger Baldwin of the American Civil Liberties Union. Davis stated that there was a "general misapprehension" about the Myers report, and that it was no more than an investigation of specific complaints against certain landlords. He compared it to a record of a criminal case, which of course could not be made public.[11] Davis told Baldwin it was regrettable that the public had drawn the conclusion that the report was a survey of general conditions and that AAA had been put in the position of seeming to suppress a document of general public interest when such was not the case. Davis assured Baldwin that a general analysis of tenancy conditions in counties "where relief has shown an increase" was being made and that the results would be made public "just as promptly as the facts can be filed." [12]

Norman Thomas' *Plight of the Sharecropper* was published during the furor over the Mary Connor Myers report, and in it Thomas challenged Chester Davis to make the report public. When the book circulated through AAA, Paul Porter, AAA Information Chief, forwarded it to Alfred Stedman, his counterpart in the USDA, with instructions to "note the challenge." Stedman replied that "sometime I hope the AAA gets around to my idea that this is a spot to move off." [13]

In late February, 1935, Drew Pearson and Robert S. Allen reported in their "Washington Merry-Go-Round" that in the Mary Connor Myers report Henry Wallace and AAA officials had hold of a bear's tail. They described a press interview in which Wallace commented that tenancy conditions had been "greatly exaggerated." Reporters then asked Wallace if that were true, why did he refuse to make the report public. Pearson and Allen said that what was secretly worrying the agricultural "generalissimos" was the knowledge that nationally known liberals had become interested in the plight of the sharecroppers

[11] The 1934–35 cotton contract required all signers to expressly waive the right to have records pertaining to the production sale of cotton on the farm kept confidential. Thus, there were no legal barriers to making Mrs. Myers' findings public. USDA Form No. Cotton 1a, *Cotton Contract, 1934–35,* NA, RG 145.

[12] Chester Davis to Baldwin, March 2, 1935, Myers File, NA, RG 145.

[13] Routing slip attached to *Plight of the Sharecropper,* Thomas File, NA, RG 145.

and had launched a drive on Capitol Hill for a Congressional investigation.[14] Eventually, the Senate Committee on Agriculture demanded to see the report, and Seth Thomas took a copy to a closed meeting of the committee.[15] What happened at this meeting has never been made public.

The steadfast refusal of AAA to release the Myers report served only to convince many people that it was a general report on tenancy conditions and that it was being suppressed because it was damning to AAA. Years later, Chester Davis admitted that "it might have been better tactics to release it for what it was,"[16] but this is a moot question since the report contained much that could have been used by AAA's critics. In the context of the purge of the liberals in AAA, the tactical soundness of publishing the report seems questionable.

Despite the solid front now presented by AAA to the public, the fight concerning tenancy still went on behind the scenes. USDA economist Mordecai Ezekiel, although definitely one of the liberals, had survived the purge because of Wallace's high regard for him. Even before the purge Wallace had instructed Ezekiel to look into tenancy matters, and one of Ezekiel's approaches was to have a county agent in a typical county conduct a minute survey of the effects of the acreage reduction program on tenant displacement. He chose a county in eastern Texas in which there were 614 cotton contracts. The agent's investigations showed a slight increase in the number of sharecroppers and a small decrease in share-tenants in the county between 1933–1935. He explained the increase in croppers by saying they had probably moved from the cities and had no farming equipment. The decrease in share-tenants he attributed to increased land ownership by this group. From these facts, the agent concluded that there had been no great effort by the landlords "to sidestep or cheat" their tenants.

The agent found that 65 per cent of the landlords had recognized their "three-fourths" tenants as managing share-tenants; however, he admitted many of them held the view that no tenants were entitled to share in rental benefits. The agent reported that because some tenants had received rental payments,

[14] *Washington News*, February 20, 1935.
[15] Myers to author, October 6, 1959.
[16] Chester Davis to author, August 21, 1959.

they were boasting that there was more profit in renting land than owning it. He warned that some landlords, who had been coerced into granting the status of managing share-tenant in 1934 by threats from their tenants to burn improvements on the farm, would not allow themselves to be so influenced in 1936.[17]

Evidently, Ezekiel was not wholly pleased with the agent's report. He wrote that the purpose of rental payments was to yield all producers parity prices and that tenants should share in them.[18] However, he incorporated some of the information gained from the agent into a set of far-reaching recommendations made to Chester Davis. Ezekiel felt it was too late to do anything about the 1935 contract except through interpretation of the existing provision. He wrote Davis, "We will probably have to stand by the contract, as signed." However, he strongly recommended careful scrutiny of the 1936 contract in order "to provide more liberal treatment to tenants than had been afforded them . . . thus far." Specifically, he recommended that the qualifying phrases in paragraph 7 of the contract be deleted and that the definition of managing share-tenant be broadened to include all two-thirds and three-fourths tenants. He also suggested that the administrative rulings be changed so that landlords could not require their standing-renters [19] to pay their rent in cotton exempt from the Bankhead tax as was the practice.[20]

Davis sent Ezekiel's suggestions to Cully Cobb for review, and Cobb took them apart one by one. He said they had been presented many times before, especially by the Legal Division, and discarded as "administratively impractical and utterly . . . unreasonable." Cobb felt that it would be impossible to require landlords to keep even the normal number of tenants without qualification because of the financial reverses suffered by landlords and the difficulty in determining what the normal number was. Moreover, Cobb said, such a policy would prevent landlords from replacing "shiftless" tenants with better ones. This last argument by Cobb was particularly specious since a landlord could replace bad tenants with good ones under the interpretations put on paragraph 7 by Wallace's Memphis telegram without lowering the number of his tenants.

[17] C. C. Morris to Ezekiel, January 9, 1935, NA, RG 145.
[18] Ezekiel to Morris, January 14, 1935, NA, RG 145.
[19] Tenants who paid their rent in a fixed amount of cotton.
[20] Ezekiel, Memo to Chester Davis, January 31, NA, RG 145.

Cobb maintained that managing share-tenants should not be defined as two-thirds or three-fourths tenants because there were many other types of arrangements commonly made which this definition would exclude. He also pointed out that use of this definition would result in a "Belt-wide demand" that all contracts be rewritten, which would be an intolerable situation. In answer to Ezekiel's suggestion that landlords be prevented from requiring rent in tax-free cotton, Cobb said there was already a rule calling for punishment of a landlord who attempted to collect an "undue" amount of tax-free cotton.[21]

But Cobb's word was not final, and Ezekiel continued to look into tenancy matters on behalf of the Secretary. After investigating the distribution of benefits from the cotton program, the economist reported to Wallace that the gross income from lint cotton of farmers in general increased 50 per cent from 1932 to 1934. On tracts of land where the farming was done by managing share-tenants, the landlord's income increased 62 per cent and tenants' 44 per cent. On land where there were nonmanaging share-tenants, the landlord's income increased 74 per cent and the tenants' 27 per cent. Farms using sharecroppers had an increase of 97 per cent for the landlords and 27 for the tenants.[22] These figures showed the unfairness of the program to the lower classes of tenants and probably had some effect on the tenant provisions of the 1936–39 cotton contract.

In the months that followed the purge, the news of the reign of terror in Arkansas was so unfavorable to AAA that the agency and the Secretary were forced many times to defend their position. Chester Davis on a tour of Southern agricultural areas, told reporters that the real problem among the sharecroppers was not abuse of the cotton contracts by landlords but the general decline of the cotton industry. He explained that sharecroppers were inclined not to understand the terms of the cotton contract, especially when they got the idea that landlords were required to keep the same tenants.[23]

Later, after the Birdsong incident, Davis found it necessary to write President Roosevelt explaining the tenant situation. He said that a detailed study was being made of the effects of the cotton

[21] Cobb, Memo to Chester Davis, February 6, 1935, NA, RG 145.
[22] Ezekiel, Memo for the Secretary, March 5, 1935, NA, RG 145.
[23] *New Orleans Sunday Item-Tribune*, March 21, 1935.

program on the displacement of tenants, and that these efforts were being accelerated in view of the events in Arkansas. Davis assured the President that the landlords had been told repeatedly that they must live up to their obligations under the cotton contract. He outlined the procedure whereby a landlord was required to sign a certificate of compliance before receiving final payment of benefits and how a landlord's payment was withheld if there was any evidence of a "net displacement" of tenants since 1932. Davis said the mechanism for investigating tenant disputes had been strengthened and that AAA was taking positive action to hold to a minimum the labor displacement caused by the cotton program. However, the Administrator wanted the President to understand that AAA was not responsible for the tenancy problem and could hope to do little about it. He wrote, "these conditions . . . as you know, are of long standing and are not the result of the AAA cotton programs." [24]

A flood of mail arrived at AAA in the spring of 1935 complaining of injustices to tenants. These letters were usually answered by the Cotton Section, but on one occasion, Paul Porter, USDA Information Chief, found W. J. Green's replies so unresponsive that he wrote a reply himself and mailed it without sending it first to the Cotton Section "for further scrutiny." [25] Even Rexford Tugwell found it difficult to answer his correspondence concerning the tenancy problem. He received a letter from an old friend and colleague, literature Professor Mark Van Doren of Columbia University, who had talked to a Negro sharecropper brought to New York by the STFU. Van Doren enclosed a letter from the cropper's wife in Arkansas which demonstrated "how desperate and dangerous" the situation was, and he suggested that an investigation of affairs in Arkansas might "work wonders." [26] Tugwell thanked him for his concern and admitted that the trouble in Arkansas was "bothering us greatly and we are very puzzled to know what to do about it." [27]

In March, 1935, Secretary Wallace appeared before the Senate Agriculture Committee during hearings on the Bankhead Farm Tenancy Bill and wholeheartedly endorsed the measure. He traced the development of the tenancy problem in the United

[24] Davis, Memo to the President, March, 19, 1935, NA, RG 145.
[25] Porter, Memo to Mr. C. B. Baldwin, April 15, 1935, NA, RG 145.
[26] Van Doren to Tugwell, March 26, 1935, NA, RG 16.
[27] Tugwell to Van Doren, March 30, 1935, NA, RG 145.

States and acknowledged that AAA might have made the problem temporarily more severe. He declared that neither AAA nor FERA could hope to cure the tenancy evil but said the Bankhead Bill was a big step toward that goal.[28]

As usual, Wallace's utterances were much more liberal than his actions; however, his politically wise endorsement of the Bankhead Act drew fire from certain areas. One outraged Michigan businessman demanded to know how the Secretary had become committed to reforming farm tenancy, a condition which had existed "since the Indians were kicked out of place." He asked if farmers were to become and remain the "special pets of political America," and if the city man and taxpayer were to be forever the "victims of class legislation." What the farmer really needed, he claimed, was "rest from political interfering—and lots of it." [29]

The AAA found after the purge that it had a few loose ends to tie up. One of them was the matter of official records. In March, Gardner Jackson charged in a letter to Senator Burton K. Wheeler that the files of AAA had been stripped of the more revealing materials concerning the purge.[30] How Jackson learned of this is anyone's guess, but he was probably right. The records of AAA turned over to the National Archives are notably sparse for the period immediately before and after the purge. Correspondence mentioned elsewhere does not appear where it should. The Mary Connor Myers report, for instance, is not present. The letters of dismissal sent to all the purgees are not in their correspondence files. Evidently, the bosses of AAA wanted no reminders of the unpleasant experience.

As soon as possible after the purge, AAA was reorganized along lines more acceptable to Chester Davis.[31] The offensive Legal Division was uprooted and placed under the Solicitor of the Department of Agriculture. The Commodities Division disappeared and the various commodity sections were elevated to the rank of division. In general, it was a more streamlined and efficient organization and one less likely to have internal friction.[32]

[28] USDA, Press Release, March 5, 1935, NA, RG 145.
[29] John H. Schouten to Wallace, March 7, 1935, NA, RG 145.
[30] Jackson to Wheeler, March 11, 1935, File 1737, NA, RG 145.
[31] See Table 4 on p. 186.
[32] Nourse, Davis, and Black, *Three Years of AAA*, p. 58.

TABLE 4

REORGANIZATION OF AAA, FEBRUARY, 1935

DEPARTMENT OF AGRICULTURE
Office of Secretary

BUREAU OF AGRICULTURAL ECONOMICS

AGRICULTURAL ADJUSTMENT ADMINISTRATION
Office of Administrator

FEDERAL EXTENSION DIVISION

Cotton Producers' Pool

Solicitor of the Department

Division of Consumers' Counsel

Division of Program Planning

Division of Information

Division of Marketing and Marketing Agreements

Division of Finance

Division of Tobacco, Sugar, Rice, Peanuts, and Potatoes

Division of Cotton

Division of Grains

Division of Livestock and Feed Grains

The new Solicitor was Seth Thomas, brought in by Wallace because he "understood both law and agriculture and political practicalities" [33] and perhaps because he was a fellow Iowan. Thomas was a sharp contrast to Jerome Frank. When Robert Mc-Connaughey of the Benefit Contract Section of the old Legal Division ruled that the government could give legal advice to tenants in suits against landlords, Thomas reversed the ruling. McConnaughey, one of the few remaining liberal lawyers, argued that the government was under compulsion to see that the contract was fulfilled, and if a dispute arose out of failure of one party to do so, the government might give legal advice or even assistance to the other party.[34] Thomas denied this and said it was not the duty of his department to advise individuals although these rights were based on government contracts. Even if county agents or county committeemen were accused by a tenant of fraud or misrepresentation in connection with AAA programs, Thomas said, it was a matter of legal action between individuals. The new Solicitor also made it clear that a managing share-tenant could not use as grounds for suing the government the fact that he had not been allowed to sign a contract.[35]

Thomas' seemingly harsh ruling became an issue in the presidential campaign of 1936, when John P. Davis, secretary of a Washington-based Negro protest organization called the Joint Committee on National Recovery, charged that the federal courts, aided by the legal opinions from the Solicitor of Agriculture, had declared that tenants had no right to take legal action against the government to require enforcement of the cotton contracts.[36] Shortly thereafter, a representative of the Republican National Committee called on the Solicitor and asked to see the pertinent legal opinions. He was told that the Solicitor made opinions for the Secretary of Agriculture and other bureaus and they were not ordinarily made public.[37]

Another charge made by John P. Davis was that the government had refused consistently to take legal action to prevent

---

[33] Wallace to author, June 13, 1959.
[34] McConnaughey, Memo to Mr. Seth Thomas, May 1, 1935, NA, RG 16.
[35] Seth Thomas, Memo to Chester Davis, May 8, 1935, NA, RG 145.
[36] John P. Davis, "Let Us Build a National Congress," Campaign pamphlet quoted by Mastin White, Memo for the Files, July 23, 1936, NA, RG 145.
[37] Mastin White, Memo for the Files, July 23, 1936, NA, RG 145.

illegal evictions, which left the tenants with no rights which the
landlords were bound to respect. Davis referred especially to the
case of *West vs. Norcross* in Arkansas courts,[38] and this case
seems to confirm his allegations. Jerome Frank considered entering the case on the side of West, who represented a group of
STFU union members evicted by Norcross, but after the purge
AAA steadfastly refused to have anything to do with the case.
The tenants lost because the Arkansas Supreme Court held that
tenants were not a party to the cotton contract and had no right
to bring suit to enforce it.[39]

Final disposition of the Norcross case in AAA, which revolved
around much the same issues as *West vs. Norcross*, was made
largely by default. The recommendations of Margaret Bennett
and Jerome Frank that Norcross be prosecuted for violating the
contract were ignored, and Norcross' final parity payment was
made. Chester Davis consented to this procedure because both
Mary Connor Myers and the Cotton Division reported that Norcross had more tenants in 1934 than in 1933.[40] Secretary Wallace's
policy of "the-same-number-but-not-the-same-tenants" declared
in the Memphis telegram made it clear that Norcross had not
violated the contract if he had more rather than fewer tenants. In
exonerating Norcross, AAA also disregarded the fact that he
had evicted only union members and that before the purge the
Legal Division had ruled that union membership, in itself, was
not sufficient cause for eviction.[41]

The victory of the Cotton Division in the Norcross case, and
the purge, had a salutary effect on the Division's attitude toward
the tenant problem. With most of the urban liberals now gone
and the Legal Division shoved completely out of AAA, members
of the Cotton Division could advocate reform measures without
seeming to give in to the enemy. J. Phil Campbell was the first
to do so. On February 13 he recommended that because FERA
had agreed to provide crop loans to tenants whose landlords
could not support them during the next winter, it would now be
feasible for AAA to announce that it actually expected all landlords to retain the normal number of tenants in 1935. But Camp-

[38] *Ibid.*
[39] 80 (2d) *Southwestern Reporter* (1935), pp. 67–70.
[40] Myers to Chester Davis, February 12, 1935, NA, RG 145; and Green
to Chester Davis, February 14, 1935, NA, RG 145.
[41] LaFayette Patterson, Memo to Mr. Christgau, January 22, 1935, NA,
RG 145.

bell wanted it made clear that AAA was not responsible for current displacements of tenants in the South. This he blamed on "forces let loose by the depression." [42]

The Cotton Division next made a move that would have come as a great surprise in AAA a month earlier: the Division recommended the creation of a landlord-tenant relations unit. However, this was not the landlord-tenant committee which Alger Hiss and Jerome Frank had advocated. It was to be attached to the Cotton Division and headed by W. J. Green. There would be a staff in Washington to handle cases forwarded to AAA and a unit in each cotton state to adjust cases on the spot. The state units were to work under the control of the State Directors of Extension and in close coordination with county agents and committees. Heads of state units would be chosen from "distinguished county agents or . . . district agents." In Washington, an advisory committee of three men from the South "who command [ed] the respect of all groups" and who understood conditions in the South, would provide counsel.

The Cotton Division further recommended that a legal unit be set up within the Office of the Solicitor of Agriculture to handle cases arising out of cotton contracts. Specifically, the legal unit would take care of cases involving cancellation of contracts, civil action to recover payments made before breaches of contract were discovered, and criminal action for fraudulent statements made to obtain benefits under the contract.[43]

An idea for a survey by county agents and county relief directors to determine the extent of tenant displacement due to acreage reduction also received the endorsement of the Cotton Division. In fact, the leaders of the Division felt it would prove them right.[44] In addition, Cully Cobb recommended to Chester Davis that AAA "proceed more vigorously" in prosecuting the violators of the contract and AAA regulations. He said that, although some convictions for criminal violation of the contract had been obtained, more were possible. He pointed out, however, that most prosecutions to date had been for abuses by landlords

[42] Campbell, Memo to Mr. Tolley, February 13, 1935, NA, RG 145.

[43] Cotton Division, "Recommendations for Organizing to Deal with Landlord-Tenant Complaints," Landlord-Tenant File, NA, RG 145; and Cobb, Memo to Chester Davis, February 14, 1935, NA, RG 145.

[44] Cobb, Campbell, and Green, Memo to the Administrator, February 14, 1935, NA, RG 145.

and that violations by tenants should also be looked into. Said Cobb, referring to noncriminal infractions of the contract, "Suspending payments on contracts and actually canceling contracts is the only way to get prompt action." [45]

Another idea sponsored by the Cotton Division was to have a conference in Washington of extension directors and district agents from cotton states to formulate plans for dealing with tenant problems. Subsequent conferences would be held in the states with county agents and committeemen attending. The Division desired no publicity for these conferences, but it wanted to publish the results of the survey of the effects of acreage reduction on tenant displacement in order to "answer the unfavorable statements that are being made." [46]

Naturally, Chester Davis was amenable to the suggestions of the Cotton Division, since to accept them would make the purge of the liberals look less sinister. He ordered the reforms to be carried out, and the Cotton Division set them in motion. However, it should be noted that the changes, if anything, strengthened the control of the Cotton Division over tenant affairs. Moreover, the cotton men might have changed their attitude toward the handling of tenant problems, but their views on tenant rights remained the same. For example, W. J. Green as head of the Landlord-Tenant Relations Unit could be expected to favor landlords over tenants in the interest of expediting the cotton program, and the conference of extension directors was not likely to produce any general condemnation of tenancy policies.

One action recommended by the Cotton Division proved to be a real administrative headache. It was the survey of the effects of acreage reduction on tenant displacement. The Division had high hopes for this survey, and their optimism seemed confirmed when W. J. Green was chosen to head the work. In each of eleven Southern states, the Directors of Extension and the Federal Relief Administration selected a man with no previous experience with AAA or FERA to supervise the survey. They usually chose someone from the faculty of a land-grant college in the state. These supervisors became temporary federal em-

[45] Cobb, Memo to Chester Davis, February 14, 1935, NA, RG 145.
[46] Cobb, Campbell, and Green, Memo to the Administrator, February 14, 1935, NA, RG 145.

ployees and were given clerical staffs to assist in the work.[47] Their first job was to pick three to six counties in their state to be investigated. In a letter to all supervisors, Chester Davis cautioned them to work with open minds and not to champion the cause of either the tenant or the landlord.[48]

The survey was limited to tenants who were on farms and covered by cotton contracts in 1933 or 1934 and who were currently on relief, plus landlords against whom complaints had been made. Working closely with county relief officials, the surveyors made a list of contract-farm tenants on relief, and then got out to interview them and their landlords. They used a schedule for tenants which required the number in the family, the color, the race, and the county, state, and township of all residences for the past four years. It also listed the type of tenure, whether or not the tenants were replaced when they left, and whether the tenants who replaced them were lower in status. The form asked if the tenant had been allowed to use the rented acres for producing food and feed and the number of acres used. Another schedule for the landlords who showed a net displacement in tenants asked them the number of families on their land for the last four years and the reasons for eviction.

The data collected from the landlord and tenant schedules were summarized into a state report and forwarded to Washington, where a committee headed by W. J. Green synthesized all state reports into a general one. When completed, the Green Report found that "little, if any" relationship existed between cotton acreage reduction and the number of tenants and former tenants on emergency relief. The statistics of the report revealed that only 8.2 per cent of those on relief in the fifty-two counties canvassed were tenants from cotton contract farms. In order to determine if the survey was valid, Green ordered an additional study of all contract signers and their tenants in twenty-three townships throughout the South. According to Green, the results of this study were "practically the same" as those of the survey of relief-roll tenants.[49]

The total of cotton contracts in the counties surveyed was

[47] "Letters to Relief Administrators, AAA-FERA Survey," File 119, NA, RG 145.
[48] AAA-FERA Survey, File 119, NA, RG 145.
[49] AAA-FERA Survey, Introduction, File 119, NA, RG 145.

92,340. There were 594 contract violations on these farms revealed by the relief-roll survey and 176 turned up by the township survey. Over 14,000 tenants were interviewed in the relief-roll survey and 7,585 in the township study. In the counties selected, there were 175,000 relief cases, of which 14,319 were tenant farmers. Comparing the contracts in force with the violations revealed by the two surveys, Green concluded that the cases of net displacement by landlords accounted for only .6 per cent of relief-roll tenants and .2 per cent of all tenants. About 81 per cent of relief-roll tenants made use of the rented acres to grow food and feed.

Perhaps the most significant figures gathered by the survey were those showing the movement of tenants, for these indicated the extent of evictions. The statistical summaries of the Green Report were limited to the movement of tenants across state, county, and township boundaries. Moves within townships were not shown; however, it is possible to use the statistics presented in the various state reports to arrive at figures for all types of tenant movements. For instance, although the Green Report boasted that tenants moved no more across boundaries in 1935 than in 1933, the statistics for all kinds of moves show that in Arkansas 37.1 per cent of tenants moved in 1933, 45.5 per cent in 1934, and 43.4 per cent in 1935. This means that every year, more than 800 families in six counties in Arkansas were forced to move. The figures for Oklahoma (these are the years of the "Grapes of Wrath") show in the state report that as many as 66.6 per cent of tenant families moved in 1935, and in Missouri the percentage reached 68.4 in 1934.[50]

When landlords who had violated the contract were asked their reasons for evictions, 24 per cent blamed crop failure, 14.2 per cent named "financial difficulties," 11.2 per cent attributed it to "unemployment," and 4.1 per cent said the tenants fired had an insufficient working force (too small a family). Of the tenants who were asked why they were on relief, 28.1 per cent said it was because of crop failure, 14.4 per cent blamed "unemployment," 28.4 per cent attributed it to "financial difficulties," and 3.7 per cent said they could not find a farm. Only 1 per cent blamed AAA's acreage reduction.

[50] AAA-FERA Survey, Statistical Summary; and Arkansas, Oklahoma, and Missouri Reports, File 119, NA, RG 145.

One set of meaningful statistics was the percentage of moves made by tenants involved in contract violations by landlords. Full figures were not given on Arkansas, but in Oklahoma 92.7 per cent of such tenants on relief made some type of move in 1934. In all the counties surveyed, 71.4 per cent made a move. A large part of them were sharecroppers and laborers.

Another vital phase of the survey was the determination of how many tenants on contract farms had been lowered in status or replaced. This information came from the tenants themselves, and because of fear of reprisal or sheer ignorance it may not be completely reliable. Nonetheless, in the entire Cotton Belt, 37.5 per cent of relief-roll tenants were replaced in 1933, 47.1 per cent in 1934, and 43.1 per cent in 1935. The percentage of those who had their status lowered was 4.5 in 1933, 28.9 in 1934, and 42.6 in 1935. And yet, Green was able to write that "the foregoing figures show definitely that there has been no wholesale displacement and change in status of tenants," even though the sample on which he based his assertion was only .8 per cent of all tenants on cotton contract farms.

In his conclusions, Green cited examples of unusual cases in which an apparent violation of the contract might not in reality be one. He also pointed out that on farms studied by the township survey, there was an increase since 1932 in the number of tenants in every category. From this he concluded that there had been a steady increase in the number of farm families covered by the cotton contracts and that there was no indication of an "abnormal change in status" of tenants on these farms.

One thing absolutely essential to the validity of the Green Report was the assumption that tenants on relief could be used as a representative sample of all tenants affected by the cotton program. In order to establish this point, Green offered the explanation that 14,319 families who were tenants on farms covered by cotton contracts ended up on the relief rolls of the fifty-two counties studied. This, in itself, was a damaging statistic, but Green was forced to use it. He neglected to add that there were 29,574 other tenants on the same relief rolls.[51]

Probably the most revealing part of the AAA-FERA study was the township survey. In this, the entire township was covered and contract landlords and their tenants were interviewed. The

[51] AAA-FERA Survey, Conclusions, File 119, NA, RG 145.

Green Report made few conclusions about this survey, except where they could be used to support the findings of the relief-roll study. One important statistic which Green did not mention but which can be computed from various data scattered through the report is that 20 per cent of all tenant families living on contract farms had been involved in apparent contract violations. In Arkansas it was 24 per cent. Moreover, deductive reading of the statistics indicates that 1.3 per cent of all tenants on contract farms had been lowered in status in 1935. Projecting these percentages to the tenants on all contract farms in the South, a hypothetical total of 8,376 families would have been demoted in status and 400,000 would have been involved in contract violations in 1935.

The overall tenor of the Green Report was to take pride in the fact that the conditions of tenants and sharecroppers had deteriorated only slightly since AAA began. But this viewpoint, in itself, was an admission that the government program for cotton had not helped tenants and croppers, a notable failure since the Agricultural Adjustment Act was designed to benefit *all* farmers. Certainly, the economic position of most landowners had been improved by the cotton program, and yet Green felt it was no discredit to AAA that more than half of the cotton farmers, the landless ones, were only a little worse off!

The Green Report was intended for publication, but there were so many flaws in it that several people in AAA objected. William T. Ham, an economist in the Bureau of Agricultural Economics, was given the task of writing a criticism of the report. Ham's commentary turned into a hatchet-job. He questioned whether the displacement under the cotton program was as small as Green stated and added that net displacement was only one problem among many.

Ham's fundamental criticism was that the Green Report had a "narrow range of . . . subject matter" and that limitations imposed by the procedure and deficiencies in planning made the report unsatisfactory. He felt critics were likely to assert that the report made a constant effort to give a more favorable impression of the cotton program than was warranted by the data. To prove this, he cited Green's conclusion that tenants evicted and not replaced made up only 1.5 per cent of tenants on relief. Ham asked, "Why compare the number of violations with the *total* number of tenants on relief rather than with the numbers of *contract* tenants on relief? In the latter case, the percentage would be 4.5 per cent." Again, the Green Report stated that tenants and former tenants from cotton contract farms made up only 8.2 per cent of the total relief cases in the fifty-two counties. Obviously, said Ham, it would have been more to the point to compare the relief-roll tenants from contract farms to the total of relief cases from rural areas, which would yield a figure of about 16 per cent. Ham commented: "One suspects that the reason was to avoid the higher percentage which would result." Even Ham did not care to point out that the tenants on relief from contract farms made up 32.6 per cent of all tenants on relief and that in Arkansas the percentage was 68.9 and in Mississippi 73.2.

Although at first glance the township survey might seem the most valid, it too was criticized by Ham. He explained that only twenty-three townships were surveyed, and that even if they were selected at random, which he doubted, this sampling was too small to be reliable. He feared that the county agents and supervisors who picked the townships to be investigated, chose those in which the cotton program had been administered well in order to reflect credit on themselves and AAA. Ham's fears on this score appear well-grounded in the light of some of the correspondence which took place between Washington and the various state supervisors. For instance, C. A. Hughes, supervisor in Arkansas, wired the Cotton Division during the early stages of the study that there was "no cause for alarm." [52] Later, he wrote that "the Arkansas extension people" (who picked him as supervisor) were concerned that the survey be conducted in a manner that would "incite no additional unfavorable publicity" concerning tenant troubles in Arkansas. [53]

Another discrepancy found by Ham was the impossibility of learning from the landlord and tenant schedules whether the information had been gained by interview with the individual or from the relief rolls. He also questioned whether an ordinary displaced tenant would know if there had been a contract violation in his case and if he had been replaced by a tenant of lower status. Ham criticized the readiness of the surveyors to

[52] Hughes to Green (Telegram), May 11, 1935, File 119, NA, RG 145.
[53] Hughes, "Progress Report," File 119, NA, RG 145.

take the word of landlords about the number of families on their land. Works Progress Administration officials had told him that little credence could be put in the verbal statements of landlords on this score. Also, Ham felt it was "incredibly naive" to ask landlords guilty of contract violation the cause of their evictions and then use the data gained without pointing out the limitations involved.

Ham conceded that relief-roll tenants were probably "as fair a sample as could readily be secured" of tenants adversely affected by the cotton program, yet he felt the assumption that all displaced tenants eventually appeared on relief rolls was "doubtful." He pointed out that in some Southern areas, Negroes could not get on relief and that sharecroppers as a class did not appear on the rolls in as large a proportion as they did in the general population. The BAE economist concluded that relief rolls did not give a true picture of the situation of the cotton tenants.

Ham accurately defined the main grievances of the Southern tenants under AAA's cotton program as displacement involving reduction in status and/or eviction, forced reduction in acreage of cash crops, and failure to receive a fair share of AAA benefits. The Green Report considered only the first of these, and Ham felt it was false of Green to claim that his survey was "fair and unbiased" and a general assessment of the effects of the cotton program on tenants. Ham feared that if the Green Report were published it might be justly accused of being "evasive and misleading" because it considered only the problem of net displacement. The real problems, said Ham, were what happened to displaced tenants and to tenants whose status was lowered. In addition, he held that violations of the cotton contracts were seldom matters of outright eviction, but rather "a resort to numerous and varied arrangements prejudicial to the interest of the sharecropper." The Green Report, according to Ham, ignored these practices.

Ham suggested to his superiors that if the Green Report was released to the public, it should be carefully identified as a study of net displacement and nothing else. However, he seriously doubted that publication of the study would benefit AAA in any way.[54]

In view of Ham's comments, Alfred Stedman, Head of AAA's

[54] Ham Commentary on Green Report, File 119, NA, RG 145.

Press Section, informed Chester Davis that it would be "highly inadvisable" to publish the Green Report because of its "marked departure from the objective inquiry" which Davis had originally ordered.[55] Paul Porter, USDA Information Director, commented that while the Green Report was completely favorable to AAA, it should not even become a reference source in the BAE library because of its "admitted deficiencies." Administrator Davis confirmed their opinions by ordering the report to be pigeonholed.[56]

The fiasco of the Green Report was a heavy blow to the Cotton Division, but in the summer of 1935 the Division received another. A clerk in the Correspondence and Filing Section of the Division became concerned about the accumulation of letters concerning cotton contracts which was piling up in his office. He had no contract files to put the letters with, and when his superior refused to be bothered about the letters, he took them in two large bundles to the section in the Cotton Division charged with tracing lost contracts. The tracing section attempted to find the 1,200 contracts involved and learned that most of them were in the office of the Comptroller, where contracts were kept after payments on them were started.

It developed that most of the contracts had been paid, and that many would not have been if the misplaced correspondence had been in the files when they were processed by the Comptroller. Immediately, the Administrator ordered an investigation which lasted more than eight months and caused considerable excitement in AAA. Special investigators appointed by Davis held hearings and questioned dozens of people, including Cully Cobb, E. A. Miller, W. J. Green, and George Bishop. As the full story emerged, it became evident that members of the Cotton Contract Clearance Section of the Cotton Division had been stripping papers from the contract files which might bring the contracts under suspicion when they were processed for payment. Many of the letters removed were complaints from tenants.

Numerous witnesses from the Clearence Section testified that they had been instructed by their superiors, including W. B. Camp, Assistant Chief of the Cotton Division, to remove unfavorable correspondence such as tenant complaints in order that the contracts might be approved for payment without difficulty.

---

[55] Stedman, Memo to Chester Davis, February 4, 1936, NA, RG 145.
[56] Porter, Memo to Miss Lacy, May 6, 1936, NA, RG 16.

There were two types of cases in which this was done. One was when the person doing the file stripping felt the landlord involved was honest and entitled to payment. The other was any case in which the Landlord-Tenant Relations Unit, W. J. Green, E. A. Miller, and J. Phil Campbell, had approved payment. Evidently, there was a gentlemen's agreement that after the Landlord-Tenant Relations Unit had passed on a case, all materials which might impede its final approval by the Comptroller were removed from the file. The effect was that all decisions of the LTRU were final, and there was no opportunity for review by any authority outside the Cotton Division.

The defense offered by the Cotton Division was that the Comptroller's Office had been uncooperative in turning over contracts about which there was some question. In looking into this countercharge investigators found a bundle of requests for the return of contracts in the Comptroller's Office which had never been acted upon. E. A. Miller and others also claimed that the Comptroller had caused a bottleneck in the processing of one million cotton contracts, and that out of desperation the Cotton Division developed the expedient of removing damaging papers from the contract files so that they would go through without a hitch. They said none of the people involved had acted out of dishonesty but only from a desire to expedite the adjustment program.

The first case of file stripping, which set the precedent for all the others, concerned a landlord who had signed as having only one managing share-tenant. Letters in the file on this landlord stated that he had more than one, indicating that a new contract might have to be signed. However, a clerk in the Clearance Section took fourteen letters out of this file concerning the other tenants and sent the contract to the Comptroller's Office where it was approved and payments started. The clerk who did this testified in the hearings that he discussed the matter with E. A. Miller, who authorized this procedure. Miller stated that he may have given that impression, but he had not intended to do so. Soon this practice was being used quite frequently. On several occasions, when contracts were returned by the Comptroller disapproved, the Clearance Section sent them back with the objectionable correspondence missing and they were then approved.

Mastin G. White, Solicitor of Agriculture, reviewed the entire case of file stripping in the Cotton Division and recommended to Secretary Wallace that all the information gathered be turned over to the Attorney General because of possible violations of federal codes dealing with destroying, concealing, removing, or attempting to conceal government documents. However, Wallace decided not to follow this suggestion. Perhaps he feared the scandal it would cause, especially since the landlord-tenant issue in AAA was already so touchy. To be sure, the top officials of AAA and USDA took immediate action to stop the practice of file stripping, but there is no evidence that they did anything to rectify the injustices which may have been done to hundreds of tenants because their complaints never got outside the Cotton Division.[57]

But this was not the end of the Cotton Division's troubles. As the Division was laying plans for the 1936–39 cotton contract, it ran afoul of the Comptroller General of the United States, J. R. McCarl. The General Accounting Office, headed by McCarl, learned that AAA had been making parity payment to landlords to be distributed to their tenants and that the agency was planning to continue this in 1936. It was the same practice to which Alger Hiss objected in writing the 1934–35 contract. There was great concern in the Cotton Division that McCarl might force individual payments to all tenants, which would have caused much more work for the Division but which have been joyously welcomed by many tenants.[58]

In early October, word came from McCarl that separate payments would have to be made to landlords and tenants under all of AAA's programs. Frightened by the prospect of an almost certain outcry from Southern landlords, the Cotton Division drafted a letter for Secretary Wallace's signature explaining their viewpoint. They stated that they planned to use trust agreements in 1936 whereby tenants authorized their landlords to collect parity payments for them. In 1934 and 1935 such agreements had been used although it had not been necessary for all tenants to consent to them; however, the Division assured McCarl that in the future all tenants would be required to sign the trust

[57] White, Report of Investigation of Irregularities in Processing of Cotton Contracts, n.d., File 31, NA, RG 145.
[58] Porter to Callender, November 2, 1935, NA, RG 145.

agreements. The Division's letter carefully explained that it was essential to use the trust agreements in certain areas of the South because if the tenants were paid directly their landlords might withdraw all credit and some irresponsible croppers might skip out with the payments without settling their debts to their landlord. This would leave insufficient labor. In answer to the rather obvious argument that tenants could be paid separately after the harvest, the Cotton Division said weakly that this would "involve other difficult problems," meaning probably that the landlords would be opposed to this also.

The Cotton Division's letter pointed out that making payments directly to tenants would tremendously complicate the work of county agents. In many cases, tenants and croppers lived many miles from the county seat and had no means of transporation. The truth was that most tenants would have gladly walked the distances to get their checks, but the Division did not mention this fact. Another problem mentioned by the Division was that tenants would be hard to identify since many had no identification papers and could not sign their names. Evidently it never occurred to the Division to have the county agents go to the plantations and distribute the payments as the landlords identified their tenants. Anticipating that someone might suggest mailing checks to tenants, the letter said "this class has inadequate addresses."[59]

Of course, the purpose of the Cotton Division's letter was to convince the Comptroller General of the necessity of continuing the trust agreements. However, it is not likely that Secretary Wallace ever saw the letter drafted for his signature. Chester Davis realized that the letter revealed clear bias, and he knew also that it would not pay to bandy words with the General Accounting Office. The GAO was a part of the legislative branch, created and maintained by Congress. Had the order to make separate payments come from the Department of Treasury of the Bureau of the Budget, AAA might have appealed to the President, but to defy the GAO would have been risking the wrath of Congress. Accordingly, Davis wrote McCarl that every effort would be made to comply with his requirements. He indicated that it would be possible to make separate payments to tobacco tenants even though there were about eighty tenants for every

[59] Draft of letter, Wallace to McCarl, November 2, 1935, NA, RG 145.

100 contracts. But in the case of cotton tenants, Davis said that, although constant attempts had been made to develop a practical plan for direct disbursement, "we have been unable to do so." He asked the Comptroller General to reconsider his decision and let AAA make payments to trustees under the cotton contracts in 1936 with the understanding that thereafter AAA would comply with his wishes.[60] McCarl turned down Davis' request, but the Cotton Division solved the problem by making joint payments to landlords and tenants. This procedure meant that both landlord and tenant had to endorse the checks.[61]

Despite its earlier difficulties, the Landlord-Tenant Relations Unit proved to be a moderate success, at least from the Cotton Division's point of view. Eventually, the unit perfected a method of processing complaints which worked smoothly. Most tenant complaints were handled by county committees with a standardized report made in each case to the state committee. If a case could not be decided locally, a field representative from LTRU went from Washington to settle the matter working closely with the state committee. During 1935, tenant complaints continued to be much the same as before—lowered status, eviction, failure to receive AAA payments, and unfair county agents and committees—but the number of these complaints gradually declined. In addition, AAA was slightly more inclined during 1935 to take corrective action. For instance, some county agents and committeemen were fired for favoritism to landlords.[62]

The Landlord-Tenant Relations Unit was also able to gain acceptance of several of its recommendations in the 1936–39 cotton contract and accompanying regulations. At the Unit's suggestion, the program contained a formula for distributing rental payments which gave landowners 37.5 per cent and the person furnishing the workstock and equipment 12.5 per cent, with the remaining 50 per cent divided between landlord and tenant according to their usual arrangement. Thus, a sharecropper would get 25 per cent of the rental as compared with nothing in 1934–35, and a share-tenant would receive 50 per cent whether or not he was a managing share-tenant.

Another recommendation by the LTRU was that benefit pay-

[60] Chester Davis to McCarl, October 28, 1935, NA, RG 145.
[61] USDA Form CAC No. 2, 1935, NA, RG 145.
[62] Report of LTRU, November 1, 1937, NA, RG 145.

ments be made directly to the person managing the farm, which was an improvement over previous policy, although it still excluded sharecroppers and many share-tenants. Recognizing that it was hopeless for the government to try to "freeze" the status of tenants, the LTRU suggested this policy be abandoned in 1936–39. Instead, it was recommended that county committees have the power to allow landlords to keep fewer tenants than normal or to lower the status of their tenants if they could satisfy the county committees that it would be "economically impracticable" not to do so. Under this plan, county committees would have the power to disapprove contracts if the landlords did not treat their tenants fairly.[63] On the surface, this policy might seem reasonable, but in the hands of the planter-dominated committees of the areas like northeastern Arkansas, it could become a means of completely circumventing the intent of the Adjustment Act.

All of these recommendations by the LTRU were incorporated into the 1936–39 contract. However, Mastin White, the new Solicitor of Agriculture, raised some serious objections concerning them. In fact, White seemed to be experiencing some of the difficulties which Jerome Frank once had. Perhaps it was because the legal mind simply could not tolerate such intangible phrases as "economically impracticable," "each tenant's fair share," and "an equitable distribution." White removed many of these phrases from the contract only to have them put back by the Cotton Division. Also, he objected to requiring all contract signers to name a beneficiary since other contracts did not do so. He intimated that landlords might abuse this by having themselves named beneficiaries of their tenants, evicting them, and then collecting their benefit payments. Despite his protests, the contract required beneficiaries.[64]

Generally, the administrative ruling which went with the 1936–39 contract followed previous policies. There was a slightly improved definition of a managing share-tenant, but not the one Mordecai Ezekiel suggested. Only managing share-tenants could sign the contract, and no contract would be accepted if it appeared there was a side agreement which might deprive one

[63] Recommendations of the Landlord-Tenant Committee, n.d., NA, RG 145.
[64] White to Chester Davis, November 27, 1935, NA, RG 145.

party of the benefits due him. Each tenant was to receive a "fair share" of the available acreage,[65] and much more discretion was left to county committees in making acreage allotments.[66]

The cotton program for 1936–39 was all set and the sign-up campaign was in its beginning stages when judicial lightning struck AAA. The Supreme Court on January 6, 1936, in the case of *United States vs. William Butler et al., Receivers of Hoosac Mills Corporation,* invalidated the Agricultural Adjustment Act of 1933. Justice Roberts, speaking for the Court, held that the Adjustment Act, in setting up a plan to regulate and control agricultural production, unconstitutionally invaded the rights reserved to the states. He said that the processing tax was merely incidental to the regulation of agriculture and could not therefore be based on the constitutional right of Congress to levy taxes. He added that contracts with farmers for the reduction of acreage were outside the range of federal power since such agreements could not justly be said to come under the power of Congress to provide for the general welfare of the country, and since the contention that such agreements were not coercive was a fiction. Roberts further held that the widespread national emergency did not confer on Congress the powers reserved to the states or any powers not granted by the Constitution.[67] In a stinging minority opinion, Justice Stone berated the inconsistency of the majority's position and warned against a "tortured construction of the Constitution." Justices Brandeis and Cardozo also dissented.[68]

The AAA was not destroyed by the Supreme Court's action. The men who ran the agency picked up the pieces and continued to operate. Within a few weeks Congress appropriated enough money to meet the obligations incurred under the Act of 1933, and on February 29, it passed the Soil Conservation and Domestic Allotment Act. The new law provided crop controls and benefit payments for the ostensible purpose of soil conservation, but the old goals of enforced scarcity and parity prices were still there.[69]

[65] USDA, Form No. CAC 2, 1935, NA, RG 145.
[66] USDA, Form No. CAC 1, 1935, NA, RG 145.
[67] 296 *U.S.* 1 (1936); and 102 *American Law Records* 914 (1936).
[68] James Smith and Paul Murphy (eds.), *Liberty and Justice* (New York: Knopf, 1958), p. 407.
[69] Murray Bennedict, *Farm Policies of the United States,* 1790–1950 (New York: The Twentieth Century Fund, 1953), pp. 349–353.

In fact, the Hoosac decision may have been something of a blessing in disguise to AAA because it hastened a transition which had long been planned. This was a change from the temporary emergency phase of the adjustment programs to more permanent policies which gave a larger place to soil conservation and improved farm management.[70]

The tenant provisions of the 1936 soil conservation program for cotton were little changed from what had been planned originally.[71] However, 1936 marks the beginning of a new era in the New Deal's handling of tenant problems. The agitations of the Southern Tenant Farmers' Union, the troubles in Arkansas, and the tenant difficulties encountered by AAA had their effect on the more positive future policies of the Roosevelt Administration such as the Farm Security and Resettlement programs.

[70] AAA, *Agricultural Conservation, 1936, A Report of the Activities of the Agricultural Adjustment Administration* (Washington: U.S. Government Printing Office, 1936), p. 1.

[71] Tolley to McFarlane, April 6, 1936, Landlord-Tenant File, NA, RG 145.

Conclusion

Nearly two million Southern tenant farmers and their families, living in the direst poverty, constituted one of the most perplexing problems facing the United States in the 1930's, and yet during the hectic Hundred Days of 1933 the matter seemed far less imminent than the general economic distress which beset the country. Thus, when legislation to assist recovery of American agriculture was written and passed, no guarantees were made that tenant farmers would share equitably in the government aid, and the larger problem of reforming the Southern tenancy system was entirely ignored.

Moreover, little concern for tenants was shown by the leaders of the Agricultural Adjustment Administration in planning the cotton programs. The cotton experts in AAA were intent on reviving the cotton economy by a voluntary program of acreage reduction involving what they hoped would be a minimum of red tape. They should have realized that a drastic decrease in cotton acreage would be disastrous to Southern tenants, but if they did they refused to let the knowledge deter them.

The cotton experts in AAA understood Southern tenancy well, and rather than attempting to reform the system—a task for which they had little enthusiasm and no authority—they accepted it and adapted their plans to it. They made the landlords the administrators of the cotton program to their tenants, and they saw to it that the landlords received a far greater share of the government benefits than did the tenants. To have done otherwise would have seriously disrupted Southern tenancy structure. It is a tragedy that the system was not disrupted at precisely this time, for the opportunity was golden. Never in its long and cruel history had tenancy been more vulnerable. If, for instance, AAA had made equitable payments for acreage reduction directly to tenants, the money would have given the tenants greater independence and bargaining power with the landlords and might have begun the destruction of the tenancy system. The leaders of AAA argued that they had to favor the landlords or too few would agree to reduce acreage and there would be no program, but one suspects that in 1933 and 1934 the landlords were desperate enough to accept government aid no matter what strings were attached.

The favoritism of the AAA toward landlords brought a storm of protests from tenants and liberal groups. The huge agency responded only with makeshift corrections and half-hearted reforms; it could do no more because once the cotton programs were set, AAA was stuck with them. This dilemma points up one of the most serious difficulties in government planning. When drastic new programs are undertaken, there may be unforeseen problems for which there are no solutions. Only when administrators remain flexible and Congress maintains a watchful eye on new programs, can most unforeseen difficulties be overcome. The administrators of the cotton programs, especially the agrarians of the Cotton Division of AAA, were amazingly rigid, and Congress showed little interest in the plight of tenant farmers throughout 1934 and 1935.

As news of tenant evictions and uprisings became more and more frequent during 1934, the liberals of AAA, particularly in the Legal Division, realized that the agency had an opportunity to reform tenancy or at least do something to help the tenants. When the young lawyers started working toward these goals it caused a schism in AAA which threatened to disable the entire agency. The struggle reached a climax when the Legal Division, with great impracticality, attempted to reinterpret the cotton contract so as to guarantee the tenure of every tenant on a contract farm. Such a policy would have been difficult if not impossible to enforce, and Chester Davis and Henry Wallace were left with the alternatives of changing AAA into an agency of reform or of getting rid of the liberals. They chose the easier path and purged Jerome Frank, Gardner Jackson, and the others.

The position of Davis, Wallace, and Cully Cobb throughout the tenant controversy was that the Agricultural Adjustment Act was not intended to reform the system of Southern tenancy. This was true, but to take the attitude was begging the question. The declared purpose of the act was to increase the purchasing power of *all* farmers. It did not exclude tenants and sharecroppers. The real question is whether AAA was completely fair to tenant farmers in the planning and execution of its cotton programs. The answer is no. The liberals, in their own inept way, were simply fighting to protect the tenants from exploitation under the unfair cotton programs. It was a heavy blow to tenant interests when the liberals were fired.

After the purge the tenant problem receded somewhat into the background, although it remained the largest single headache of AAA. There were some signs in 1935 of a softer attitude in the agency toward tenants, even by the agrarians; moreover, there was a slight improvement in tenant policies. The proposed program for 1936, for instance, seemed to be moving in the right direction, and the Landlord-Tenant Relations Unit was finding a few solutions to the thorny matter of handling tenant complaints. But AAA still had a long way to go.

In the spring of 1936, Senator Frederick Steiwer of Oregon, the keynote speaker of the 1936 Republican National Convention, launched an attack on AAA in the Senate. He charged the agency with "wholesale frauds and . . . misrepresentations," the objects of which had been to plunder the United States Treasury and to "deprive the sharecroppers and tenants of the benefits that had been intended for them." The Senator presented as evidence dozens of affidavits taken in sixteen counties of Texas which indicated various types of malpractice, especially in the distribution of Bankhead Act tax exemptions. Steiwer had hardly begun his broadside when he drew fire from various Southern senators who wanted to know the source of the affidavits. They eventually forced him to admit that the statements were collected by a former employee of AAA who had since been indicted for fraud and was probably now in the employ of the Republican National Committee.[1]

Before Steiwer could nail home the points he wished to make, one of the Democrats' ace hatchet men, Tom Connally of Texas, caused a diversion by attacking Steiwer personally. Connally charged that Steiwer had Vice-Presidential ambitions and added that the Oregonian, like many other Republicans, had clung tenaciously to President Roosevelt's coattails in the perilous days of 1933 ("and some say he got under the President's coattails"), but now that the country was saved Steiwer was turning against the Administration and trying to discredit it. Said Connally, "Whenever you find one case of wrongdoing in the Agricultural Adjustment Act, you will find 100 poor farmers who have been benefited and lifted up from the very dregs of poverty. . . ."[2] When Connally had finished, Steiwer was glad to drop the whole matter.

As indicated by Senator Steiwer's experience, it was almost impossible to talk about AAA without getting involved in the worst kind of partisan politics. If the Republicans attacked the agency or its programs, the Democrats came to its defense. It was that simple. A similar situation existed within AAA: if the liberals proposed, the agrarians opposed without even considering the merits of the idea. By the same token, any suggestion of the agrarians was automatically suspect to the liberals. There was even less understanding at the grass roots between the tenants and the landlords, where the differences led to violence and bloodshed.

Today, it is possible to look at matters more calmly. And yet, because of biased and conflicting sources, it is still difficult to make sound judgments. For instance, the extent of AAA's responsibility for the displacement of tenants in 1933, 1934, and 1935 cannot be determined precisely, even from the best sources. The conclusions of each study, both government and private, seemed to depend on which group made it and what it hoped to find. The best that can be said is that the number of evictions was tragically large and that AAA's tenant policies not only gave the landlords a motive for evictions but offered the tenants little protection against them.

[1] U.S., *Congressional Record*, 74th Cong., 2nd Sess., 1936, LXXX, Part 10, 10512–14.
[2] *Ibid.*, pp. 10521–32.

Perhaps the hardships to some tenants caused by AAA's tenant policies were offset by the general improvement in the cotton economy which helped many tenants. Here again no pat answer is possible. Certainly many tenants benefited from the government payments and the increase in cotton prices, but many others suffered by the acreage reduction. It must also be added that the landlords profited from the cotton programs much more handsomely than did the tenants.

What was the overall effect of AAA on Southern tenancy? Although the Census of Agriculture of 1935 showed a continuation of the fifty-year-old pattern of growing tenancy throughout the country, it also indicated a significant decline in tenancy in the principal cotton-growing areas of the South. In fact, the decrease was confined almost exclusively to Southern cotton and tobacco counties. Some of the cotton tenants who lost their status had become wage hands on the same plantations or other farms, and some had moved to the towns and cities. Many were on relief. Very few who were former tenants had become landowners, and in most cases the displaced tenants had moved down the agricultural ladder.[3]

Combining the facts about the decline of cotton tenancy with a knowledge of the workings of AAA's cotton program leads naturally to the conclusion that AAA failed to benefit great numbers of Southern tenants and even harmed many of them. In a way, AAA accomplished an unintended reform in helping to drive tenants from the land, because those evicted were forced to seek new occupations and most of them eventually found a better life. However, it was usually years before they could make the adjustment, and in the meantime they suffered terribly. A great, humanitarian nation as rich as the United States can find better ways to achieve such reforms.

[3] Turner, *A Graphic Summary of Farm Tenure*, p. 25.

Bibliographical Note

Manuscript Collection

Much of the material used in this study came from the records of the Agricultural Adjustment Administration now in the National Archives in Washington, D.C. These records are in the Agriculture and General Services Branch of the Archives designated as Record Group 145. The files most used were the letters and memoranda of the Cotton Division, the Legal Division, the Consumers' Counsel, the Comptroller's Office, the Office of the Administrator, the Central Files, the Landlord-Tenant Relations Unit, and the correspondence files of the various individuals concerned. Also utilized were the numerous publications of the AAA concerning the cotton programs and tenant policy, the press releases, the transcripts of public speeches by officials, and the various published and unpublished reports and studies made by AAA.

Another important source in the National Archives was Record Group 16, the files of the Secretary of Agriculture. The materials used from this group came largely from the correspondence and memoranda of the Secretary, the Under-Secretary, the Assistants to the Secretary, and various staff members. Also, the incoming correspondence of the Secretary from farmers, other government officials and Congressmen, and the general public proved to be a valuable source of information. Still another source in the National Archives was "Trouble in the Cotton Country," a *March of Time* film made in 1936 and on file in the Film Library.

Other manuscript and unpublished sources included the George N. Peek Diary and Papers, Western Historical Manuscripts Collection, Columbia, Missouri; the Thomas Collection, papers of Senator Elmer Thomas of Oklahoma in the Division of Manuscripts, University of Oklahoma Library, Norman, Oklahoma; the records of the Southern Tenant Farmers' Union now on file at the Headquarters of the National Agricultural Workers Union in Washington, D. C.; and the records of the Oklahoma Extension Service, Stillwater, Oklahoma.

Index

Byrd, W. E.: receives letter from planter, 122; asked for advice, 138; recommends Arkansas investigation, 139; interpretation of paragraph 7, 142

Caldwell, Erskine: 8, 17, 167
Camp, W. B.: 45–46
Campbell, J. Phil: and Amberson, 101; and STFU delegation, 103; as "agrarian," 105–106; on Adjustment Committee, 128–129; advocates reform, 188–189; in file stripping, 198
Campbell, Sid: 160
Cape Girardeau, Missouri: 77–78
Capone, Al: 103
Carpenter, C. T.: and C. H. Smith case, 96; and A. B. Brookins case, 97–98; appeal for AAA legal aid against Norcross, 138; and Rodgers trial, 157; terrorized, 159–160
Carraway, Hattie: 131
Cash-tenant: definition of, 6
Census of Agriculture, 1935: decline of tenancy, 209
Chambers, Whitaker: 108
Childs, Marquis: 150
Christgau, Victor: on certificate of compliance, 73; as part of efforts to create landlord-tenant committee, 132; interpretation of paragraph 7, 142; resignation, 148
Civil Service Commission: AAA not under, 23; Senate debate on AAA not under, 32
Civil Works Administration: 85
Cobb, Cully: in formulation of cotton acreage program, 45; on tenant policies, 53; in formulation of 1934 cotton program, 54; on landlord-tenant relations, 56; 1934–35 contract approved, 58; on Bankhead Cotton Control Act, 62; on tenant

injustice, 68; installs check-writing machines, 71; instructions to landlords, 73; reaction to complaints, 98, 121; Miller's report, 100; opinions on STFU and Arkansas problem, 101; meeting with STFU delegation, 103; as "agrarian" leader, 105–106, 114; as Chief of Cotton Section, 114; charges Communism, 114; employs Negroes in Cotton Section, 114; views toward liberals in AAA, 115; theory on increased tenancy, 115-116; and D. P. Trent, 118; comments on Adjustment Committee, 128; against landlord-tenant committee proposal, 132–133; upbraided by Appleby, 137–138; on Norcross case, 138; and Mary Connor Myers, 139; interpretation of paragraph 7, 142, 144; summary of position on tenant problem, 151–153; comments on second STFU Washington delegation, 172; reaction to Ezekiel report on tenancy, 182–183; prosecution of violators, 189–190; in file stripping, 197–198; conclusions on, 207
Commissary: 11
Commission on Farm Tenancy: 14
Committee on Minority Groups: 122-123
Committee on Violations of Rental and Benefit Contracts: landlord-tenant complaints and decisions, 126–127; case of Tchula Plantation tenants, 127; case of Twist Brothers Plantation tenants, 127; questions jurisdiction, 128; R. H. Polk case, 131; landlord-tenant committee proposal to abolish, 132; trouble over complaint handling,

134–135; Norcross case, 144; report from Miller and Hudson, 144–145
Commodities Division: 42, 45, 52, 57, 73, 118, 132
Commodity Credit Corporation: 50, 116
Commonwealth College: 92, 158
Communist Party: and Claude Williams, 92; and STFU, 93, 94, Chambers-Hiss case and in AAA, 108–109
Compliance Committee: 128
Compliance Section: 130
Comptroller's Office: 106, 116, 126
Connally, Tom: 208
Consumers' Counsel: 38, 106, 108, 112, 149
"Contracted acres": 45
Corn-Hog Section: 122
Costigan, Edward: 162
Cotton Belt: definition of, 3–4; churches of, 92; Cully Cobb's opinion of Communists in, 114; district committees on 1934 tenant payment complaints, 127–128
Cotton Division: victory in Norcross case, 188; advocates reform, 189; calls conference on tenant problems, 190; file stripping, 197; defense of file stripping, 198; difficulties over making tenant parity payments to landlords, 199–200; and trust agreements, 199–200; on 1936 program, 202
Cotton Exchange: 34
Cotton Option-Benefit: 45
Cotton Pool: operation, 44, 45; and Oscar Johnston, 116; allowed to pay tenants directly, 127; and R. H. Polk case, 131
Cotton Section: tenant income, 13; tenant tenure, 13–14; tenants on relief, 14; program planning, 42; cotton plow-up,

45; acceptance of "offers," 47; division of cotton payments, 52; attitude toward tenant farmers and cotton payments, 52; 1934 cotton program, 54–56; rental payments, 70; form for contract signers, 72; instructions to landlords, 73–74; certificate of compliance form, 74; tenant evictions stand, 78; appeals by tenants, 80; STFU delegation in Washington, 103; and Margaret Bennett, 111; Cully Cobb's ideas on, 114; Negro employees, 114; tenant increase, evictions, displacements, 115; tenant complaints, Cobb's ideas and policies, 168
"Cotton Week": 46
Cox, A. B.: 77
Crittenden County (Arkansas): 95–96
Crop Production Loan Unit: 51
Cummings, Homer: 174

Davis, Chester: in fight for farm parity, 19; selected Chief of Production Division, 38; ideas on AAA, 39; and cotton acreage program, 45; and division of cotton payments, 52; and landlord-tenant relations in cotton program, 57; 1934–35 cotton contract approved, 58; letter on payments to tenants, 69; defines managing share-tenant, 70; instructions to field workers on fair distribution of checks, 72; on certificate of compliance, 73–74; on landlord-tenant status, 78; actions with regard to meat-packing code, 113; as referee between AAA liberals and agrarians, 117; and D. P. Trent, 118; on AAA as agency of reform, 126; policy on enforcement of cotton contracts, 127–128; memo